TRUST ME
I'M
EXHAUSTED

Dr Harry Stone

© **Dr Harry Stone, 2024**

Dr Harry Stone is hereby identified as the author of this work in accordance with section 77 of the Copyright, Designs and Patents Act 1988

All rights reserved. No part of this work covered by the copyright herein may be reproduced or used in any form or by any means – graphic, electronic or mechanical, including photocopying, recording, taping, web distribution or information storage and retrieval systems – without the prior written permission of the author.

British Library Cataloguing-in-Publication data

A catalogue record for this book is available from the British Library.

The author is a consultant in the NHS who has recently retired. He had roles in General Paediatrics, Respiratory Paediatrics and Medical Education.

Dr Harry Stone is a pseudonym. Patient and staff names have been changed to protect the anonymity of hospitals, doctors, nurses and patients in this story. The story is based on a true-life experience.

The opinions expressed in the book are those of the author. The dialogue should not be assumed to be verbatim. The book reflects the author's present recollections of experiences over time. The author and publisher do not accept any responsibility for any offence or medical advice taken from this memoir. Names of persons and places names have been changed to provide anonymity.

Thanks to Ian Pike and Kitty Walker for their advice and counsel.

ACKNOWLEDGEMENTS

During my training I had the privilege to meet amazing patients and work with inspiring doctors and nurses in the NHS (National Health Service) and abroad in South Africa and Australia. I dedicate this book to my family whose love and support I cherish.

Illustrations in the book all by Author using watercolour and pen. Front cover "Medicine takes it toll "

Self-portrait

CONTENTS

ACKNOWLEDGEMENTS 3
CONTENTS 4
PREFACE 7

THE JOURNEY BEGINS 12

CHAPTER ONE: WHEN YOUR HARD DRIVE JAMS 13
CHAPTER TWO: THE BIRTH OF AN NHS DOCTOR 18
CHAPTER THREE: THE REALITY ZONE 23
CHAPTER FOUR: SURGICAL TRANSITION 40
CHAPTER FIVE: DELIVERY IS EVERYTHING: GETTING NOTICED 45
CHAPTER SIX: REJECTION AND THE BLEAKNESS OF LIFE 49
CHAPTER SEVEN: WELCOME TO THE FRONTLINE. SHO IN A&E 53
CHAPTER EIGHT: UNEXPECTED MOVE TO CHILDREN'S MEDICINE 63
CHAPTER NINE: GENERAL PAEDIATRICS BECKONS 66
CHAPTER TEN: LIFE BEYOND HOSPITAL – DOWNTIME 73
CHAPTER ELEVEN: BEGINNING OF LIFE – NEONATOLOGY 78
CHAPTER TWELVE: NHS TURMOIL AND LIFE ON ONE HUNDRED-PLUS HOURS A WEEK 85
CHAPTER THIRTEEN: ON TOUR TO THE HEART OF THE SOUTH 88
CHAPTER FOURTEEN: ISLAND LIFE FOR A YEAR 97
CHAPTER FIFTEEN: LONDON EXPERIENCE – SENIOR SHO NEONATOLOGY 106

STEPPING OFF THE NHS TREADMILL AND INTO THE RAINBOW NATION 113

CHAPTER SIXTEEN: STEPPING INTO A DIFFERENT WORLD – SOUTH AFRICA 114
CHAPTER SEVENTEEN: FOLLOW THE DUSTY ORANGE ROAD TO BOULDER ROCK HOSPITAL 117
CHAPTER EIGHTEEN: STEEP LEARNING CURVE – MEDICAL OFFICER, RURAL HOSPITAL – ONE YEAR 121
CHAPTER NINETEEN: GETTING UP TO SPEED 128
CHAPTER TWENTY: EDUCATION, EDUCATION, EDUCATION 133
CHAPTER TWENTY-ONE: DILEMMAS AND MISUNDERSTANDINGS 136
CHAPTER TWENTY-TWO: BEING LATE 140
CHAPTER TWENTY-THREE: SURGICAL CHALLENGES ON-CALL 142
CHAPTER TWENTY-FOUR: REALITY – EXOTIC MEDICINE AND ADMINISTRATIVE NECESSITIES 145

    CHAPTER TWENTY-FIVE: RECOGNITION BY THE SOUTH AFRICAN NURSING COUNCIL AND GREEN PAINT 149

    CHAPTER TWENTY-SIX: STRANGE REQUESTS 152

    CHAPTER TWENTY-SEVEN: SOUTH AFRICA – A WORLD IN ONE COUNTRY 154

    CHAPTER TWENTY-EIGHT: REALITY OF LIFE IN SOUTH AFRICA 159

RETURNING TO NHS REALITY 165

    CHAPTER TWENTY-NINE: BACK TO THE FUTURE – AWAKENING 166

    CHAPTER THIRTY: NORTH OF THE WATFORD GAP 168

ESCAPE TO THE "RIP SNORTER" DOWN UNDER 175

    CHAPTER THIRTY-ONE: ESCAPE DOWN UNDER 176

JOURNEY'S END IN SIGHT 188

    CHAPTER THIRTY-TWO: BACK TO REALITY 189

JOURNEY'S END 194

    CHAPTER THIRTY-THREE: END OF THE ROAD 195

    CHAPTER THIRTY-FOUR: EPILOGUE – FIXING THE NHS 200

REFLECTION ON THE JOURNEY OF HUMANITY 202

    CHAPTER THIRTY-FIVE: A SYNOPSIS OF IMPORTANT ASPECTS OF MEDICAL PRACTICE 203

    CHAPTER THIRTY-SIX: POSTSCRIPT – MEDICAL STUFF 218

    CHAPTER THIRTY-SEVEN: FINAL SALUTE 243

    CHAPTER THIRTY-EIGHT: HELPFUL REFERENCES 245

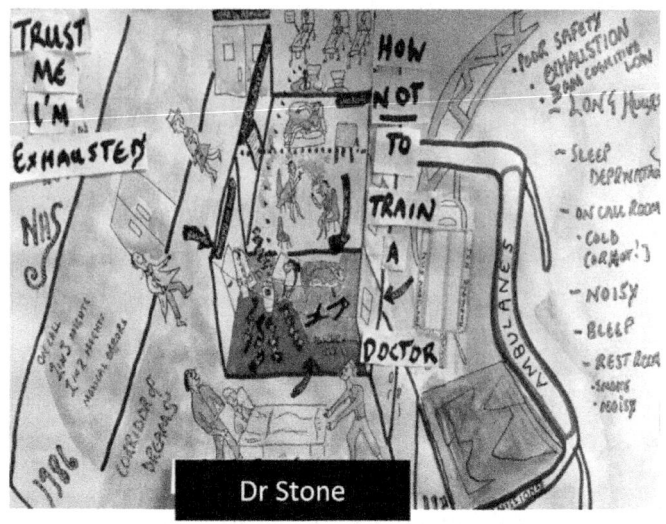

"Corridor of dreams"

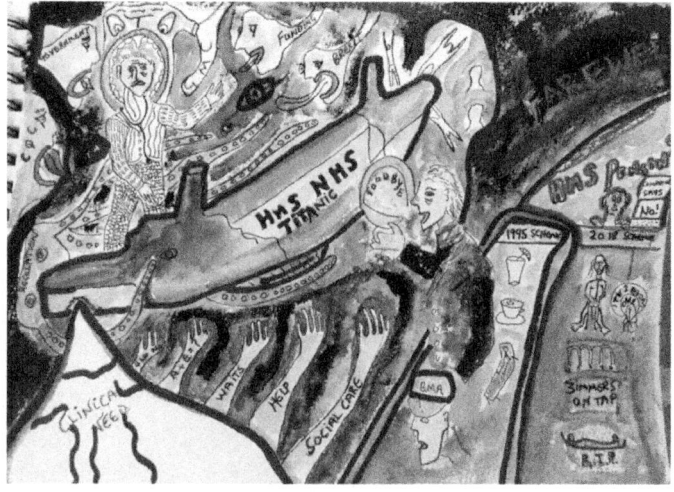

"NHS Titanic on collision course with iceberg of clinical need."

PREFACE

A road traffic accident plunged me toward an abyss of no return. This near-death experience and subsequent hospitalisation made me reflect on my life, in particular my medical training to become a hospital consultant and my experience as a patient in the present-day NHS. I recall my journey from qualification as a doctor in 1986, entering the NHS in a baptism of fire, to becoming a consultant in 1998, battle- scarred but nevertheless, a survivor.

The story of my NHS odyssey from junior doctor to consultancy has relevance to today's health service. It provides an insight into the present-day deep disillusionment felt among many doctors about their profession. My experience of being on the other side of the fence as a patient in an NHS hospital, revealed to me the ongoing struggle to provide a humane system of care in an understaffed and challenging clinical environment. It has made me reflect on the importance in healthcare to strive for the 'holy trinity' - consisting of valuing staff; state-of-the-art safe medical practice; and humane, compassionate patient-centred care.

As a young doctor trained in the mid-eighties (at the height of Thatcher's Britain), I inhabited a clinical landscape akin to the 'Wild West' when compared to today's regulated clinical arena. This was an era where 'doctor knows best' pervaded patients' expectations and the medical profession often accepted suboptimal care as 'that's just the way it is'. Challenging this acceptance was discouraged.

Today society quite rightly expects doctors to be competent professionals who work in partnership with their patients. The outdated "doctor knows best" mantra replaced by patient-doctor joint decision making and informed consent. Today if a medical error or adverse incident occurs there is an expectation of honesty and transparency from staff to patients and families involved. Staff are expected to inform patients as soon as possible after an incident putting patient safety first. This is known as duty of candor.

The eighties was the decade that heralded the advent of the hospital manager and marketplace in the NHS[1]. This changed the NHS, introducing a competitive financial ethos within the healthcare system. The power and influence of managers, since these changes, has increased year on year. Senior managers now take on significant clinical responsibilities and drive through unpopular changes, but often, without clinical accountability.

This lack of accountability has been laid bare by the recent case of a neonatal nurse convicted of murdering babies in her care. Senior managers ignored consultant concerns about the nurse, who seemed to be the common factor in the deaths of babies on a neonatal unit. The senior managers seemed to have prioritized avoiding reputational damage, over patient safety concerns. There is now a call for an independent regulatory body to oversee NHS managers. [2]

Back in the 1980s, junior doctors faced a harsh clinical environment. Training was characterised by sudden immersion of doctors into a high-risk clinical arena, without a comprehensive induction. It was akin to being thrown into the deep end of a swimming pool without a buoyancy aid and seeing if you could swim. A toxic cocktail of excessive hours, chronic sleep deprivation, poor supervision and inadequate senior support compounded this. The training mantra was 'See one, do one, teach one'. This is a far cry from today's junior doctors' training backed by regulation, including statutory work-based assessments, logbooks, close consultant clinical and educational supervision and compulsory induction.

It was an era that seemed to disregard the priority of patient safety and informed consent. This encouraged a "gung-ho" attitude to procedures and treatments. My view is backed up by the many scandals that have been uncovered in recent decades, e.g., the Bristol Royal Infirmary children's heart scandal (2001)[3], the Alder Hey organs retention scandal (2001)[4] and the failings at the Mid-Staffordshire Royal Infirmary revealed in the Francis Report (2013)[5]. The clinical care in this era was often detrimental to both patient and doctor safety and wellbeing. In short, the clinical arena was a cauldron of clinical risk in which doctors and nurses could be broken physically and mentally. Training became an experience to survive, rather than cherish. It was in retrospect, not the way to train a doctor. There were some positive aspects gained from such a challenging environment, but not many. Junior doctor camaraderie was strong and in view of the long hours, patient continuity was good. However, I must emphasize, that some doctors working in the 1980s in this dysfunctional clinical environment, developed high risk behaviours and attitudes toward patient care. This outdated approach lingers still in a few senior doctors.

The General Medical Council (GMC) have identified expected professional skills and behaviours of a doctor.[6] These are both laudable and helpful, in defining what conduct is expected of a doctor. However, the expectation of the GMC does not always align with the reality of the issues faced by doctors working in a pressurised understaffed NHS.

My story covers the good, the bad and the ugly aspects of medical practice. It reveals the fallible underbelly of training in the NHS. In addition, it documents my experience of acute NHS care as a patient. This was a sobering experience. While grappling with my cardboard urine bottle, I witnessed the flaws in our system of healthcare. It made me feel extremely vulnerable and at times scared. There is a worrying disconnect between frontline medical and nursing staff and management. Patient care can suffer because of this conflict, a casualty caught in the crossfire of differing agendas.

Writing this story was not easy to do. Many encounters described still concern me, both professionally and personally. The present-day NHS is under unprecedented pressure. It is facing huge issues such as the post CoVid backlog of patients needing treatment; an ageing population; growing social and health inequality; limited funding and staffing shortages. This is against a global backdrop of conflict, climate change and an ongoing energy crisis. We need sustainable solutions to fix out healthcare system.

To understand the reality of the present and plan the future direction of The NHS we need to learn from the past.

On the one hand, to become an NHS consultant was tough and challenging; on the other hand, it was also undeniably interesting and at times great fun. I track the course of my training, crisscrossing the north-south divide in the UK with spells in South Africa and Australia. This has allowed me to witness other health systems where user pays. This sheds light on the beauty of the NHS, which is free at the point of delivery irrespective of income.

I hope this memoir captures an era of consultant training that began at the height of Thatcher's Britain. I hope it can help inform the future direction of training and patient care in the NHS. I feel this story is important to tell as there are imminent dark storm clouds threatening our healthcare system. These clouds include staff burnout and disillusionment, understaffing, team fragmentation, management bullying, abusive patients, poor pay and ever-increasing patient demand. All these factors are contributing to record numbers of doctors and nurses leaving the NHS[7]. As a patient the reality of acute care in the NHS is alarming. Patients are having to endure waits in ambulances on arrival to hospital, waits in A&E to be seen and waits to be admitted to a hospital bed. Corridors are becoming makeshift wards and are being accepted as the norm. This sad situation denies many vulnerable patients any dignity or humane treatment[8]. We desperately need to change the course of *NHS Titanic* as it steams onward toward the iceberg of poor patient care and safety. I hope this memoir can help alter its direction by highlighting ways to improve patient care, staff training and wellbeing.

The book is divided into three broad sections.

Firstly, is the memoir tracking my NHS odyssey from a doctor starting in the NHS (1986) to becoming a consultant (1998). It also recalls my experience as a patient receiving acute care in the present-day NHS.

The second section is a synopsis of medical practice which will be useful for those without a medical background. This can be read prior to the memoir if needed.

The third section is a series of clinical vignettes that I feel are important to provide an understanding of important aspects of being clinically astute in the swamplands of medical practice.

Finally, I list useful references that may be useful. They are annotated in the text.

Let the memoir commence!

COMPARISON OF DOCTOR ISSUES 1986 versus 2024

House Officer 1986	Foundation Doctor 2024
1. 100 hours+ per week 2. Induction absent / minimal 3. Stable firm structure, good camaraderie among juniors. 4. Out of hours specialty middle grade based in hospital. Sleep Deprivation severe Live in & On Call rooms available Doctors mess availiable Canteen open all hours Pay 1/3 out of hours. 5. Teaching : "See one, do one teach one" Adhoc approach 6. Written documentation X Ray films 7. Medical errors : Hidden, acceptance "That's just the way it is " 8. Long hours gave patient continuity 9. Adhoc supervision	1. EWTD (European Working Time Directive) limits hours to 48hours per week. Shift work and blocks of nights 2. Induction Mandatory 3. Fragmentation of firm structure. 4. Out of hours isolation-skeleton team covering specialties in hospital Seniors not in hospital. Shift working & antisocial hours. Lack of rest areas with access to vending type food only. Many commute Premium pay out of hours. 5. Teaching: Mandatory attendance and follows a curriculum Staffing issues can affect attendance 6. Electronic: multiple poor software platforms to deal with (multiple passwords) 7. Duty of candor System of reporting: Datix. Aim for non-blame culture and transparency Still tendency to blame 8. Multiple handovers, poor continuity. 9. Clinical & educational supervisor Mentor system, work-based assessments.

THE JOURNEY BEGINS

"The hardest part of any journey is the first step".
John W Hayes

CHAPTER ONE:

WHEN YOUR HARD DRIVE JAMS

I lie still. A wave of lethargy crashes over me. I am detached from my surroundings, yet aware of voices and 'Puff the Magic Dragon' emanating from the CD player of the upturned car. I try to move but my body feels completely numb.

"Here. Put this on your head," comes a friendly, concerned voice.

I place the towel offered to me over my skull and feel a burning sensation followed by aching pain. A warm liquid flows down onto my forehead; it is blood seeping from my bleeding scalp wound.

"Are the kids, OK?" I hear myself ask.

My family stands away from me, ashen-faced and in shock, looking like a scene from a Victorian photograph; still, bereft of colour, serious and austere.

"They're fine. You just lie still," replies the reassuring voice of the towel bearer.

I lie on the grass verge where a silence of anticipation, like that before the opening night of a theatre performance, hangs uneasily in the air. Slowly the silence dissipates as I become conscious of the wail of sirens in the distance. Muffled voices begin to gather round me, but they are overwhelmed by a whirling noise that grows ever louder. A green-clad paramedic clutching a large red rucksack settles down next to me. He begins to question me, upbeat and positive.

"Hi, Harry. Do you know where you are?"

"Yes," I mumble.

"Where d'you work?"

"At the hospital."

"What do you do there, Harry?"

"Consultant paediatrician."

"Busman's holiday for you, eh? I'm just going to immobilise your neck."

I feel a stiff collar being slipped under me, the Velcro crackling as it is secured. Next, a plastic mask is placed over my mouth. The paramedic examines me – airways, breathing, circulation, disability and exposure… a familiar sequence I had been teaching just one week ago. I am turned delicately, and a hand runs down my back.

"Ow!" *Suddenly a searing pain rips into my consciousness.* "That hurt?"

I nod and feel a scratch on my hand, as an intravenous line is inserted. Fixation to a spinal board soon curtails my movement and a sensation of floating upward into the air and moving with a cacophony of heavy breathing from my stretcher-bearers, takes me toward the air ambulance.

"Ever been in a helicopter, Harry?" "No," I grunt.

"Well, that's how we're taking you in, so enjoy the ride. OK?"

I rise into the helicopter, hearing the clicking of straps. I look up at the sky, bright blue with perfect white cauliflower clouds. The throbbing thunder of the helicopter soon fills the air, and my world starts rotating. A feeling of serenity descends upon me as we rise upward. I feel like closing my eyes and drifting away, offering myself up to some greater being.

Suddenly, my thoughts are jolted as a gloved hand moves into my field of vision, giving me the thumbs up sign. I reciprocate.

Must stay focused, must survive, I keep telling myself.

I now enter my place of work, yet this time in a horizontal position allowing me to inspect the finer details of the hospital's-stained tile ceiling. In the resuscitation bay I listen as a comprehensive handover is given from the ambulance crew to the waiting trauma team, clad in their blue, pajama-like theatre clothes. The oratory passes to the clear, commanding voice of the surgical registrar, the leader of the trauma pack.

"Just going to check you over again," *he announces with regal authority.*

He repeats the A, B, C, D and E sequence but, for thoroughness, E now includes a rectal examination. A perk, I suppose, of being part of the system. His team then set about me, taking blood and siting intravenous lines. The junior doctors are task-focused and professional. The attention I receive is intense for the first thirty minutes and I find this reassuring.

I still have severe pain in my back and start to feel uncomfortable, desperate to alter my posture, but the restricting collar and hard board make movement impossible. A wave of agitation passes through me, and I start to think about the possible causes of the pain in my back. I immediately settle on the worst possible scenario.

"What if I've dissected my aorta?"

I start to panic and notice my heart rate begin to rise on the monitor. I immediately alert my fears to the team around me.

"Let's give him some pain relief," says the sister.

A warmth and calmness spreads through my body, replacing the agitation, as morphine gets to work. Now further embedded into the system, I move to the CT scanner and then, on return, to the resuscitation area, the focus of the staff swiftly shifting to another bed and admission. The trauma team is flitting purposely between patients, like bees collecting nectar from flowers. The staff are focused, professional and caring. I have fractures of my third and fifth thoracic vertebra and am offered more morphine, which I greedily accept.

A confident, tall doctor approaches me.

"I've come to stitch you up," he announces in a clipped, South African accent.

He goes about gathering the equipment to suture me, as the nurses are too busy to help.

"How long you been here?" I ask.

"Three years, but don't worry, I've stitched many heads back in South Africa."

He draws up the trolley he had just prepared then adjusts the light to illuminate my blood-caked scalp and then he expertly dons his apron and gloves with a flourish akin to a pianist playing a trill. Bending attentively over me, he starts the procedure. I feel the wet flow of cleaning fluid on my head and the sting of local anaesthetic.

"How d'you like it here?" I blurt, pinching my skin under my gown in anticipation of pain.

"OK, but I'm on a shift system, no one likes it. I finish at six."

I relax as the wound is slowly closed and my mind begins to wander and analyse the conversation.

The implementation of the European Working Time Directive (1998) has restricted junior doctors' hours so no doctor can work more than thirteen straight hours in a stint and the working week is restricted to less than forty-eight hours, the result of a strict shift rota. This is so different from my experience of working a hundred-plus hours a week as a junior doctor. In my own department, everything has changed. There are many more junior doctors; they are regularly appraised, and teaching is mandatory. Consultants are now hands-on and involved in day-to-day care. As I touched on earlier, the old way of 'see one, do one, teach one', the era I trained in, has been replaced by supervision, standard operating procedures, guidelines and work-based assessments, which truly is so much better for both patients and doctors.

"Don't get enough proper experience on these hours, though," he admits. I wince as another stitch is inserted outside the area of the local anaesthetic.

This was a common complaint from junior doctors and had some validity. The reduction in working hours following the European Working Time Directive (EWTD) has led to less doctor continuity with patients and reduced hands-on experience. This, however, must be balanced against the present day more structured supervision of juniors so that they learn the right way to practice. I start shuddering with apprehension as I reflect and recall my own junior doctor experiences in the mid-eighties. It really was just all about 'see one, do one, teach one'.

I wait in the resuscitation area for six hours watching the activity around me. CoVid is still stalking the hospital and I huddle down on my trolley bed. The plastic screen separating me from the chaos on show, frames my vista. Patients, old and young, litter the department in various degrees of distress. Doctors and nurses try to act focused and driven, tragically forced to ignore the cries for help and the obvious lack of space. The cubicles in Resus and Majors are full, so patients are accommodated on beds and chairs that line the thoroughfares. The staff avoid eye to eye contact, trying to do their best. Patient confidentiality is impossible as doctors and nurses' interview and treat patients in full view of everyone. A queue — that unique British obsession — has formed to get into A&E. Corridor medicine, a feature of today's resource-strapped NHS, is in full swing. My family, having also been in the crash, are assessed with thankfully no serious injuries, and sent home.

At last, I move to the admissions ward in a six-bed bay. I transfer from the trolley to a comfortable hospital bed and from here can observe, overnight, the system I know so well. Four nurses set about trying to catheterise a morbidly obese lady in the opposite bed who has just been hoisted there by lifting equipment. Next to me a junior is discussing dizzy spells with a chatty, but rather deaf, old woman. The repetitive nature and increasing volume of the interrogation is thankfully mitigated when, the doctor asks the woman to turn her hearing aid on. An elderly man peers out from beneath his bed sheets with a young male nurse sitting next to him, encouraging him to sleep. I know that having suffered a head injury I will need four-hourly, neurological observations overnight and note that the nurses are late with my first set. This worries me and I start to feel alone and vulnerable. What if I deteriorate without being detected? I call one of them over and remind her of my needs.

The nurse smiles.

"You're fine. We'll do them if we need to." But I DO need them! I scream in my head.

"I really would feel better if you could," I say.

"Don't you worry. We're keeping an eye on you," the nurse replies firmly, then leaves.

I am forced to just accept her reassurance. You're on your own here, I think to myself. I am now focused on surviving the night. I really was scared at what faced me, having no agency or control over my predicament. I simply had to trust the system but knew from my experience as a doctor that it was pretty much broken.

My mind again begins to wander, but this time I close my eyes and become lost, recalling my era of training during the mid-eighties. It was the height of Thatcherism. Division pervaded the political and cultural discourse with a very clear north-south split and deeply divided local communities. Music from that era echoes round my head: the New Romantic movement, Duran Duran, Billy Bragg, The Jam and The Specials… Soft Cell. I am fully transported back to my entrance into the noble profession of medicine.

CHAPTER TWO:

THE BIRTH OF AN NHS DOCTOR

I awoke hot, sweaty and smelling of stale beer. I looked at my watch its 7 am. I forced two glasses of water down my neck and left my companions in their alcohol-fueled slumber. The drive back to the hospital started well until I hit the morning traffic queues. The breeze in my face from travelling freely along the dual carriageway with the car window down had been invigorating, but now that I was stationary, a less than pleasant feeling arose from my stomach. I suddenly felt incredibly hot and a passage of bitter, acid liquid rose towards my throat. I panicked, stopped, and quickly leant out of the door, depositing my stomach's contents onto the tarmac below. I then immediately kicked into survival mode, repeating to myself, "Must get to the hospital quickly and lie down."

Boston's 'More Than a Feeling' starts blasting out of the radio, as I struggled to find a parking space. Finally, in desperation, I forced the car up onto a grass verge and ran into the hospital, clinging to my white coat. It was 8.55 am and the departing house officer was there to greet me.

This was the pinnacle of five years' training and an investment of one hundred thousand pounds, allowing me to finally call myself a doctor in the NHS. I had trained and qualified as a doctor. The focus of my world was now a District General Hospital where I was to start as a medical student locum house officer in medicine. I was apprehensive but excited to finally see what working as a junior doctor would be like. However, my ability to be responsible and have self-control, I knew was my Achilles' heel. This was exemplified by my current hangover. I had vowed to stay for one beer the previous night and to then get a good night's sleep in readiness for my first day. In the blink of an eye, however, I had found myself locked in the local public house with a pot-bellied, jaundiced landlord listening to my fellow medical student singing Irish ballads. The joviality of the moment seeming to have the greater pull than my plan to get an early night in view of my medical student locum. The consequence of my poor self-control was that I had become completely intoxicated and spent the night fully clothed on my friend's floor. I was now bleary-eyed, shattered and about to start work as a doctor.

"You the medical student locum?" "Yes," I blurted out.

"Everything's quiet enough. Here's your ward bleep and the crash bleep."

I took them and he was gone. A fresh feeling of panic gripped me and then another familiar feeling arose from my guts. I ran to my on-call room, emptied the remaining contents of my stomach into the toilet and then staggered over to the bed. I lay there praying God, please don't let the crash bleep go off.

For ten minutes all was silent, and calm returned to me. I would be OK if I could get a little sleep, I told myself.

Then suddenly the room echoed with a piercing shriek and a voice akin to Big Brother roared out "Cardiac arrest, ward 24!" Then, just in case once was not enough, it repeated itself.

Terror struck me. I pulled on my white coat, my badge of honour and made sure that several newly purchased books covering every emergency known to man were wedged securely in my pocket. I headed out of the on-call room and down the stairs to the main corridor. The bleep went off again, right in front of passing nurses. I started moving hesitantly to my right, realising I had no idea where ward 24 was. The nurses, seeing the panic in my eyes, pointed in the other direction and sniggered, hopefully because they could sense my fear and not because they were close enough to smell me.

"Thanks," I blurted and started to move to the left with a hesitant gait.

I was still gripped with panic. What if I arrive first? That was my ongoing nightmare.

Then, as if manna had fallen from heaven, I saw another white coat moving quickly in front of me. Must be the registrar, I thought, and suddenly my movement became more confident, and, like a good eight hundred-metre runner, I slid effortlessly into his slipstream.

"You the locum?"

"Yes," I replied proudly.

"Best follow me, then."

We ran quickly to a stairwell. "Up here's the back way."

We both hit the stairs at great speed but on the third flight we're confronted with tarpaulin-type plastic sheeting blocking our path.

"Shit! Building works."

Then, the registrar leapt onto the outside of the bannister and catapulted round the tarpaulin. I took a deep breath and followed his example.

We finally arrived on ward 24. I was breathing heavily and very light-headed.

"Over there!" shouted a nurse as she pointed to a bay at the opposite end of the ward.

This was it! In the bay the rhythmically billowing curtains were drawn round the bed as frenetic activity occurred unabated from the confined space within. The registrar moved beyond the curtains, and I followed. The sight that confronted us was of a huge gentleman, adorned with greying locks, prostrate on the bed. A young house officer was leaping up and down on his chest, while a nurse tried to deliver oxygen via a facemask. The registrar appeared to take the chaotic scene fully in his stride, and immediately restored order to the resuscitation. Cardiac arrest was confirmed on the monitor, the patient intubated, and the house officer instructed on cardiac massage. I looked on in awe. My wonder was short-lived when the curtains were thrust back to reveal a short, stocky, fearsome looking sister, attired in the customary dark blue uniform.

"This one's not for resus." The sister announced curtly.

The registrar turned.

"Why in God's name was a resus call sent out then?"

The house officer looked sheepish and went bright scarlet.

"Look," said the sister, producing the patient's notes where you could clearly see written 'DNR – Do not resuscitate. Terminal bladder cancer'.

She then turned to her colleague.

"We should get them all tattooed with 'DNR' on their forehead and just to make sure, tattoo 'Can't you bloody read?' on their chest!"

We all stopped what we were doing, and the registrar instructed myself and the house officer on how to intubate the sadly recently deceased patient. This part was a boost to my ego as I managed to do it first time and the registrar promised that I could practise a central line insertion if there was another arrest. This way of teaching was common practice and clearly gave junior doctors hands-on real-life experience in resuscitation techniques. It's not done these days, as practicing intubation and central line insertion on recently deceased patients is no longer considered ethically acceptable. Teaching these resuscitation technical skills now occurs on mannikins in a simulation centre.

Certainly, my baptism of fire that first morning as a locum made me realise that I could never have a repeat of this current hangover again and would need to be a lot more responsible going forward. My tendency to live for the moment, hoping all would be well, would just not cut it anymore. They were lessons I needed to heed and key components in practicing good medicine. Strangely, the cardiac arrest, although terribly sad, was also utterly exhilarating and I looked forward to the next one. I was now fully focused on any opportunities to improve my advanced resuscitation skills in life support. The act of intubating and inserting lines in the dead patient as a practice was never questioned at the time. The prevailing mantra was "That's just the way it is". The respect and humanity of death in this era was surpassed by the desire to perfect resuscitation techniques. Justification for this was improving our technical prowess may save the life of the next patient.

Briefly, I drift back into consciousness as the tea lady offers breakfast at 7.00 am. Cereal, together with limp, barely browned toast, are the choices that I eat with gusto. I had survived the night and had noted the observations were done at six-hourly intervals. At least they made some sort of effort, I mused to myself. This then became the pattern that followed, as days turned into weeks and I slowly became institutionalised following the routines of the ward, my free spirit slowly replaced with the NHS rhythm of observations – tea and meals on repeat every few hours. I am stripped of any individuality, wearing a tablecloth-like gown, fastened round me by impossible-to-undo back drawstrings. I am now just a barcode to be scanned before the four-hourly observation by the nurses. The four-hour rule is fully adhered to during the day. Most nurses are taking a mechanistic approach to their tasks, and I soon limit my interaction with them to simple pleasantries, holding out my arm without instruction when they approach. This reminds me of my house officer post when the workload was such that the temptation became to forget all human aspect of healthcare and just to see patients as tasks to be completed. My mind begins to move into my subconscious as I vividly recollect that first post as a house officer. As the ward juggernaut ploughed onward regardless with the daily tasks of care, feeding, toileting, washing, medication, ward rounds and observations, I have plenty of time to look back on those hugely hectic years.

CHAPTER THREE:

THE REALITY ZONE

I arrived at the District Hospital the evening before starting my house officer post. The hospital accommodation was a newly built terraced dwelling shared with four other doctors, three of whom I knew well and had trained with: Chris, Jane and Nick. The other inmate, Clive, was a senior house officer (SHO) in Surgery. He seemed initially friendly but soon revealed his obsessive and domineering personality traits.

Having heeded the lesson from my medical student locum, I went to bed early. However, I could not sleep, waking every hour in anticipation of starting work as a real doctor. The post I knew would be challenging as it was in one of the busiest hospitals in the region. The main attraction for me, was the expertise I would gain from a demanding job. I was enticed by the knowledge that one of the consultants was a professor of cardiology. A professorial post I felt would be prestigious and help in applications for future posts.

My medical student locum had taught me to take work seriously and prioritise it over everything else. Since the locum I kept ruminating about my cardiac arrest experience in the form of a recurring dream. The dream jolted me awake most mornings and comprised of the patient at the end of the arrest sitting up and ripping out the endotracheal tube and central line, before grabbing my arm and screaming: 'Don't you have any respect?'

I awoke at 6 am sweaty with palpitations. The continual feeling of butterflies in my throat prevented me from eating any breakfast. I pulled on my white coat, freshly ironed for the occasion, and started to laden it with what I deemed essential cargo. Emergency medicine handbooks, a pocket diary, a stethoscope, a tourniquet and in the lapel a red pin. The pin was something I never used but was considered useful in the assessment of visual fields by neurologists.

"Up early, Harry?" Chris mocked, still in his pajamas. "And look at your crisply ironed white coat. Very impressive!"

"First time for everything," I retorted.

"Even got the old red pin in your lapel. Harry, man, you seem to be prepared for everything. Bet that hasn't seen the light of day since your neurology firm."

"It's my lucky charm," I replied. "Reckon it'll protect me against the dark side."

Chris then pointed at all the books stuffed into my pockets. "What do you need those for?"

"Just in case," I mused.

"You're the only doctor I know who comes with a library card," and with that he retreated to his bedroom to get ready for his day.

I sat for half an hour while the others got dressed. Finally, we left the house and as we did so, I turned to my housemates, "NHS, here we come!"

On arrival at the hospital, our respective SHOs met us. I was working for three consultants, but only ever met two during the entire post. The two I did meet I saw later in first week on their ward rounds. The absentee consultant, to my disappointment, was the cardiology professor. He worked at another hospital in the town. He rarely ventured to the District Hospital to see patients admitted under his name. He acted arrogantly, leaving these patients' day to day care to his senior registrar. I never met him and yet, as other juniors had forewarned me, he was willing to give me a reference when I left the post. This falsehood, a reference being sent from someone whom I had never met, started to prey on my mind. It began to destroy my faith in the integrity and transparency of the profession. This absence of consultant input into day-to-day care of their patients was common at that time, with senior registrars acting in their place.

Today, the senior registrar grade has completely gone, and consultants see every patient under their care. All junior doctors also have consultant mentors, so the absence of consultant presence, something I repeatedly experienced while training, is now, thankfully, a historical footnote.

The SHO I had been assigned was a blond haired, well spoken, athletic looking man called Simon. He quickly produced a list of thirty patients scattered throughout the hospital for me to see, most of them on ward 69, the respiratory ward.

He introduced himself.

"Hi, Harry, my name's Simon Merriott, SHO for general medicine. You'll be working for three consultants; Dr Bailey, he's great and understanding; Dr Doli more serious; and Professor Satori, who you'll never see as his patients are managed by his senior registrar, Will. He's great, though."

I was desperate to question Simon about the absentee Professor Satori but he was in full flow.

"We're as mad busy as always right now," he said. "All patients need to be seen every day and bloods done…" he paused, "…Oh and, by the way, we're on acute take tomorrow."

He showed me the various ways to get to all the wards spread throughout the hospital campus.

Ward 69, the respiratory ward, was a single-storey, prefab, wooden building with a veranda, dating from World War II. It was set two hundred metres from the main hospital building and looked out over a green lawn. The ward housed patients with smoking-related cancers, chronic obstructive airway disease, asthma and occupational lung diseases such as silicosis, and pneumoconiosis.

The ward, whatever the weather, had a welcoming party of men huddled by the entrance on the verandah smoking whilst attached to oxygen supplementation. They displayed great skill in taking one breath from the oxygen mask or nebuliser and then several puffs from their cigarettes. The ward inside was packed with endless rows of elderly patients clinging to their gurgling oxygen supplies. Most of the patients looked frail and extremely old. In fact they were only in their fifties and early sixties. Today this would be considered comparatively young.

"One other thing... we give all intravenous drugs in the hospital out of hours. There's always a house officer on call for this and you'll get to enjoy that pleasure soon enough. That's it. Good luck. I'm due in clinic, so page me if you need me." And with that Simon smiled and left.

Nowadays new doctors spend a full week shadowing the junior doctor in post. During this week they receive a comprehensive induction programme including meetings with their consultant mentor. In 1986, starting work felt very much like being thrown into the deep end of a pool without a buoyancy aid to see if you would sink or swim, with absolutely no regard for patient safety.

I started to introduce myself to the patients and commenced routine tasks such as bloodletting and re-siting of intravenous lines. They are plastic tubes inserted into veins for access to the circulation. They are essential to give drugs and fluids intravenously. My locum experience meant I was familiar and competent at these basic procedures. This was something I was particularly pleased about. At lunch, I heard that one house officer, an Oxford graduate, had been found trying to insert an intravenous into a vein downwards away from the heart. This was a highly dangerous elementary error.

In the afternoon I was shown by my registrar how to do a pleural biopsy. This was an advanced procedure that involved a special needle inserted aseptically into the chest to obtain tissue from the lung. The tissue could then be tested for cancer or tuberculosis (TB). After the procedure the registrar said I could have a go at the next one. This brought me a stomach-churning feeling of anxiety. This was, after all, only my first day. The expectation that I could handle such a procedure with little experience was somewhat overwhelming.

By the time it got to 5 pm, my official finish time, I still hadn't seen all patients under my care. I therefore ploughed on regardless reviewing notes, writing blood forms, labelling bottles and sourcing needles for the bloodletting in preparation for the next day. At 7 pm, I finally left, returning home extremely hungry, exhausted but delighted to have survived my first day!

The next day I went into the hospital early, a necessity to keep up with the clinical work. I arrived at 7 am and began the bloodletting for the day. The exchanges with patients were already getting shorter and more to the point, as time pressure started to pervade the huge lists of tasks to be completed before the ward round began.

"Morning, Mr. Smith, I'm Dr Stone. Just need to take some blood I'm afraid," I said jovially to the first patient.

"Can't it wait? I'm having my breakfast," complained Mr Smith.

"Need it now, I'm afraid. Won't take long," I replied firmly.

I started to move the table that protruded over his bed to allow access to his arm. Hospital tables are like relics from the Stone Age with limited maneuverability. This table resisted my attempts to move it, until it suddenly gave way. The table catapulted to one side spilling its breakfast cargo - toast, cornflakes, yoghurt and tea all over the bed. Despite the mess I persevered taking blood. I apologised to the bewildered patient for the mess and retreated to the relative safety of the nurse's station.

My introductions from then on became shorter and more direct. My focus became on completing the morning bloodletting tasks rather than engaging with the patient.

"Just need to re-site your intravenous line Mrs Repton." "Hello Mr Lloyd, just need to do a heart tracing."

"Need to listen to your chest, sorry."

"Arm, please. I'm going to take blood."

During the morning my bleep had begun a metamorphosis from a sedate, intermittent, pleasant interruption into a raging monster, continually pulling at my coattails. The main subject of the bleeps related to the intravenous drugs (IVs). The IVs that should have been given at 6 am were now overdue by three hours. I finally caught up by 11 am, an hour before the next quota of IV drugs had to be given.

I was bleeped again. This time it was the Admissions unit, so I sped off to the main hospital, feeling very important but also quite nervous. This was to be my first 'fresh patient'. The patient had suffered a dense stroke. He was unable to communicate. I spoke with the family for some time gathering a history and tried to reassure them that everything would be OK. I was in full flow explaining his care when I was bleeped again. The dreaded IVs again ! I tried to not seem hurried but made a quick exit from my deep conservation with the family to speak with the nurses about IVs that were due.

All afternoon, I had to balance seeing patients with asthma, gastrointestinal bleeds, dizziness and myocardial infarcts, with the incessant demand for IVs. The on-call day moved seamlessly into the evening. I was joined by my SHO.

We clerked patients alternately like a tag team. The admission ward rapidly filled up with new patients. Those admitted earlier in the day were now decanted around the hospital to make space for yet further new admissions. Our clerking had to be rapid and succinct. The volume of patients meant we had to carry out investigations and administer treatments in rapid succession.

Medical history taking, I began to realise, is the bedrock of medicine. I learnt that taking a careful case history of patients was particularly important, especially on the respiratory firm. Respiratory disease could be caused by exposure to various noxious agents at work such as coal dust in miners, asbestos in roofers and china clay dust in cup handlers!

I also realised locality and distance was hugely important to most patients.

"Any relatives nearby?" I would ask.

"My sister's in Beesham but we hardly see her anymore. It's too far," would be a frequent response.

To my surprise Beesham was only a few miles away.

By 11 pm we had twenty-five patients admitted and still the admissions were coming in thick and fast. At midnight I met my SHO at the night-time cafeteria on the hospital campus. I had not eaten all day, but was soon tucking into greasy bacon, beans and chips. After this sustenance, it was straight back to clerking admissions.

At 2 am I managed to make it to the on-call room situated on the admissions corridor. I have never found these rooms conducive with sleep. I laid on the bed and within five minutes my rest was interrupted by a bleep from the ward about an imminent admission. As I lay back down, I drifted off to sleep knowing my slumber would be short lived. The on-call room was strategically positioned to prevent rather than encourage sleep. You would be woken by the sirens and flashing lights of an ambulance arriving with a patient. This was followed by the sound of chirpy ambulance staff unloading their precious cargo. And then by the creaking of the wheels of the ancient patient trolley conveying the patient to the ward. I would often lie still in a state of suspended anticipation listening to these sounds waiting for the inevitable bleep from the ward to see the new arrival. If this was not enough disturbance the on-call room, was conveniently sited next to the staff rest room. This meant the chatter of nurses on their break percolated constantly through the walls. The bed consisted of a firm foam mattress clad in two well used sheets and a blue thin blanket. The room was hot, heated by antiquated radiators that were permanently on which made the atmosphere stifling.

At 3.30 am I was bleeped to see another admission. I wandered onto the ward and started clerking an elderly lady who reminded me very much of my own grandmother. A wave of fatigue washed over me, but I managed to fight it. Again, it came and soon the monitors became blurry, and I felt warmth envelop me. A hand on my shoulder suddenly startled me. It was a nurse.

"Wake up, doctor!"

I had fallen asleep on the lady's lap. She had waited five minutes to see if I would wake of my own volition and then rung the emergency bell. I had hit rock bottom but am pleased to say that never again have I fallen asleep on the job!

Sleep deprivation and its negative impact on cognitive functioning is now well recognised. At 3 am a doctor's thinking and decision-making is at its lowest ebb. Doctors are often unaware of this. It is worrying that doctors at 3 am despite their tendency to cognitive impairment, have more confidence in their decision making than at any other time of day or night. Clearly this is concerning for patient safety. Today this issue is slowly being addressed to mitigate risk for patients of poor clinical decisions. The skeleton service covering our hospitals at night does not help. This consists of a few senior nurses and very junior doctors without good senior medical support covering unfamiliar wards and patients throughout the hospital. Adjusting Work schedules and rotas to incorporate rest periods early in a night shift have been shown to improve performance of doctors. There is still some reluctance to accept the need for rest periods especially from senior nurses and doctors. This reluctance goes to the heart of the issue which is about attitude among senior staff and managers. The senior staff who themselves have endured long hours portrait junior work schedule as easy in comparison to their abusive experience as juniors. Seniors ignore the science of cognition and changes to schedules are not prioritised. Interestingly if we were discussing cognition and an airline pilot, we all without exception, would want the pilot to be rested and supervised when flying a plane with 500 passengers at 3 am!

Any junior doctor from any era will tell you there is something magical about the dawn. It is usually a time of calm and, of course, usually heralds the end of a brutal shift. That first night was no exception, I watched the transition to a new day, while chasing results and checking patients. I felt so tired. I should have been heading home after such a frenetic busy sleep deprived night. But no, the shift did not end till 5 pm. The early morning calm was just a prelude to the climax of the previous twenty-four hours endeavor- the consultant ward round.

At 8.30 am, Dr Bailey introduced himself. He was a middle-aged portly man who wore circular spectacles. He was clad in a tweed suit that emanated a smell of tobacco. He concealed a pipe strategically in his trouser pocket. I noted he always washed his hands between patients but wore a long-sleeved shirt with cuff links and a college tie throughout the ward round.

His attire today is replaced with short sleeved shirts, no ties and vigorous hand washing between patients.

I led him to see the first patient, accompanied by the ward round entourage, consisting of an SHO, registrar and senior nurse. The patient was the man with the dense stroke who I had clerked in at the beginning of my on-call stint. I relayed his history and the clinical findings. However, before I had time to finish, Dr Bailey had pulled back the curtains surrounding the patient.

"So, we are maintaining regular obs. but I have seen the patient deteriorate significantly overnight," I continued.

"You can say that again. He's dead!" Dr Bailey muttered quietly. He then nodded to the registrar who went off to talk to the relatives.

I felt utterly traumatised but for now I had to keep my emotions in check. We were weaving our way through the ward at speed, back and forth between the patients who all seemed to be deteriorating rapidly before my eyes. I really was panicking about losing another one. At 12.30 am we broke for lunch with a plan to reconvene in an hour to complete the round. At lunch I met the registrar who had been dealing with the relatives of the man who had died.

"Nothing you could have done," he said. "Just remember, always paint a picture that's blacker than it is. If the patient survives, the relatives will thank you for saving them. If the patient dies, they still thank you for trying to save them against the odds." I thought they were very profound words and have always remembered them.

The round eventually finished at 3.30 pm when I had to go off to see my other consultants' patients as well as carry out jobs from the round. I finally left the hospital at 7.30 pm, utterly shattered and functioning purely on autopilot. This state of mind became a common occurrence during this six-month post. I drove to a supermarket and just about managed to guide a trolley round, grabbing nothing more than processed junk that I might be able to eat quickly. Back at the house I discussed the day's events with my housemates over a few beers. The alcohol ameliorated the fatigue and finally I was anaesthetised enough to collapse into an uninterrupted well-earned slumber.

The next day in I had sixty patients under my care scattered across the hospital campus. To see them all everyday became an impossible challenge. I remember one poor gentleman that I failed to track down for three days. I eventually found him on one of the Psychiatric wards. Jobs came in thick and fast; the ward rounds very much the domain of the registrars and SHOs.

Patients saw me as the visible member of the team, so put their trust in me. I remember vividly an occasion when I got a pleural biopsy result showing advanced cancer in a sixty-year-old man, an ex-teacher. I informed the SHO who told me to tell the patient the result as he was busy. With great apprehension I spoke with the teacher and his wife. I tried to do everything right. I found a room separate from the ward and discussed it with the nurses prior to the disclosure, but the nurses were then too busy to join me for the actual chat. It was one of the worst moments of my life, breaking such huge news alone. To my surprise, the couple simply thanked me for letting them know and for being so honest with them. I recoil with horror now. To think back on just how inappropriate, it was for someone so junior to deal with such a matter.

Breaking bad news is something taken far more seriously these days. Senior doctors lead these conversations, and it is recognised that allowing time, careful preparation and full support to deal with the inevitable emotional responses, are key to handling it properly.

The next day after lunch I got a bleep to attend the mortuary. This was sited opposite ward 69 but was very much unmarked. The building looked more like a converted garage. I pressed the intercom and announced my arrival.

"All right, doc," came the cheery voice of the mortuary assistant. A very jovial, thin man, draped in a green apron over a white suit and wearing oversized wellies, ushered me into the inner sanctum. There, much to my horror, I spotted the patient who had been missing from my morning round, lying on the concrete slab with his inner organs exposed. The pathologist who was huddled over him peered up toward me.

"Any history on this one?"

"Err, heart failure… or was it pneumonia?" I replied, desperately searching back through my memory bank.

"Want me to tell you?" he asked unceremoniously, before removing the lungs and squeezing them out, fluid gushing forth. "Poor bugger drowned," he pronounced. I was fully deflated, but I certainly learnt to know a patient's history inside and out before even entering the inner sanctum of the mortuary again.

Today, doctors rarely attend post-mortems. This is largely due to a change in pathology services and the loss of its prominence in medical training. Although a really challenging experience, I feel it's loss from routine training is disappointing.

I was now on a one-in-three rota with either an on-call night for admissions or second-on, which entailed giving IVs and covering those patients already admitted. My first scheduled second-on call fell on a weekend. That Saturday morning, I was awoken by my bleep. Bleary eyed and half-conscious I rang the hospital and was put through to a nurse.

"Six o'clock IVs due ward 64," she announced with some force.

"OK." I peered at my watch it was 8 am, my shift started at 9 am.

"I will be with you soon "I said through gritted teeth.

This was taster of the day to come as second on. I moved from ward to ward giving out IV drugs. On some wards the nurses had everything laid out already and would help by identifying which patients needed IV medication. On others, my arrival seemed to be met with utter disdain.

"You're late… IVs are in the cupboard – haven't had time to get them out. Here are your drug charts."

The giving of the IVs became utterly mind-numbing and inevitably led to me taking short cuts. 'Infuse slowly over five minutes' became 'push hard over thirty seconds'. By 7 pm, having done the late 6 am round, then the 12 am, the 2 pm and the 6 pm IVs throughout the hospital, I was bleeped to an unfamiliar ward. I attended and was told that chemotherapy was to be given. I was not familiar with the administration of these drugs and told the nurse who had handed me the drug charts.

"I'm not familiar with giving chemo" I said hesitantly.

"The sister who does it is busy, so you'll just have to make it up. Doxorubicin and methotrexate, please."

I consulted my *British National Formulary* and started to prep the drugs. When I had finished the nurse peered round at me in the side room on the ward.

"Those goggles and apron were for you to wear," she sighed.

I left disgruntled and dissatisfied. I felt like Pavlov's dog my bleep wedded to the IVs. I had no time to reflect as I found myself on the phone almost immediately to answer the next bleep.

Every house officer was furious about this system of IV giving. I therefore drew up a letter on behalf of all the house officers outlining to the management the patient safety issues related to doctors giving all the IVs. The letter was signed by all the juniors and led to a meeting with the medical director of the hospital. He thanked us for our concerns and agreed that the present system 'was not optimal'. This was rather understating things. He said he hoped to rectify things during our six-month post. I felt exhilarated that he promised to change things and proudly fed back his comments to my colleagues. Once again, I was to be disappointed about senior medical consultants keeping their word. The IVs were not rectified during my time there. The resolution of this issue only came a year later when a patient on ward 69 died following a delay in the administration of an IV. This disaster was predictable and avoidable but at last led to nurses giving routine IVs.

The screeching noise of a medicine trolley drags me back into the present. It's the medication round and a nurse, dispensing drugs, enters my bay alongside a senior sister daubed in a red vest covering her uniform, saying 'Do not disturb. Medicine round'. They approach each patient. The intravenous drugs have been carefully drawn up and checked.

Today, doctors rarely give IVs as nursing staff now mostly do it. Trained practitioners only, give chemotherapy, not a passing junior doctor. These drugs are pre-prepared by the pharmacy and never drawn up on the ward. The complaint to the hospital hierarchy about the IVs was the first time I had felt agency. All the juniors who signed the letter were hopeful change would occur during our six-month posts. It however was not forthcoming. The medical director, knowing we were only there for six months, just pushed the issue into the long grass. We did inform the juniors that followed us about the changes the medical director had agreed. However, to our frustration, yet again, it was still not implemented. It took a death of a patient and the family to lodge a complaint for change to finally occur. Once again, the integrity and honesty of the seniors in the profession, in my eyes, was becoming questionable.

I took some more painkillers gratefully and sailed back to reflecting on my early years.

During my first shift as second on call I was summoned to a geriatric ward late at night. I had been asked to certify a patient, so I trudged upstairs.

"Over there," a nurse said, pointing to the far dimly lit and rather forbidding reaches of the ward. I grabbed the notes, managed by some miracle to find an ophthalmoscope that was working, and headed to the end of the ward.

The patient, a man who had cancer and had lost his hair during chemotherapy, was hidden behind drawn curtains. I peered round and surveyed the scene. He was sitting up still and bathed in the moonlight pouring in from the window. This, combined with the low rhythmical rumble of snoring in the adjacent bed, gave a serene air to the situation. Nevertheless, it did not take much for me to see that he was no longer with us. I fumbled for my stethoscope, trying to focus on certification of death. I leant forward to place my stethoscope on his chest and, as I did so, he fell forward onto me.

"He's alive!" I gasped and sat on the bed trying to push the patient away.

My heart was pounding but I felt a ripple underneath me and realised he was being nursed on a waterbed. The act of sitting on the bed to examine him had displaced the water on one side and as a result propelled him toward me. I quickly tried to regain control and dignity for the patient and then carried out the certification, my heart in my mouth.

On my return to the nurses' station, I was greeted with muffled laughter.

"You OK, doctor? That must have given you a shock!"

My six months in this District hospital was a steep learning curve, but very much a case of learning through experience. Teaching was infrequent since everyone was so busy. The comradeship between junior doctors was great but associated with ladles of cynicism. Looking back on it now, the six-month post was far removed from anything experienced today. We regularly had forty-plus patients with nothing more than the backup of a registrar in another hospital, and so frequently ended up taking responsibility beyond our training or experience. The consultant contact was intermittent, despite regularly working one hundred-plus hours per week. The administration of IV drugs was still a major bugbear and was tantamount to abuse.

My housemate, Chris, once said to me when he had sixty patients in the hospital at one time and was on-take:

"This is just like being at war."

"No," I responded, "we chose to do this."

Life outside work (yes, there was some!) revolved around trying to blot out what was going on at the hospital. I drank, partied and took in the wonders of the town I now called home. I was chronically sleep deprived. I remember once going to the local rep theatre with Jane and Chris to see *Amadeus,* but by the end of the play, both Chris and I were fast asleep. This scenario was often repeated in cinemas and any place that was warm and dimly lit.

During my time in the post, I broke up with a long-term girlfriend who was also a doctor. This was difficult, but in view of the intensity of the work, something of a relief. The demands of the post were such that time off was fully focused on recovery and seeking numbness through alcohol. New relationships were hurried and not well thought out. My resilience to mitigate the emotional challenges of the post left no room for developing a meaningful liaison. This led to short relationships, which eventually fell on barren land.

I got involved with a junior doctor revue, which we performed in a local theatre. The sketch, I was involved in, summed up much about the system for junior doctors at that time and was based on a government heroin addiction broadcast. I appeared on stage as a well-attired, junior doctor and announced,

"I'm on a one-in-six, I can handle it."

I would then appear again more dishevelled.

"I'm on a one-in-two. Just got a bit of a cold at the moment. Can't sleep but what the hell? Who needs it?"

I then appeared totally dishevelled, black under my eyes with white talc over my face and hair.

"I'm on a one-in-one. My SHO is dead in the next on-call room. My registrar is lost, presumed dead and my consultant has never been found. I can handle it...", then a pause with a lingering harrowing look at the audience, "...can't I?"

Then a *Big Brother*-type voice would say,

"You think you can control Medicine till Medicine controls you!"

Despite the ongoing issues, the experience at the end of the six months gave all of the junior doctors a great deal of confidence with emergency situations. On my last on-call, I recall being bleeped up to the Psychiatric wards for a cardiac arrest. The ward was beyond ward 69, and having sprinted, I found I was the first of the arrest team to arrive. One of my fellow trainees from the Midlands Medical School was fumbling around with the resuscitation alongside a nurse. I took control, confirmed an arrest on the monitor, instructed them on cardiac massage and intubated the patient.

"Well done," came the voice of the registrar behind me.

The outcome was sadly unsuccessful and so we all practised intubation and insertion of a central line.

I have come a long way, I thought. I have met my nemesis of being the first on the scene and conquered it.

My final memories of the District Hospital were of being on-call on the last night and having to start work as a house officer in Surgery in a neighbouring city the next day. I tried to change the rota at both hospitals to give me a break but that was apparently unacceptable. I then went to the mess party to say goodbye and was left with the image of the SHO dancing to Duran Duran, a beer in one hand, cigarette in the other, with the 'ward and crash bleep' clipped to either ear.

A lot has changed since my house officer post for the better. Today there are reduced hours and better training and supervision in the daytime. However, out of hours especially at night junior doctors often feel isolated and undervalued. This is due in part by the 'Hospital at night scheme'. This initiative was instituted to reduce doctors hours to comply with theEuropean Working Time Directive. It has led to a skeleton team made up of junior doctors and senior nursing staff covering the whole hospital at night with a shift pattern of working. The result has been junior doctors working more antisocial hours and having less visible senior support out of hours. This has meant less interaction of juniors with their allocated consultant or clinical team. When arriving on a night shift, juniors often find that they do not know who the consultant covering is or any of the patients!

The long hours culture I experienced in my house officer post did have some benefits. There was better peer group camaraderie, patient continuity and senior doctor team interaction. Socialisation was easily available through the doctors' mess and canteens. During a night shift, differing specialities would meet up and your network of doctors would be wide and varied. Today, out of hours food is usually from a vending machine and doctors' messes are either non-existent or poorly attended as many doctors now commute to work rather than live in. The well-being of doctors is becoming of paramount importance in the present clinical arena. Feelings of being hungry, angry, lonely and tired at work are common complaints among juniors. Some flagship hospitals have started addressing the issue with an initiative known by the acronym HALT. [7] Solutions to this crisis include reinvention of the medical team or firm-junior doctors need feel valued within a team. There is a need to improve sociability of rotas; provide ready access to healthy cooked food twenty four seven; establish rest facilities and easy access to mental health support. Doctors after a night shift should be able to rest on site before travelling home especially if driving. Every year doctors die from road traffic accidents on the way home from a night shift. Many seniors are not fully committed to a well-being agenda for junior doctors. They question the resilience of juniors, calling them 'Generation Snowflake'. This is misplaced, as the issue for junior doctors is the toxic workplace conditions and NOT individual doctor's resilience. There is a need for all staff to address this well-being agenda urgently. If we do not, we risk disenfranchising a whole generation of doctors.

I suddenly wake again as a young woman dressed in a white coat approaches my bed. It's 7.30 am and her manner is thoughtful and curious.

"Dr Stone, I'm Bella, the pharmacist. Just want to check your medicines." She is well-spoken, polite, focused and makes good eye contact.

She methodically goes through my meds, questioning me thoroughly and explaining her role in checking through everything I am currently taking. I am impressed and realise that, as a doctor, I was never really that aware of her or her colleague's role on the ward.

My lack of knowledge about other professionals' role on the ward is a common issue with doctors, nurses and allied health professionals. All healthcare professionals inhabit the same clinical arena but act like differing tribes instead of forming a cohesive team. It can be described as 'pseudo team'; in other words, the professionals may look like a team but show very few characteristics of one. This seems strange as it is known teamwork is essential for effective patient care. The reality of building a cohesive team remains a major challenge even today. Doctors and nurses and pharmacists are trained separately so rarely interact meaningfully until they meet in the workplace.

The pharmacist who had given rise to this thought sat at my bedside talking to me at some length. I noted that she had taken the time to listen and talk, unlike the doctors and nurses who are always busy following the ward agenda.

I ask about discharge medications and potential delays to discharge. Often on my paediatric ward, the discharge medications would often be late arriving. I beg for my medications to be ready early on my own day of discharge. I explain that when I am well and back at work, we can do an audit on the children's ward together and she is particularly enthused at the prospect. When we finished talking, the nurses commenced another set of observations and I return to my dream world and my first house job in surgery.

Chapter Four:

Surgical Transition

My next port of call was to be at another district hospital. I was to be a house officer for three months in urology and then three months in surgery. At 9 am on that first Sunday morning I found my way to the Surgical ward. On arrival, a senior sister met me and coolly announced that there were eleven urology patients and six breast patients to be seen. I tried to look enthusiastic but realized it was going to be a marathon clerking session.

The urology patients were, for the most part, elderly gentlemen with prostate problems. The clerking was very repetitive, mostly involving a steady flow of questions about the strength of their urinary stream. 'How frequently do you go? Do you have urgency? Can you hit a wall at one yard? Do you dribble?' These questions echoed round the ward. One of my predecessors had been reprimanded for lining up all the gentlemen with prostate problems, opening all the notes at once and asking the above questions just once, while noting their responses in turn! Despite the repetitive nature of the history-taking, I found I quite enjoyed the morning talking to these pleasant and interesting men.

I was expected to consent the patients, but of course had little familiarity or experience of the procedures being proposed or the likely complications. I tended to focus on issues regarding the anaesthetic, as this was one area I could understand, repeatedly using the phrase:

"You consent for anything deemed necessary to be given to help you should there be any life-threatening complications?"

All the patients signed without question.

Once again, I shudder at the thought of this and thankfully, nowadays, the emphasis is very much on informed consent taken by the surgeon operating.

By the end of the morning, despite feeling tired, I was satisfied with the work I had done, however, just as I was about to go for lunch, the sister explained that all the urology patients now required bloods and those over sixty (all eleven of them) would need an electrocardiogram (ECG). An ECG is a heart tracing which assesses the rhythm and conduction of the electrical activity of the heart. My own heart sank, but I began bloodletting and putting the antiquated ECG machine through its paces. At 5 pm I finally finished on the Urology ward and moved onwards to the Female Surgical ward.

This ward had a completely different feel to Urology. The most striking thing I noticed was the age of the patients. They were all young women. It was visiting time when I arrived, and draped around each bed were families, often young children and anxious husbands. One woman, only thirty-two years old, was particularly striking in that her head was fixed in flexion with her chin stuck down on her chest. She had breast cancer with a secondary spread in her cervical spine and had had metal rods inserted to try and stabilise the spine, but these had become infected.

I gathered the notes for the six women due for breast lump removal and began clerking. This time each consultation was packed full of tension. The women would ask me questions, which I felt impotent to give an adequate answer to. I was expected to consent the patients but this time my bravado, which had been with me on the Urology ward, completely deserted me. I rang the registrar and explained that I was not happy to consent the patients: 'Don't worry, we always go over consent again', he had reassured me. And so, with that stock phrase, 'Sign here, but someone will go through it in more detail tomorrow', I consented them all. The next day the list started early, and I later discovered that no one had actually had time to go over the consent.

Once again, during this era, senior doctors failed to understand the issues involved. Thankfully, this landscape is very different today and much of the work I describe is now carried out properly in a pre-admission clinic.

My initial three months were spent working with a Mr Payne, an aristocratic gentleman who always wore smart suits, a yellow tie and smoked cigars, even in the operating suite. The pace of the ward was slow compared to that at the General Hospital. The peaks of activity for myself occurred the day before his routine operating list when patients for surgery were admitted. Ward rounds with Mr Payne were leisurely affairs. He would introduce himself to all patients on the ward whether they under his care or not! If the patients were not under his care, he would simply say "Lovely to meet you but we must pass you by".

In theatre he was slightly more animated, but still retained a leisurely and regal approach. His operations to remove a kidney (nephrectomies) were renowned to be prone to bleeding. I assisted him with one such operation and, having removed the kidney, it was obvious that there was still much oozing of blood into the abdomen. He then looked up at the clock and announced, 'Times like this, you have to just have a steady nerve and close up'.

This he did and two hours later the registrar was not unsurprisingly taking the patient back to theatre to stem intra-abdominal bleeding. Meanwhile Mr Payne was operating at a private hospital on the other side of town. On the ward round the next day Mr Payne visited the patient on the Intensive Therapy Unit (ITU). The ITU doctor gave a comprehensive account of the intense post operative care the patient required including the lifesaving units of packed cells and clotting factors. Mr Payne listened, then simply muttered,

"Still like to see some more red stuff going in."

On a positive note, the main lynchpin of the urology team was a senior registrar called Will. He did some teaching and provided structure to the job. The SHO on the firm, on the other hand, was a very arrogant, red-faced doctor who had moved down from Scotland. He considered this hospital terribly provincial and at every opportunity would expound his experience under a famous Scottish-based surgeon. Senior and junior medical staff alike found him hugely irritating and the impact on the team was unlike anything I had encountered before. He was, in my opinion, technically a good, young surgeon but his arrogance, insensitivity, offhand manner and inability to empathise or listen to fellow staff caused much team anguish. Unfortunately, this surgeon seemingly had no insight into his negative impact and the consultants supervising him, apart from muttering behind his back, never addressed the issue of his behaviour. In fact, the mutterings mainly consisted of how they could try and ensure he moved out of the region as quickly as possible.

My experience of working with him simply hardened my own belief in myself, giving me a strong feeling of worth and agency. I was determined not to be bullied and so stood up to him when he made unnecessary demands, which were frequent. This strategy worked well, and I think he grudgingly accepted and respected my non-acquiescence. At the end of the three months, he invited my fellow house officer and I round for a meal at his home. I realised, talking to him outside work, that he had no insight at all on how he was perceived. These issues continued unaddressed and never once seemed to hinder his progress through the system to consultancy. At consultant level, issues with his behaviour did eventually come to a head leading to serious consequences, but lower down the ranks he progressed totally unchallenged.

Today, annual appraisal for all doctors is mandatory. If it had been in place at that time it would have clearly highlighted the behavioural issues much earlier in his career. It may have even allowed him to address the problems or, if not, have at least thwarted his progress through the system. I am convinced that corridor mutterings, with the attitude of 'let's just make him someone else's problem', now belong to a bygone era of consultancy, thank goodness.

Urology, being a specialist area of practice, is dominated by repetitive procedures but with hugely interesting patients. I would be called on occasions to see elderly men with enlarged prostates who had gone into acute retention of urine. These patients would be in extreme distress, but the passage of a urinary catheter could transform them. One elderly, ex-Spitfire pilot said, after the relief of his retention,

"You must love this job. You've just worked a bloody miracle!"

Excitement then hit the Urology ward with the admission of a patient for a sex change operation. Clifford was going to become Cherry. Clifford, when he arrived, was six foot tall with jet-black hair and a very visible outline of facial stubble. He was admitted to the female part of the ward and, within an hour, had an entourage of female urology patients gathered around, examining various toiletries scattered across the bed. He then changed into a long, flowing dressing gown, which seemed rather at odds with his very masculine bandy-legged gait. The operation engendered extreme interest among the nursing staff. On the day of the operation the nurses took turns to attend theatre as voyeurs. Post-operative care included twice-daily insertion of a dilator into Cherry's newly fashioned vagina. This was something that I carried out on my last weekend in Urology before moving on to my surgical firm.

Back in my new world as a patient, I drift in and out of sleep watching the ward pass by and thinking how much things had changed. This causes me to reflect to the next stage in my medical career and the house job in Surgery that follows.

Chapter Five:

Delivery is Everything: Getting Noticed

The surgeon on my general surgery firm was the one and only Mr Meakins. He had a reputation of being grumpy but fair. He had a very gnarled appearance with a wrinkled, ruddy face, slit-like eyes and a growl of a voice. His senior registrar, a swashbuckling Australian surgeon named Mr Smith, who was not only knowledgeable and great at surgery, but also an excellent communicator, led his firm. The firm's speciality was gastrointestinal and general surgery, and the week was very regimented but not so busy as to be unmanageable.

My major role was to set up the main operating list of the week every Wednesday. This involved working through the patient list to check the necessary investigations had all been done in time for the patients having their operation that week. There was never an issue with lack of beds or operating theatres time back then. The flow of patients was rarely disrupted, unlike today!

Nowadays operating lists are controlled by managers. The surgeon may never of met the patient they are operating on and not necessarily see them for follow up. This disconnect between surgeon and patient is a worrying trend and I feel needs to be reestablished. Surgery is more than just a technical procedure and continuity of care pre and post op is important for patient's confidence and trust in the service and for professional development of the surgeon.

During this post I got my first exposure to the outpatient clinics which I found hectic but fun. I also was scheduled each week to assist Mr Meakins. My main role in assisting during operations was to hold tightly on to a liver retractor. This held the liver away from the abdominal cavity. I would be hanging onto the retractor for hours . Mr Meakins during the operation would be continually moaning and intermittently yanking at the retractor saying,

"For God's sake, hold it properly, boy."

Apart from these utterances in theatre he otherwise said very little to me during most of my time on the firm. However, this changed with one event, a hospital cricket match.

In my last week on the firm, the annual cricket match between the two rival, local hospitals was to be played. Mr Meakins was the captain of our hospital's team and during a ward round he asked if I played cricket at all.

"Yes," I replied.

"Bat or bowl?" he grunted.

"Bowl."

"Good. We're desperate for bowlers. You're in."

So, one evening that week the match was played. The neighbouring hospital batted first, led by a raging consultant surgeon in thigh pads, helmet and with a crowing public schoolboy voice. Mr Meakins looked at him with contempt, turned to me and, with more animation than I had seen throughout the firm, said to me,

"Give it your best, son."

I ran in. The following moments seemed to pass by in slow motion. The ball hit the deck, moved between his bat and pad then hit the top of the middle stump. It was one of those champagne moments, arms flying up in the air with delight. Mr Meakins, for the first time, metamorphosed into a smiling, ebullient being.

"Well done, boy. Fantastic!"

The next two balls beat the bat and then I took another wicket with the same response, this time with much patting of my back. Then with the following over I repeated the exploit, taking three wickets in all.

Mr Meakins came over to me, beaming. "Better take you off or we won't have a game."

I was duly rested. Towards the end of the allotted twenty overs, the last wicket pair from our rival hospital were at the crease, with the surgeon's fourteen-year-old son seconded into the team, batting at number eleven. I was brought back on, and, in view of the boy's short stature and age, I bowled two gentle deliveries at him.

Mr Meakins was at first slip and, just as I was about to bowl the next ball, he juddered over to me.

"Stop messing about and give him a fast one," he growled.

The dilemma did not take much thinking about. I ran in and let fly, the boy moved out of the way and the wickets splattered. The following week on the firm, Mr Meakins was almost jovial and started to ask me with keen interest about jobs I would now be applying for as an SHO.

I awake again, startled by some commotion on the ward. An elderly man I share the bay with has started to wander about after his male nurse had taken a short break from his one-to-one overnight supervision.

I watch in horror as the patient walks over to another elderly man opposite me and urinates all over his bed. Straw-coloured urine cascades over the floor. I urgently press the red call button by my bed. The nurses respond, leaving their note-making behind a bank of computers. They herd the man back to his bed, call his minder and instruct a cleaner to mop the floor, the nurses sadly receiving a good deal of abuse from the man who has dementia. I am shocked that morning when I later find him urinating over my own bed. I feel scared and vulnerable once again so vent my outrage with the senior nurse.

"This is very common, I'm afraid," she says in a matter-of-fact way. "No one cares about us. We only see managers when it suits them and the doctors are only here for such a short time as they have patients scattered all round the hospital."

She is burnt out and her eye contact is of a resigned, defeated look. She then points to the plastic screens separating the nurses' station from the ward corridor.

"Took five months to get them installed. Our powers that be really are useless."

"Didn't you raise it with Mr Rangoon?" I ask. Mr Rangoon being the CEO of the Hospital Foundation Trust.

"He doesn't care unless it's anything that might involve a photo shoot. You've seen the state of A&E, haven't you?"

It completely appears to me at that moment that because the doctors flit in and out of the ward, never seeing the abuse and challenges faced by nursing staff, that these are not noticed let alone acted upon. I sit on my changed bed and slip into an uneasy morning slumber while recalling the next stage of my medical journey as I struggled to secure a SHO post.

Chapter Six:

REJECTION AND THE BLEAKNESS OF LIFE

Senior House Officer posts are the next stage of training following on from successful completion of a year as a house officer. *This can be a stressful time for many young doctors, as it is the time that they deviate from a pre-ordained path and their peer group. Some doctors will choose a path to train as a surgeon, others a physician and so on. I chose to train as a physician despite my bruising experience at the District hospital.*

So, I started applying to medical rotations throughout the U.K. including the District Hospital where I had been a house officer. On reflection I was surprised I applied to a hospital where I had experienced a post with such abusive demands. I think this has parallels with abusive domestic relationships where the victims will return to it despite the known patterns of behaviour and risks, they will endure.

This process of securing my next post was the first time I had to deal with rejection since applying for medical school. Either I was not shortlisted for jobs, or I attended the interviews and was unsuccessful. I travelled to interviews in Ipswich, Exeter, Stoke and Nottingham, but all were in vain. I would set off full of hope and expectation, then after the interview, wait, sometimes for several hours, only for the administrator to, one by one, ask the successful candidates back in, my name forever seemingly absent. In desperation at the lack of success, I started to apply for Casualty jobs. Once again, I headed off to far-flung interviews in London, Manchester and Birmingham. During my interview for a job at Dudley Road Hospital (now City Hospital), I was even asked if I knew any Hindi or Punjabi, since eighty percent of the population served by the hospital spoke these as their first language.

"No," I replied, "but I'd be willing to learn."

This was a desperate response and, quite rightly, a Punjabi-Speaking candidate got the job.

I therefore finished my house officer role and returned to the family home in South London, now fully unemployed. Unemployment was, to my mind, almost impossible to comprehend. I kept seeing friends who, after many applications, finally got posts, so I persevered. I was finally rewarded when I received a call for an interview at a northern city hospital. The interview went well, much as most of the others had in the past. However, this time I was the only candidate at the interview. I felt rejection this time was totally untenable. I will never forget the elation I felt when they did offer me the job. I had attended fourteen interviews and at last had struck lucky!

Understandably, my frustration with attending so many interviews had, however, taken some toll on my confidence and well-being. At one stage I was at such low ebb that I wrote this note in a recently rediscovered diary: 'I have finally reached a point in life where I face being utterly alone. How did it come to this? I seem to be struggling to just survive when I want to achieve. But how can I achieve with this constant pressure and demand of being a doctor in the NHS. At twenty five years old, my hands shake as I write this, I am at rock bottom, in debt with no job, split up with my girlfriend and seen my friends get posts scattered across the U.K. What will become of me?'

This note reflected my realisation that the training was all-encompassing. My last long-term relationship had ended at the beginning of my post at the district hospital. The demands of being on call for both of us, with one-in-three-night rotas, with associated sleep deprivation, difficulties in coordinating time off and a significant distance from each other were simply too overwhelming and destructive to ever survive. Our relationship floundered and when it was over it was something of a relief for the two of us.

For me, the demands of the job had meant that relationships were becoming superficial distractions, sporadic and never based on firm ground. At the District Hospital, downtime was now just a blur of alcohol-fuelled parties and pub outings with trophy relationships. This I knew was wrong, but my persona of caring and empathy for humanity had been left behind in the hospital wards and theatres. This loss of empathy and the realisation that the pathway ahead remained so tough made me deeply unhappy. As the note showed, I felt totally alone with no true, close friends. Who do you counsel when you have reached such an impasse? Luckily, the answer for me was family. I rang my sister and told her about my relationship breakup.

"Come see me, Harry," she said, inviting me to visit at her college in Oxford. Thankfully, the two days I spent in company with my sister and her friends were just what the doctor ordered. We laughed, drank and reminisced. It even reinvigorated me enough to sustain ploughing on at the district hospital and meant I was able to cast away to history the negativity of a broken relationship and my general malaise.

The year I spent as a house officer saw an era of huge responsibility in the clinical arena, or 'swamplands' as we called it – responsibility unfairly thrust upon newly qualified doctors without adequate support, induction or supervision. My seniors were aware of this but varied in their levels of sympathy. In the past, they had also been exposed to similar conditions themselves with heavy rotas and so, frustratingly, they saw it as being 'just the way it was'.

I learnt mainly by experience, my main mentors being the registrars and SHOs around me. Their approach, however, was often pretty gung-ho. For example, they 'taught' us, just the once, how to do a cardioversion of the heart for an arrhythmia and then expected us to go solo the next time. One senior SHO was renowned for turning away admissions, infamously sending home a civil dignitary with herpes simplex encephalitis. When he was the admitting registrar on call, he always prided himself in trying to divert patients away.

"Matthew, I've got a sixty-year-old man with central crushing chest pain and ST elevation in Lead 2, 3 and AVF. Wondering if you could take him for us?" This was a classic heart attack confirmed by the changes on the ECG and should have been his responsibility to deal with.

I could hear Matthew's heavy breathing over the phone. "How raised?"

"Never mind that. I'm telling you; he must be admitted."

I wake briefly as another round of tea is dished out in the bay.

Today a very different system is in place for inducting and training new NHS doctors. There are foundation training schemes, which run for two years, with four-month rotations in differing departments. This does give some stability to doctors but can lack the flexibility of stand-alone training posts, available in my era. An on-line, national application process, with interviews, does the foundation programme allocation of posts. It is usually only considered necessary when applying for speciality training. During the programme there is protected teaching, regular mentoring and work-based assessments with consistent feedback. Appraisals are 360-degree and include input from nursing staff as well. There is a guardian of safe working to deal with working hours, breaches and concerns. Doctors also have a clinical and educational supervisor; such a chasm between today's support and that experienced in the mid-eighties for house officer posts.

The bleep of an infusion pump alarm metronomically provides a piercing backdrop to the bustle of the corridor adjacent to the bay. No one responds to the alarm emanating from an unresponsive patient lying opposite me, who had already been marinated in urine earlier in the day. It is only me who reacts.

"Can you not hear that?" I ask a passing nurse. "We'll get to it as soon as we can," she replies.

Two hours later, the alarm still reverberates like some form of torture. Hospitals are noisy places. Recovery from your illness or injuries quickly becomes secondary to surviving the tortuous hospital environment. I bury my head into my pillow and drift back into my recollections of being a SHO in casualty.

Chapter Seven:

Welcome to the Frontline. SHO in A&E

The hospital was in the north side of the city. It was nestled among lonely banks of terraced houses. The land between the buildings was a wasteland of rubble, a result of past house clearances. The houses that still stood were alternately occupied and unoccupied. The unoccupied houses were boarded up with metal grilles which gave a menacing feel to this encasement of property. The whole vista effused chaos, deprivation and a loveless, forgotten terrain. The only shops close by were small newsagents and off-licences. The off licences were like banks. Their secure glass walls on the interior allowing only viewing of the alcohol and goods available. A drop box counter system allowed exchange of goods for money. The food on offer was mainly of the tinned variety, as this was not a place where anything fresh belonged. The whole ambience was an austere reality of an area which had seen better days.

My hospital accommodation was a room on the tenth floor of a block looking out over the wasteland, sharing a shower with an adjoining room. I had access to a communal kitchen with the eight other residents on my floor. The car park was at the base of the tower block but within the first week of living there, several cars had been stolen and one was completely burnt out. This shocked me but the locals were completely unperturbed. In that area, Ford cars were known as 'Ford takeaways'. Car theft and damage seemed rife, so locking up vehicles rapidly became an obsession.

The main social area was a pub opposite my accommodation block, which was a solitary building standing defiantly among the surrounding wasteland. The pub was a throwback from the Victorian era with a series of partitioned seating areas inside. It was a small pub seemingly full of endless private snugs. It was here that most medical and ambulance staff first met in the early evening to socialize. Often after a few drinks they would move on to sample the city's nightlife. The landlady's ancient attire and countenance made her seem very much part of the old building. She was elderly and had a hunched posture with her hair bound up in a bun, covered in a black knitted hairnet. Her voice, unlike her frail appearance, was booming, commanding and piercing. She was able to cut through any pub banter or dissent sent her way. Her scouse accent reverberated all night among the general hubbub of the punters drinking at the bar.

I spent many early evenings in this establishment. One Friday evening, a gang of workmen were drinking at the bar, totally caked in red brick dust acquired from the old school they were demolishing. The knocking down of this building meant that the pub was literally the only building standing in the vicinity of our accommodation. The resultant vista was truly like an apocalyptic scene from a World War II air-raid strike. The gang of workmen, that evening were soon fuelled up with pints of beer. They began to entertain anyone who would listen to them with familiar songs. The climax of the evening being a rendition of Tom Jones' 'Delilah' with everyone in the pub joining in. A communal expression of joy!

Casualty was certainly also a place to see 'Joe Public' in all his glory, an endless variety of conditions and clientele presenting. The booking system divided patients into Majors, those with life-threatening injuries or illnesses, and Minors for the rest. In Minors, the system of allocation of patients to doctors consisted of a pile of green cards stacked in a box. They were in chronological order with the patient's details and presenting complaint scrawled at the top of the card. The next doctor free would take the top card and call for the corresponding patient.

The presenting complaint was usually self-explanatory. For example: 'Injury to hand'. A few, however, took a while to ascertain, such as: 'Strange in manner'. This usually meant a patient with a psychotic mental illness or intractable psychosocial problems. These cards could sometimes spend ages in the box as doctors kept putting them under the top card to try and avoid seeing those patients.

The 'regulars' were a group of patients that were well known to the department, usually in the 'strange in manner' category. Initially, the new influx of doctors would spend a lot of time taking a full history and examination from these patients, but as time went by, their repeated attendance correlated with less and less information being recorded from their visits.

One day I came on duty at 8.30 am to be greeted by the receptionist saying:

"There's a man in here and he's not too well."

I wandered into the waiting area where a huddled figure in a worn, threadbare, dark jacket was sat propped up against the wall on one of the orange, fluorescent plastic seats, alongside several other patients. I approached him.

"How we doing?" I heard myself saying, as I picked up his cold hand.

He slumped forward and I struggled to keep him upright on the chair.

"Get a wheelchair and help, quick," I whispered to the now distressed receptionist.

Soon a small posse was gathered around. He had no pulse and was ice-cold.

"This way, Sir. We'll look after you now," I announced for the benefit of the other patients, as we wheeled him round to Majors and into the 'brought in dead' room.

He had clearly died some time ago. Apparently, he was a regular who had been seen the night before, after a fall. The doctor had then discharged him but, by then, he had missed the last bus home. The reception team had taken pity and agreed he could stay in the warm waiting area till the bus service resumed first thing in the morning. The receptionist taking over the next day was then alerted to his presence from a waiting patient who was concerned that the man did not look well and had not moved for some time. The doctor involved with his discharge was extremely worried he had missed something vital such as bleeding around the brain (a subdural haematoma). This is a slow accumulating blood clot, which can press on the brain and cause death, especially common in the elderly following a fall. The post-mortem, however, showed that he had died of a heart attack.

This episode emphasised the importance of consistently being thorough in clerking patients and never ignoring symptoms, even with the regulars.

Another type of regular attenders were 'the addicts'. Unfortunately, drug addiction was a common problem in the city. Some addicts would attend casualty and feign severe distress in the hope they would receive an opiate as pain relief. The nurses were hyperaware of this issue and were always looking for suspicious behaviour that indicated an addict just seeking an opiate hit. I did experience this type of regular and it taught me a lesson to always listen carefully to nursing staff concerns.

I was in Majors one day, when a young man presented with severe abdominal pain. After a morning of dealing with vague symptoms, this man, despite appearing to be in significant distress with his pain, gave a very clear history. He described pain radiating from the left loin to the left groin, colicky in nature and a score of nine out of ten on the severity scale. The history flowed as quickly as I asked the questions. *Renal colic*, I thought, and on autopilot I inserted a ventflon, took blood for investigations and then, despite the nurse expressing reluctance to give opiates, I gave intravenous pethidine as pain relief. I left the patient feeling very satisfied with the consultation; I had diagnosed his condition in good time and treated his pain promptly with an opiate, as the pain is known to be severe in renal colic. On my return ten minutes later, he was gone. The nurse smiled ruefully at me and said,

"I thought I recognised him, he's a regular. Another opiate addict, I'm afraid."

"Oh," I blurted, "I missed he was an addict."

"Yes, you did," the nurse said firmly. "I tried to warn you but you didn't let me tell you."

The whole of humanity passes through casualty from cradle to grave with no class divide, and among the staff there was a team approach to the onslaught of 'Joe Public', especially on a Saturday night. Most nights, but especially on Saturday after 10.00 pm, nearly every attendance was alcohol related.

The casualty was positioned near enough to the city centre for it to be considered a legitimate nightspot. From around midnight to 2.00 am we would see the results of fighting, usually related to an overzealous bouncer from a certain nightclub. The victims would attend casualty with head wounds and broken hands. These young men would be alcohol-fueled and lippy. The nursing staff that dealt with these patients, however, were hardened campaigners.

"I'm ****ing dying, Doc! ****ing dying," would echo around Minors.

The nurse would retort, 'If you're going to die, could you at least do it quietly!'

When asked about how they acquired their injuries the reply was consistently similar:"I was jumped, Doc!"

We tried to process individuals injured in fights as quickly as possible. This was to try and prevent fights resuming while in the hospital. This was especially crucial in those patients injured in fights with bouncers at local nightclubs. Delays in dealing with these injuries, which were often due to the long waits for an X-ray, meant there was a strong possibility that patients would meet the bouncers they had been fighting with while waiting in the X-ray queue. Reunions of bouncers and their victims resulted in fights often reoccurring in the hospital.

Another phenomenon I noticed on Saturday nights were women attending Casualty as supposed emergencies brought in by ambulance. On arrival, these women would suddenly announce that they were now feeling better and leave the hospital. Their use of the ambulance service as a glorified taxi ride was beyond belief.

I encountered women and men who were usually drunk displaying very undignified behaviour. I remember one woman in her twenties that I interviewed responded to my enquiries about her symptoms by squatting down in front of me and urinating on the floor before walking out of the room. This woman was clearly very troubled, exhibiting high-risk self-demeaning behaviour. Some of these women attending and acting strangely would depart via the X-ray queue. Here they would stop and try to pick up a willing male punter for a close encounter. On several occasions I lost track of a patient sent for X-ray when they hadn't returned from X-ray. The 'patient' was found in the car park outside the hospital engaged in an act of intimacy and exchanging bodily fluid.

In view of the violent threats from these attendees there was always a security guard on duty. I got to know one guard very well. He was called Derek, a huge, burly man who took his job very seriously. Near the end of one particularly busy shift, I got first-hand experience of working with Derek. The police had brought in a man who had been 'Stanley knifed' as they put it. He was intoxicated with drugs and had been lacerated multiple times on the face, arms and chest. I felt that we should clean and Steri-Strip his wounds, then see him the next day when he was more lucid and co-operative in order to carry out delayed primary suturing. My colleague, Jane, a caring but slightly naïve doctor, overruled me and said that if a police officer stayed, she would suture him there and then. Jane did a careful job over the next forty minutes but before she could finish, the officer, predictably, had to leave to attend another emergency. I happened to be passing just as the patient became highly agitated, accusing staff of 'stealing his f****** ganja' and punching the treatment couch. At one point, he hit the couch so hard he left indentations. My adrenaline rose and I rapidly moved all the instruments for suturing to the back of the room. The patient then made a lunge for them, so I dived on top of him and, thankfully, was quickly joined by Derek. We dragged him out of the building, kicking and screaming.

Derek then spent ten minutes trying to stop him from putting his fist through the glass sliding doors. Then, just like the opening sequence of *The Sweeney*, three police cars roared up to the hospital and out jumped six police officers to arrest the patient.

"Next time, let's just Steri-Strip him," Jane admitted.

As I progressed through my Casualty post I became increasingly cynical. A man who had fallen from a ladder and ended up with fractures of his calcaneus, or heel, still insisted he had been 'jumped'. Clearly, this was to avoid explaining just what he was doing up a ladder at ten o' clock at night!

I witnessed some horrendous sights but two stand out, not just for the spectacle that I witnessed, but also for the sheer barbarity of what had occurred. The first involved an eighteen-year-old who had been out celebrating his birthday with his mates. He had got into an argument with a couple in the restaurant. The argument escalated and resulted in the eighteen-year-old being doused with petrol and set alight on leaving. He was screaming in pain with wild, frightened eyes when he reached us, having sustained sixty percent burns, another man, who was involved in gangland torture, was brought in having been 'ironed'. He had sustained full thickness burns all over his back.

Clearly, there were plenty of lighter moments. I was in Majors once, clerking a woman with pneumonia when I heard my colleague, Jane, in the next booth. Jane was having trouble obtaining a clear history from her patient since the woman she was with, who was morbidly obese, was in agony with severe back pain. Jane had ascertained that the lady had been admitted a month previously onto the orthopaedic ward with a similar issue, but it was now clearly much worse. I smiled to myself as I heard her struggling to get this woman coherent.

The patient abruptly wailed, "I want to push! I really need to push!"

I hurtled into the cubicle and before we knew it a baby girl had been delivered into the world. I took the child and wrapped it in hospital towels, then showed her to the mother and her partner. The partner did not look too amused, and I later found out that he had only recently been released from prison after a two-year sentence.

Cardiac arrests were frequent and would often be something of a relief from the routine. The most I encountered at any one time was three happening simultaneously in the resuscitation room at once. It stretched the department to the limit and resembled a bizarre game of musical chairs.

Another time, an elderly lady was rushed in following a cardiac arrest. When she arrived, it quickly became clear that she was desperately unkempt, clad in a soiled jumper, skirt and wrap-around stockings. She had been found, having had a fall at home, several days previously. A putrefying aroma accompanied her and so I braced myself to clerk her. Together, with a nurse, we were in the process of exposing her legs under the stockings, when a scream billowed out

'Maggots!' The poor woman's legs were covered in broken down flesh with maggots crawling everywhere. It was later reflected that the maggots were a good thing as they had been eating the necrotic flesh and keeping the wound clean.

Patients attending with overdoses were very common. This meant there was a frequent need for gastric washouts, a procedure to try and prevent absorption of the toxic substances taken as an overdose. A gastric washout was and is an upsetting and challenging procedure to see through. The clinically hardened senior nurses usually carried out this procedure. They displayed their honed skills in passing a large gastric tube into the stomach with some venom. One nurse would often grab the patient's earlobe as a stimulus to see how 'rousable' they were.

She would then repeat endlessly while carrying out the washout: "If your mother could see you now!"

The quietest time in the department was usually between 5 am and 8 am. This was when the nighttime supervisors could sit down and chat with the nurses. There were regular visitors at this time – nursing managers, paramedics and or police officers, all in search of refreshment and a listening ear. One particularly camp nursing manager once recounted an early morning phone call from a nurse on his team who was unable to attend that morning's early shift.

"She told me she couldn't come in today 'coz she'd had a terrible Chinese last night," he chortled. "I asked her – meal or man?"

The busiest time was Christmas and that year I did a full twelve-hour day shift with a colleague over the holiday period. The wait for patients could be many hours, even in Majors. One man with chest pains and a suspected heart attack had waited ages to be seen. When we eventually got to him he revealed the multiple glycerol trinitrate tablets under his tongue he'd been taking for the pain, while waiting. At this point I felt the delay to see patients was far too long, causing life-threatening issues. I discussed the problem with my colleague and she fully agreed that it was really dangerous, so we phoned our consultant for help. No help was forthcoming. This was disappointing but not unexpected. The hierarchy again seemed to take no responsibility for conditions in their department. Both my colleague's Christmas cheer and mine was replaced by nothing more than a desire for the shift to end.

The two consultants that ran the department were, in my opinion, like chalk and cheese. One was tanned, articulate and supportive, the other one cold, monosyllabic and very strange. We had weekly teaching sessions, which was a real positive of the post. The supportive consultant ran the teaching. His organisation and prioritisation of this session was helped by getting other doctors to cover our shifts to allow us all to attend. The sessions involved discussing cases and getting other departments to share common problems pertinent to our casualty clientele. This emphasised to me the importance of time with peers to reflect on your practice, alongside the matter of simply being able to share experiences with seniors as well as your own peer group.

The other junior doctors in the department ranged from prospective GPs to trainee surgeons, so there was a real wealth of collective experience. Many of my fellow doctors had trained in the region and so had settled established domestic lives. This meant that although there was good camaraderie at work, it did not always extend socially. I ended up hanging out with several physiotherapists who lived in my accommodation and together we would explore the wonders of the city's nightlife.

There was one particular nightclub that was very hospital-orientated called The Sparkling Pineapple. It was tucked down a side street on the north side of the city, the type of club where your feet stuck to the floor on entry. It was laid out over three floors, with a bar on the top floor and two dancing areas on the lower levels. It became a regular haunt and entertained most of the medical and nursing fraternity of the city. It was renown for its raucous table-top dancing. Interestingly, despite the injuries of violence in the city I witnessed in casualty, I saw none while out myself in bars or nightclubs.

I awake as an earnest junior doctor introduces himself, sitting beside me on the bed.

"Just wanted to catch up before the round. How are you this morning?" he asks brightly.

"Fine. Well, sort of." I decide to keep my ammunition back regarding the urination issue until the consultant did his round. *"Good to hear. See you later, then."*

The doctor avoids all eye contact; his body language indicating that he really doesn't want to listen, as his bleep goes off. He then makes a hasty exit without even a backward glance.

I drift again along my surreal dream highway but then have an urge to urinate, which jolts me awake. I start the delicate manoeuvre of a cardboard bottle, strategically placed beside my bed. I am delighted to be successful in filling it without any spillage.

I transfer it back to the locker beside me and then lie back, satisfied at a task well accomplished, unsure whether to call a nurse to empty it or to wait for them to pass by again. I decide to leave it and ignore the aroma now percolating my bed space. I return to my dream.

Chapter Eight:

UNEXPECTED MOVE TO CHILDREN'S MEDICINE

Toward the end of my five-month stint in casualty, I once again began the ritual of applying for jobs. I applied for medical rotations, attending interviews across the country with no success. My referee, the tanned A&E consultant, after yet another futile trip, took me to one side. He suggested I consider paediatric employment in the city, saying that he knew the paediatricians there well and if I applied I would certainly get an interview.

I had never properly considered a career in paediatrics but remembered that, as a student, I had enjoyed some aspects of caring for children. My paediatric attachment as a student did not get off to the best of starts when one of my fellow students, whilst using the ward toilet on the first day, pulled the emergency cord instead of the light switch. Several panic-stricken nurses dashed to the toilet, only to find a dishevelled, male, medical student bright purple sheepishly peering around the door. This unfortunately did not endear any of the medical students on the paediatric attachment to the ward staff. The nurses could not seem to see the funny side of the student's predicament. The result of this event on the first day was during the attachment I only ever ventured onto the wards with trepidation and great care. I did not want to further antagonise the nurses. This fear of nurses on the ward significantly reduced my exposure to paediatric cases. However, all was not lost. I got good clinical exposure seeing children in casualty when on-call. This I remember I had found exciting and greatly enjoyable.

Once the seed of a career in paediatrics had been planted in my mind, it grew and grew. I soon visited the Children's Hospital, a stark-looking red-brick Victorian building. The exterior hid a totally child-orientated interior. The walls were covered in friendly murals of leopards, lions and penguins to name but a few, each animal indicating a different ward or department. The effect was transformative, brightening up and humanising the hospital. This was in stark contrast to the sterile white walls of the adult arena I was used to. This child-friendly environment was inspiring especially the boundless enthusiasm of all the staff I met ranging from doctors to porters. They all told me how they always did their best to think about the child's perspective. This patient-focused approach had me utterly hooked. I immediately applied for a one-year paediatric post as a SHO and, to my surprise, was short-listed.

On the morning of the interview, I rushed out and bought a fresh new white shirt. My sister had sent me a booklet on interview technique, which I devoured and spurred me into the morning's purchase. I meticulously pulled out all the endless pins securing the shirt to the cardboard packaging and then donned the crisp, new shirt, the criss-cross creases giving away its recent extraction from the packaging. Thankfully, those folds were mostly hidden when I pulled on my suit.

I then positioned myself in front of my bathroom mirror and rehearsed likely questions I would be asked at the interview, such as 'Why do you want to do paediatrics? or 'Why do you want to work here?' My initial answers were hesitant and insincere, however, after several repeats the answers started to sound more fluent and genuine. My confidence levels, based on past performances, sadly, remained low. I had read the booklet further. It gave advice on how to improve body language at interviews: 'Focus on a spot above the interviewer's head' it had said. 'Always face the person addressing you and ignore the others' and 'Keep your hands by your side or folded, but away from your face'. This mirror rehearsal allowed me to visualise the interview, get my posture right and recite my prepared responses repeatedly. My preparation for the performance was complete and I felt ready for the interview battle ahead.

I was soon transported from staring at my reflection in the mirror of the windowless bathroom to a large mahogany table surrounded by eight pairs of well-dressed men and women with piercing eyes, otherwise known as the interview panel. It all went according to my pre prepared plan. I felt a passion in my answers to the usual questions and a positive feeling that lingered the usual torture techniques were then applied with a two-hour wait to hear the result. With so many failures I expected the worst. The door finally opened, and a lady addressed all the candidates waiting. I recoiled, trying not to build my hopes up too much.

"Dr Stone?" I sat momentarily in shock. I wanted to scream in celebration. I held in my feelings of joy managing a meniscal smile. I avoided eye contact with my fellow candidates and followed the messenger back into the interview room.

"Congratulations, Dr Stone. We'd like to offer you a one-year post. Six months neonatology, six of general paediatrics and endocrinology."

"I accept," I blurted out and then formally shook eight pairs of hands trying not to give away my delight.

The joy I felt then was still very much with me as a nursing assistant finally collected my bottle.

CHAPTER NINE:

GENERAL PAEDIATRICS BECKONS

I began my very first official post in paediatrics at the children's hospital. It meant I was finally able to dispense with my white coat. This, for me, was a real psychological difference, compared to the adult arena. It felt like the shedding of an invisible barrier between doctor and patient and it humanised the working environment. I was now part of a team or firm, along with a registrar, senior registrar and consultant. The interactions I had with the registrar were intense and far more satisfying than any previous interactions with middle-grade doctors. I discussed cases and was supervised doing practical procedures.

Within just a few short weeks, I felt confident and competent enough to tackle most of the necessary procedures expected at my level of training, tasks such as siting an intravenous line in a baby.

David, my registrar, was a short, unassuming man who was very protective of his juniors. He would reinterpret, in far more congenial terms, the demands from the consultant or senior registrar on ward rounds. He was always positive and kept praising me for my work. It really spurred me on and made me strive hard to please my seniors. I felt for the first time a sense of belonging and that I was valued. I now realise how important this feeling of being part of a team is and appreciated it from all staff but especially the doctors.

Despite vast improvements in working hours and conditions today, many consultants – middle-grade and juniors

– feel utterly isolated, alone and desperately unhappy. This is due partly to the fragmentation of the team or firm structure. Teams, if well run as I experienced, give doctors common goals, definite roles, support, affirmation and professional development in many ways. On the other hand, the deconstruction of the firm means doctors feel less valued by seniors and the praise they crave is never forthcoming. In today's shift work pattern, consistent team working can be difficult to achieve. Many medical consultants have retired early because of the constantly changing members of their supposed 'team'. This is no way to run an acute, high-risk medical arena and gives little continuity for patients or doctors. There is an urgent need to deliberately reinvent the firm, making them cohesive, well run and with each member undertaking an absolutely clear role, ensuring that all members feel valued and respected. Studies have clearly shown that a well-functioning medical team improves outcomes for patients and provides far better doctor well-being and professional development.

My paediatric post was certainly busy, and I was working a one-in-three rota. On admission days, I would see the patients referred from casualty to the ward by the admitting registrar. At midnight I would take over from the registrar seeing patients from casualty til 9 am the next morning.

Before midnight I was on the ward seeing patients referred by the registrar from casualty. These patients would have a treatment plan. I would re-clerk patients, carry out investigations such as lumbar punctures, urine tests and blood tests. I would then start the prescribed treatment.

At midnight my stint in casualty started in earnest and all juniors found this daunting. Often, on arrival in casualty, I would be confronted with a queue of patients waiting to be seen. Nearly all had minor illnesses or minor infections such as colds or gastroenteritis and most could be reassured and discharged. Common presenting symptoms of these children included cough, breathing difficulties, diarrhoea, vomiting, rash and high temperatures. Some registrars were very conscientious about trying to clear casualty of most of the patients before midnight, but many were just glad to finish their shift and leave the hospital.

At the beginning of my casualty shift my enthusiasm and stamina were good. Patient assessments were rapid and concise. I was confident to send many kids home. However, within a couple of hours of dealing with very demanding parents, combined with fatigue, I found my confidence to persuade mums and dads that their child was well enough to be at home would waver. 'Is it the melon-gitis, Doctor?' would ring out regularly, as parents quizzed me about their sick child. Admitting these patients became the easier option.

By 4 am to 5 am, casualty was usually cleared and it was possible to get some sleep. The residences were a significant distance away on the hospital campus so I searched for a closer place to rest. The nurses in casualty were helpful in this regard. They would make up a bed for me in interesting places within casualty including the Minor Operating Theatre. I quite regularly slept on the operating couch. This was initially disconcerting, but I soon became accustomed to it as a place to rest, partly due to my overwhelming exhaustion toward the end of the on-call night. I would frequently have a recurring dream of being operated on, often waking up to the sight of theatre lights staring down at me.

The ward rounds the morning after an on-call stint were rapid and efficient. The round moved quickly to discharge the post-midnight admissions known as 'bed and breakfast' (B&B) admissions. It is of note that the consultants were very accepting and never critical of admissions of children presenting after midnight. This B&B approach took the pressure off junior doctors making difficult clinical decisions about discharge at a time when they were tired and had distant senior support. On the morning's post-take ward round, most B&B patients would be discharged but a few would be identified as having significant issues. A period of observation and second examination is very useful in acute paediatrics. It is especially valuable when assessing the many children who initially present with concerning symptoms but who, in the main, subsequently improve and do not have a serious illness. However, unfortunately there are always a few children in the early stages of serious illness who can easily be missed.

This issue of missing significant serious illness in children was exemplified when one of my fellow SHOs saw a child after midnight and discharged the child back home. The child had a fever that he thought was due to tonsillitis. However the patient was just sixteen months old and tonsillitis was a rather tentative diagnosis as it is not that common in this young age group. At 6 am he was 'crash-called' to Casualty. The same child he had seen earlier and discharged had been brought back moribund with an overwhelming meningococcal septicaemia. My colleague was utterly distraught. He was reassured by seniors that children could appear well enough to discharge but then represent like this, even with the most thorough of assessments. This is true, but for the doctor involved, missing such a serious diagnosis was very difficult to come to terms with. He of course felt personally responsible for discharging the child with what turned out to be an evolving sepsis.

Reviewing the case now, as a consultant, it is possible if a more senior paediatrician had seen the child, they may have made a similar decision to the junior doctor to discharge the child. However, an experienced senior dealing with the case might also have been unconvinced about a diagnosis of tonsillitis in a sixteen-month old child and noted the slightly faster heart rate for a child of his age. These findings may have triggered an extra cautious decision by the senior for a second examination after a period of observation and for blood tests. Many studies have shown there is no complete foolproof way to identify all sick children. However, seniors who experience a 'gut feeling' that a child may have a serious underlying illness have been shown to be right in most cases. A gut feeling that the child is sick by a senior remains one of the best indicators of a sick child. Some clinicians correlate 'gut feeling' as compressed experience translating into a physical phenomenon. Reflecting on this now, there has been a huge campaign in improving doctors' practice when it comes to identifying a sick child, it being universally agreed that a structured approach to assessment using an ABCDE sequence is expected to be carried out on all children. These days it is mandatory that every doctor in the acute paediatric arena has attended an advanced paediatric life-support course. Senior input on the shop floor is becoming increasingly common, especially at peak times of casualty attendance, which is around 6 pm to 9 pm (out of hours). This means supervision of juniors is easier and a senior opinion is more readily available.

My colleague reflected with his close friends and understandably felt guilty. He continued to berate himself for not getting a registrar opinion and or admitting the child overnight. Interestingly, no discussion was had with the SHOs about this case from senior staff. The seniors had effectively disappeared off the radar. Certainly, as SHOs we discussed the case among ourselves and developed a conscious bias toward using the B&B model for most attendees after midnight.

Today the pressure on staff when acute patients attend Casualty is rising, especially with the reduction of the out-of-hours service in primary care. This has been coupled with a reduced bed capacity to save money, with reliance instead on ambulatory care to offload inpatient units. This change has made B&B admissions consequently difficult to implement. In my opinion this is extremely short-sighted as sending children home after midnight is fraught with risk. The money saved on reduced bed numbers has to be balanced against the need to have further senior decision-makers available twenty- four hours a day when it comes to admissions and discharges. This issue is logistically tricky as it puts a huge demand on consultants and middle-grade doctors, which is often greatly underestimated by managers. Resident out-of-hours consultants are a reality in many paediatric inpatient units and consultants will be expected to continue this throughout their career until they reach sixty-seven years of age. Is this model of coverage of out-of-hours working sustainable? I have doubts and hence, in my opinion, we urgently need to consider other ways to deliver a successful acute paediatric service. Primary care paediatricians may well be the way forward in a bid to improve the care of children in primary care and to be able to contribute to the acute service, but this new type of paediatrician based in primary care would also be uniquely placed to liaise closely with primary and secondary care.

During this particular post that I was reflecting back upon, in addition to my ward work I was required to carry out growth hormone stimulation tests every Tuesday. This was where children with short stature would attend, having not eaten for a period of time, and I would clerk and cannulate them followed by an infusion of arginine and clonidine, alongside taking blood every twenty minutes to check for growth hormone levels. These tests would take all morning. They were routine and I made a point of attending every meeting with the consultants to discuss the results. This really was the most interesting part.

Some Tuesdays I would carry out jejunal biopsies. This was to detect coeliac disease, a common cause of short stature. In those days, the procedure was carried out by passing a Crosby capsule, under sedation, into the stomach of a child and then advancing it gradually in position, hopefully in the duodenum. The child would then be transferred down to X-ray where the position of the capsule would be confirmed. The capsule would be fired, by suction, via a thin tube at the mouth, connecting with the capsule way down in the duodenum. It was always a procedure fraught with possible failure and I would spend hours practising firing the capsule. Success was only confirmed once the capsule was removed from the patient and inspected. The extraction of a small piece of what looked like gut mucosa would be highly satisfying. This would subsequently be taken directly down to the pathologist who, there and then, would confirm whether it was the right specimen. I was usually successful but did, on occasion, encounter my registrar failing and would then have to deal with the aftermath with the parents. These days most biopsies are done by endoscopy, which has a far greater success rate.

The consultant during this time was a very serious, measured man. On his ward rounds he would, having already listened to us present histories and examination findings, repeat both on all patients. This seemed to annoy both the registrar and senior registrar who would raise their eyes to the ceiling in disbelief each time. To be fair, he did pick up pyloric stenosis in a child we had admitted with vomiting, which had not been definitively diagnosed prior to the round. He also had the habit of rewriting his notes up of all the children he had visited. This clearly disempowered some members of the team, but more importantly and legally, it meant that his assessment of any child in his care was always clearly documented. This is something that as a consultant today I can appreciate. He was, despite these irritations for many of the senior team members, always calm and friendly. Everyone under him was on first name terms. I learnt a lot in those six months, having witnessed multiple emergencies and carried out many practical procedures.

Outside work time, my leisure options were limited due to the onerous rota. As I previously experienced most of my socializing was with fellow juniors. One colleague, Paul, who had trained in the city and was currently living in the residences with me, became a friend. Together we reopened the residences' bar, which had been closed for some time and we organised an opening party. It was a huge success and bred new life into the residences with good attendance from both nursing and medical staff. Toward the end of my six months, I moved into a flat with Paul near a park in the city. It was an excellent place to live and felt like a watershed moment for me seeing as it was the first time since I had qualified that I was not living in a hospital residence. The feeling was energising and gave me a sense of freedom. I re-engaged with another friend called Malcolm from university and, socially, things improved greatly. The adjacent city became exciting. I was able to visit arthouse cinemas, novelty pubs, attend the theatre and enjoy many venues featuring Irish folk music. I used to meet Malcolm for breakfast in a bar, read the Sunday papers and then stay for a few pints afterwards. I would often meet my acquaintances from the city hospital in the bars and the Sparkling Pineapple. I had finally developed a social network in the city and was ready for my next adventure.

Chapter Ten:

LIFE BEYOND HOSPITAL – DOWNTIME

The long hours as a junior doctor, meant that holidays took on paramount importance. While working at the District Hospital I went on holiday to visit friends from medical school who were working in the Channel Islands. I remember being picked up from the airport by one of my friends, Toni, in an open-top Ford Escort. It was a sun-drenched evening and the air was invigorating. We drove at some speed to a bar looking out onto a long and breathtaking, golden-sanded surfing beach. We ordered a beer and were soon sipping the amber nectar sat on the terrace and taking in the vista.

"How's the job going, Toni?" I asked.

"Look at that, Harry; just look at that!" he replied, gesturing to the sun setting as surfers with boards under their arms walked toward us clad in tight, short wetsuits. They initially looked like distant specks of humanity, actors on a jaw-dropping scenic backdrop of sky, sea, surf and endless sand. They gradually came into closer vision, hair windswept and tangled and faces beaming from their time immersed in the surf. The scene was accompanied by the constant roar of breakers crashing on the beach.

"Look at that, Harry. Look at that and think about the one in every three nights you spend at the District Hospital."

The contrast of the evening sunset over a surfing beach and the austere District Hospital with its adjacent run-down housing estates was stark.

"Cheers, Toni," I mumbled.

During my time at the children's hospital I went on a package holiday to Portugal with a fellow doctor, James, another friend from medical school. He had booked the holiday through a cleaner on his ward. We took our golf clubs with the intention to play one of the best golf courses in Portugal. This was perhaps wishful thinking since we were both fairly novice golfers, what I would describe as 'pay and display' golfers. Undeterred, we soon found ourselves, golf clubs in tow, sitting on the transfer bus at Faro Airport awaiting transfer to our hotel. The bus was mainly crammed with the older grey rinse generation who became curious about us. The cleaner, we began to realise, had booked us on a SAGA sponsored holiday.

"What do you two do?" came the dreaded question from one of the grey rinse brigade.

This innocent enquiry immediately caused us a dilemma that could determine the enjoyment of our break from the NHS. If we answered truthfully 'We're doctors', it would lead to endless anecdotes and questions about the many ailments these older holiday-makers would have and the state of the NHS, something we wanted to avoid at all costs.

"We're plumbers," James quickly replied and I nodded, digging my elbow into James' side.

"My son's a plumber," a voice chirped emanating from a woman with a purple shampoo and set hairdo just across the aisle.

For the next thirty minutes on the coach transfer to the hotel, James and myself started confabulating about plumbing with various inquisitive fellow passengers. Thankfully, their knowledge of plumbing was very limited!

The holiday was excellent; we played golf at the world-famous Penina Golf and Resort boasting three championship courses. We arrived at the course dressed up in designer shirts to give the impression of seasoned golfers, despite our inexperience. Our smart attire seemed to give the right impression and we were asked no questions about whether we had a golf handicap, which of course we did not. Our meticulous planning paid off and at 7 am we were on the first tee on a major championship golf course. In all, we played all three courses in a day, finishing at 7 pm, exhausted but very satisfied. During the midday heat while most people were retiring to the golf club terrace to have lunch, we ploughed on playing, taking our lunch on the golf course, our golf bags stuffed full of beers and sandwiches. It was a great day with the occasional sublime shot interspersed with many forgettable shots. The setting was magnificent, especially in the early evening light. We were playing the main championship course with the shadows from the tall pine trees framing the exquisitely beautiful grass-carpeted greens. The picture was completed by a speckling of golden and then crimson light through the trees as the sun set.

While on holiday we hired a car to escape the many developed tourist areas of the Algarve, which at that time had begun transforming into wall-to-wall whitewashed time-share developments. The once small quaint fishing villages were consumed by time-share phenomena with the accompanying ubiquitous Irish pubs and fast-food outlets selling chips and frankfurters.

Driving west some way from our hotel, we found a stunning fishing village on the coast called Salema. It had an idyllic beach abutting a cluster of fishermen's cottages. The fishing boats were scattered on the beach in an array of bright colours; red, blue and green. It was a tranquil scene and we spent that particular day soaking up the ambience. Several years later I returned to Salema to sadly find that the Algarve transformation had formatively struck. Salema and the cluster of cottages were now overwhelmed with whitewashed time-share mansions, its innocence lost.

On the last night we took up residence at the hotel bar and decided to work our way down the cocktail menu. Our fellow inmates all congregated with us and further U-bend plumbing stories ensued. The next morning, sitting on the bus to the airport hung over, I felt sweaty and nauseous. I leant forward, head in hands to recover and kept a very low profile. We finally arrived at the city's airport, I said goodbye to James and went in search of a bus to take me back to my flat. When I arrived at the bus station, it was announced the next suitable bus would be in an hour. By now my nausea had given away to hunger and I went in search of food.

It was a Sunday, wet, cold and everything was closed and so I began looking further afield outside the bus station. I saw, down a rather dreary street, a neon sign lit up as 'Nicky's Pub'. I lumbered toward it, golf clubs and rucksack in tow. I confidently entered through the well-used door, ascended a flight of steep stairs, through a hanging purple tinselled partition and entered a bar. I was immediately hit by the warmth and hubbub of conversation. I made a beeline for the bar and quickly ordered a sandwich and beer. Congratulating myself on finding sustenance, I then surveyed the establishment. It was packed with drinkers in various states of intoxication, but they were all men apart from a female-looking figure dressed in white but with facial stubble.

"You come on your own? You looking for anyone?" came a question to me from across the bar.

"No," I retorted. It began to dawn on me that this was a gay pub with a drag wedding in full swing. I surveyed the room, which was variably lit but pulsated with music. It was an electric atmosphere, the dance floor packed with enthusiastic writhing bodies moving to the soundtrack of 'Two Tribes' by Frankie Goes to Hollywood.

I could feel the energy emanating from every part of the dimly lit room.

"Are you here alone?" asked a man next to me at the bar.

"Yes; I mean, no." I rapidly scoffed the sandwich and downed the beer. The alcohol gave me a wave of intensity as the room's energy increased another notch with the hectic levels of gyrations that accompanied ABBA's 'Dancing Queen' that was now blasting out over the dance floor.

"You want to dance?" he asked, his hand touching mine.

"Sorry, got to go." I swiftly grabbed my rucksack and golf clubs and made for the door.

"Pity you have to go." The man was fully visible now and was sweaty, wearing a white tee shirt and courting a handlebar moustache; he looked middle-aged and drunk. The crowd was just starting their afternoon of entertainment and I was soon reacquainting myself with the cold, wet afternoon air and trudging to the city's bus station.

That afternoon I had come across men freely expressing their sexuality which, at that time, the height of the human immunodeficiency virus infection and acquired immunodeficiency syndrome (HIV/ AIDS) felt threatening. The joyous energy I felt in that bar on a dreary afternoon was such a long way from the routine long hours culture of my workplace. It made me realise that life should, at times, be fun and expression of sexuality is to be celebrated. The AIDS epidemic was a tragedy that vilified the gay community, unfairly stalking and capitalizing on the negative stigma society had placed at that time on people having same-sex relationships.

Chapter Eleven:

BEGINNING OF LIFE – NEONATOLOGY

Following my six-month stint at the children's hospital I rotated to the neonatology post. This was based in a maternity and neonatal unit in another part of the city. The maternity unit had three thousand six hundred deliveries per year and the neonatal unit had the capacity to ventilate five babies at a time. The neonatal unit was staffed by two SHOs (of which I was one), a registrar, a visiting senior registrar (attendance once a week) and three consultants of which two visited once or twice a week. Comparing this with today's statuary staffing there would be at least ten SHOs, four registrars and five consultant staff.

The key to the successful running of the unit was down to the registrar and nursing staff. The senior sisters were omnipresent and in the absence of consultants for much of the week it meant that these sisters were the main force to be reckoned with. They had strong personalities and were never shy in emphasising to junior doctors their wide knowledge, seniority and prowess at practical clinical skills.

One sister, Mollie, was particularly keen to exhibit her intubation skills at any opportunity (intubation is placing a tube into the main airway). She would often appear quite suddenly when an intubation needed to be done. She would roll her sleeves up and watch proceedings, arms crossed, showing her intent that she was ready to take over. If either myself or Sally, my fellow SHO, failed on our first attempt to intubate, she would barge us out of the way and then thrust the endotracheal tube into the larynx using forceps. Her success rate was good, but her technique lacked finesse and she did, on occasions, cause trauma to the soft tissue around the baby's airway.

Mollie's behaviour, on reflection, was understandable. At the beginning of the post the majority of the SHOs on the unit were inexperienced with many procedures, but especially with intubation.

The senior nurses saw it as their duty to intervene at the earliest opportunity to protect the baby from inexperienced doctors slow to carry out procedures. This made the relationship between doctors and nursing staff difficult. The consultants' absences, for much of the time, allowed this sort of informal policing of junior doctors by senior nurses to continue unchecked. The changing of SHOs every six months put a strain on Senior nurses. It resulted in their rather aggressive behaviour toward junior doctors which they justified as necessary to protect the babies from inexperienced staff. The robust, no-nonsense demeanor of senior nurses like Mollie toward Sally and myself made us determined to master procedures such as intubation as quickly as possible. For Mollie, every six months a new clutch of doctors arrived, and, in her eyes, most were incompetent until they proved otherwise.

This theme of predictable issues of patient safety due to junior staff changing every six months, is familiar even today. In our department, doctors change every four months. This continued changeover of doctors produces significant risk for patients. To mitigate this risk, clear guidelines and competency frameworks are now followed. This means Mollie, today, would have a competent doctor available on-site for day intubation or there would be an advanced nurse practitioner trained correctly and appraised for advanced skills such as intubation. National resuscitation courses in neonates underpin practice that have much improved matters with nursing staff and medical staff singing from the same hymn sheet.

For my first two weeks on-call, I had a senior registrar resident with me on hand for any difficulties covering the unit or attending deliveries on the Labour ward. During this six month post I became competent at the basics of ventilation of premature babies. I learnt how to insert umbilical lines, radial lines and chest drains. I became adept at intubation and changing ventilator settings. With each procedure I only ever carried out one supervised before going solo ("see one do one, teach one"). It was extremely important to learn how to put in a chest drain, since I was in the era where air leaks were common among premature babies ventilated for a condition called respiratory distress syndrome. Diagnosing a dangerous air leak was done by placing a high intensity light on the side of the chest. If the light glowed beyond its area of contact it meant an air leak was present and a chest drain was needed. I became very adept at using the light to detect air leaks early. Two weeks of supervision went quickly. Then without any discussion Sally and myself were on-call alone in the hospital doing a one-in-three rota covering the unit with a consultant available, if required, at home.

The job was tiring. On-call you rarely got any sleep. The on-call room was just adjacent to the unit and next to the staff rest room. The noise of the staff room made sleep difficult; the usual on-call room scenario. With luck and practice, within a month I became confident with intubations and chest drain insertions. I found adjustments of the ventilator initially challenging, but over the six-month post I became competent.

Our registrar, Thomas, was the lynchpin of the unit. He was a short Scottish man with a great sense of humour. He was extremely competent, a good teacher, but very cynical about the system. He carried out the rounds each day. The morning round would start with an impression of World War I pilots talking into their aeroplane radios, simulated by talking into the oxygen masks on the 'resuscitairres'.

"Roger, can you hear me?" "Roger… Roger..?"

"I've someone to introduce you to, Roger. Roger… my wife."

"OK, Roger," and so on.

Taking in the 100% oxygen and saying 'Roger' at that time of the morning always seemed to give a boost to the ward round. This was especially so after a night on call when, from around 6. am, all the bloods had to be taken from the babies to go off to the laboratory for 8.00 am. This was a mind-numbing, repetitive task with me going from baby to baby throughout the ward on autopilot.

The unit was divided into the hot nursery where the ventilated babies needing intensive care were nursed and a cold nursery for the others with a few side rooms for babies that needed isolation. I would often start the bloodletting task in the cold nursery. This would coincide with the nurses changing shift. It was quite an eye-opener eavesdropping on the nurses' recollections of the previous night's events. Both humorous and sometimes very personal anecdotes were shared among staff. One nurse, who had obviously sustained a black eye, vividly described being beaten up by her boyfriend. This unfortunately was quite a common topic of conservation and made me realise the significant scale of the problem of domestic abuse.

The uninspiring task of routine bloodletting would often make me look at the grey, drizzly morning sunrise over a housing estate and think *There must be more to life and work than this*. It was at this point that I decided I should travel and consider working in a developing country. During my time at the children's hospital, I had met students on the tropical medicine course who had been seconded to my firm. Their accounts of medicine in the developing world seemed rawer and more awe-inspiring than collecting bloods on a miserable grey morning. One English student doing the course gave me a six-page document outlining an experience he had had whilst working in a rural hospital in South Africa. It was fascinating and little was I to know at that time that I would later work in its sister hospital the Boulder Rock Hospital.

The two main consultants were very different but extremely caring when present. Dr Welby was a very intense academic man who could make the most mundane things sound both serious and exciting. Thomas knew him well and his tendency to turn down the intensity of ventilation on babies on ward rounds; the result was invariably that several hours later the babies would deteriorate and need rescue intervention. To avoid this, on occasions we would turn up the ventilation on babies just prior to his round, so placating his fiddling. The other consultant, Dr Patterson, was a tall man with a very hushed Irish voice who was a good listener, very caring, never hurried, often saying very little but always nodding empathetically. Understandably, both consultants covering a neonatal unit did face ethical decisions about the prudence of continuing intensive care in babies with overwhelming complications such as severe brain haemorrhages. Both consultants rarely followed through with withdrawal of care but for differing reasons.

Dr Welby would discuss withdrawal but, due to the limited time he spent on the unit, was unable to put in the necessary time to work through such a decision.

Dr Patterson was less inclined to contemplate withdrawal and would always recite that he met many families with children with cerebral palsy who, despite their profound handicaps, were thankful for their child's survival.

Clearly, the partnership in making decisions about withdrawal of care is something that most units today go to great lengths to discuss with all staff involved in the baby's care. This is a sea change from the more paternalistic approach I experienced during my six-month Neonatology post back in the 1980s.

During my time doing neonatology I did witness a major medical breakthrough in the care of preterm babies, the introduction of exogenous surfactant. Preterm babies often develop a condition called infant respiratory distress syndrome (IRDS/surfactant deficiency) for which many require ventilation. The condition is due to the lack of a detergent substance, called surfactant which is normally produced in the lung of the baby from thirty-two weeks gestation. This substance helps keep the air sacs in the lung open and without it they collapse. The collapse of the air sacs in a preterm baby due to surfactant deficiency leads to stiff lungs and therefore respiratory difficulties, especially in babies born at less than thirty-two weeks gestation. These difficulties worsen over seventy-two hours before slowly improving during which time the infants will often require respiratory support with ventilation. Our department was involved in the first surfactant trial. I remember one night having started ventilating a preterm infant for IRDS, the infant, predictably, began to follow a worsening clinical course. The baby fortunately was entered into the surfactant trial. I rang the research team running the trial to determine what the baby should receive. The team were based in Belfast and I was soon talking to researcher with a broad northern Irish accent. The researcher explained it was a blinded randomised placebo-controlled trial. I was to be unaware whether the baby would receive a placebo or surfactant. I administered the allocated clear liquid down the endotracheal tube into the lungs. I then witnessed a transformation of the infant that, to me, was miraculous. A grey ashen baby gave way to a pink vision and the ventilatory requirements rapidly fell. I stood back in awe at the power of modern medicine. The infant had received surfactant, which almost instantaneously improved the stiffness in the lungs and so transformed the course of IRDS.

Modern medicine always has two sides, the positive such as surfactant, which is always tempered with the negative such as the futility of applying intensive care at all costs. One neonate did exemplify this for me. He was born at twenty-four weeks premature and ran a very chronic course. He had life-threatening complications with multiple pneumothoraxes ('air leaks'), and at one time he had five chest drains in situ. His nickname, rather cruelly, was Hedgehog. A discussion about continuation of intensive care after two chest drains was muttered about, but no clear decision was made. He predictably developed severe chronic lung disease. He managed to survive three months off the ventilator but remained severely oxygen-dependent. Each ward round we would see him and make some adjustment to his medication. He would be on and off antibiotics. On he struggled, often breathless and wide-eyed with distress, struggling to interact with his parents. He was clearly significantly developmentally delayed.

That child remained on the unit throughout my post until, on the final on-call before my next post, he deteriorated. The consultant on-call came in from home and together we struggled all night to resuscitate him but, despite this, he died. I was sad and tearful for the first time at work. *All that effort for this outcome*, I thought, and *all that trauma for the parents*. I said my goodbyes to the staff on the unit feeling a failure and unhappy to be leaving on such an emotive morning. I felt sorrow welling up inside, a wave of emotion ready to consume me. I avoided the main corridor to leave and made my way down the back stairs. *Why do paediatrics for this?* I wondered to myself.

Lost in grief I was then faced by the parents coming up the stairs. I couldn't avoid the encounter. I looked at them with red eyes wiping away my tears and muttered, 'Sorry'. They both stopped and the father held out his hand. I took it and he encased my hand with a firm grip. I noticed his hard, thick skin that reflected the manual dominance of his work as a gardener. His hands that were used to weeding flowerbeds and cutting grass were now helping express the raw visceral emotion of the loss of his son. He pulled me toward him for a few seconds, tears welling up in his eyes.

"Thank you for everything. At least he had a chance, you gave us that. We got to know him. You're a bloody good doctor; keep on going."

His wife was too grief-stricken to say anything but looked at me and briefly touched my arm. I left them on the stairs and exited the hospital building, my head still reverberating with emotion. I wandered aimlessly, not focused on the quest to find my car. On the one hand, perhaps Dr Patterson was right, the parents seemed grateful despite the suffering. On the other hand, a voice deep inside me told me that the infant had suffered, and the outcome had not been dignified. The words from the parents 'You're a bloody good doctor, keep on going' rang in my ears as I drove on autopilot the length of the country to start a new post on the south coast.

I jolt awake as I recall the death of this boy. Somehow this memory has become part of my DNA and so part of me. The intense sadness of staff, my consultant and the parents was raw, deep and unsettling. Death is all around us and stalks us all. Medicine brings you close to the Reaper and I took many weeks to recover from this farewell to the city.

The bay around me is full of patients fighting the Reaper's advances. Some are close to submission. The man opposite who received the urine bath is close to the exit.

Death, as I was to find out, is something you must handle with care.

I return to my dream recalling the turmoil of long hours and little sleep, a backdrop of all my training posts. This way of living seeps into all aspects of your life. Relationships I found especially difficult to sustain and move beyond a superficial level. When I did strive for deeper meaning the demands of the clinical arena trumped everything.

I also recall another patient from a faraway land who is part of me. He now resides beyond this world and was wronged by our system in my opinion, dying unnecessarily far from home.

CHAPTER TWELVE:

NHS TURMOIL AND LIFE ON ONE HUNDRED-PLUS HOURS A WEEK

During my time in the northern city I began to witness the effects of political decisions on the NHS. Kenneth Clarke was health minister and the grading of nurses was being reformed. Nurses were graded according to the job they were doing on a certain date. It caused much divisiveness among nursing staff, with many of the more seasoned senior nurses deciding to quit the profession for perceived unfairness. The health secretary was a combative figure in those days, steamrollering through healthcare reforms despite its unpopularity. He was upset by the British Medical Association (BMA)'s campaign to oppose the reforms. The BMA produced posters saying: 'What do you call a man who ignores medical advice? Mr Clarke.'

When I started in neonatology the postnatal wards had nursery nurses. This position was subsequently abolished during one of the many imposed reforms by Thatcher's government. These nurses were invaluable in organising the efficient review of babies on the ward. Their presence meant that just two SHOs and a registrar were able to run the neonatal unit and cover the postnatal wards. The impact of having no nursery nurses was profound. Their absence led to a lack of organisation on postnatal wards. Subsequently, further doctors were required to cover the same amount of work and the mother and babies often got less attention. These nursery nurses took an interest in the babies and mothers and often had more time than the midwives to aid support for mothers in the natural adaptation of their baby's feeding.

Even today this is an issue with postnatal ward understaffing severely affecting the quality of care provided by midwives. The consequence is simply that there is less input in addressing neonatal problems. Many women now give up breast-feeding because of lack of support. We still have very low rates of breast-feeding in the UK.

Transitional care units are in place in many hospitals to fill the void of consistent care on the postnatal ward for neonates. These units deal with common problems such as feeding problems, jaundice and intravenous antibiotics. The abolishment of nursery nurses has had many unforeseen adverse effects for neonatal care. It showed me the importance of careful evaluation of changes in staffing and valuing fellow professionals. The intensity of work and the discontent in the workplace meant it was paramount to have good downtime when off work.

Outside work I enjoyed my first skiing holiday in France in France. I, Paul, and a friend called Sam, drove from the North to the Alpine ski fields in a white Mini. The first week I spent my time following a sleek, beautifully athletic French-speaking ski instructor. My learning curve was steep (just like the slopes). During the second week I skied with Paul and Sam, seasoned skiers, at differing slopes Val-d'Isère, Courchevel and Les Arcs. Skiing was something that, prior to the holiday, I had felt was overrated and a little elitist, but now I felt it lived up to its hype: I was hooked. In addition to the skiing, we drove into Italy to watch an Italian footy game in Turin. Paul and Sam were long-suffering football supporters and so had to have their football fix. The songs were predictably like the English chants and easily translatable to the non-Italian- speaking observer: 'Qui es the Bastardo in the Black?'

Work so dominated my life that relationships with women were superficial. The heavy one hundred-plus-hour rotas a week negated anything more meaningful. I did, however, become close with a fellow SHO. She was entertaining and of course we had work in common. The relationship developed during the six-month post we worked together and toward the end we were enjoying each other's company. She wanted to explore the world and had accepted her next post abroad. I knew that this move would affect our relationship but hoped our mutual friendship would last. I received some upbeat letters from her experiences travelling and from her subsequent hospital post abroad. After three months apart we agreed to go on holiday together. We travelled to an obscure village in Greece, an idyllic place, with a spectacular bay surrounded by steep cliffs covered in olive groves. The hotel looked out over the bay adorned by a strip of sand and a turquoise shimmering sea. Despite the beauty of the place, the chemistry between us did not progress. I was saddened but continued with the holiday onto the breathtaking cities of Venice and Verona. Despite such evocative destinations nothing changed with our relationship and we parted as 'friends'.

I returned on an airplane vowing to try and move on. *Life is too short*, I told myself, *to have an emotional roller-coaster holiday like that again.* I returned to the city emotionally exhausted and ill-prepared for another hundred-hour week of work. Again, the experience emphasised my failings in self-discipline in matters outside work and my indecision in pursuing and moving relationships beyond a superficial level.

Toward the end of my neonatology post, the issue of my next job loomed again. I wanted to do a paediatric speciality and looked at cardiology. In the city the junior jobs in that speciality were unpopular and so I cast my eye further afield. A job was available on the south coast. I applied and, much to my surprise, was short-listed and successful at the interview. My luck was changing.

Chapter Thirteen:

ON TOUR TO THE HEART OF THE SOUTH

I arrived at the South Coast Hospital at 4 pm, weary and emotionally drained after my long drive across the country in my newly purchased Ford Capri. On arrival, I left my luggage laden car in the hospital car park and went in search of a phone. At hospital reception I tried ringing the accommodation office. Despite it still being in office hours it took some time to get hold of someone who was aware of my arrival. Finally, after an hour I managed to speak with an accommodation officer who knew of my case.

"We want to put you in a temporary room for a week; I hope you don't mind," came the robotic uncompromising voice of the accommodation officer.

"Thanks " I replied in a resigned manner.

I was in no position to complain about this proposed temporary abode. At around 5.15 pm I picked up the room keys from reception. The keys unlocked a small room in a desolate looking tower block. It was in short depressing. I was too tired to complain. So, on auto pilot, I unpacked my car, distributing my belongings in piles around my bed. I then laid down and almost immediately fell into a deep sleep.

After several hours, my tranquil slumber was shattered by a piercing high-pitched bleep. It was emanating from an on-call room next to me. The culprit bleep belonged to an on call-doctor in the adjoining room. This repeated itself throughout the night with bleeps at 2 am, 3 am and 4 am. The next day I was exhausted and sleep-deprived. I couldn't stand another night of disturbance, so I decided to be assertive with the accommodation officer. I delivered a tirade of complaints about my temporary accommodation. This had the desired outcome and I was moved to the top floor of an adjoining tower block into a shared flat. Peace at last.

Looking back, doctors were lucky to get accommodation with posts in the hospital. The organization of the accommodation for staff however was frequently poor with allocation of flats or rooms a lottery. I learnt that being friendly and assertive to accommodation staff was important to secure accommodation that was optimal. Nowadays doctors tend to live off site and commute to work. The shift work system means on call rooms are no longer needed.

The whole atmosphere of the hospital in this coastal city was completely different to up north. It was almost like working in another country. The hospital had carpets, there were shops in the reception area and the hospital campus was situated in a residential area, which seemed tranquil when compared to the raw, barren harshness of many northern cities. I soon learnt that appearances can be deceptive. The area around the hospital consisted of private and social housing with a significant reputation for anti-social behaviour. It was here in a medical students' bar that I witnessed my first pub brawl between a group of local youths and the medical school's rugby club. It was a rude awakening that a seemingly convivial atmosphere could deteriorate so completely into chaos and violence. It was scary but fortunately the brawl was curtailed by the rapid police response.

Up north, despite the intimidating wastelands of boarded- up houses, the behaviour I witnessed in the many bars I visited was always friendly, humorous and non- threatening. This was in stark contrast to the experience of this brawl. It was threatening and exposed the human frailties of raw aggression and violence. I became streetwise, being much more aware of the clientele and the mood of bars when out in the city.

The post in the hospital was fascinating and came with significant responsibility. I worked for two consultants who were both very engaged in supporting their juniors. They relied on the three SHOs, of whom I was one, to run the paediatric cardiology ward, cover babies and children recovering from heart operations, attend outpatients and present cases to the cardiothoracic surgeons. They taught us very early on the necessary skills to provide an on-call echocardiography service to the intensive care area. This meant at night we could review infants and carry out an echo to detect possible pericardial effusions (an important and common postoperative complication to recognise). This was helpful to the consultants as it avoided them having to attend the hospital out-of-hours just to check for this complication.

One of the consultants, Dr Kwunn, was a slight, thin man of Malaysian descent who had trained in Europe and worked in America. He was an excellent clinician and teacher. He emphasised the importance of a good history and examination together with reviews of the X-ray and electrocardiogram in deciding the likely diagnosis; this would happen before carrying out the often-definitive investigation – the echocardiogram itself.

Dr Kwunn was excellent at echocardiography and when he was in full flow examining a baby's heart, he seemed to be a natural extension of the Toshiba echo machines. The echo machines were like washing machines on wheels. Dr Kwunn wielded the probe attached to the machine with grace and elegance. The clipped whooshing sounds, as he positioned the probe expertly, detected blood flow across a valve in the baby's heart and would correlate very satisfyingly with the triangular patterns of Doppler flow on the visual display. Flickering images of blue and red representing flow toward and away from the probe would appear on the colour Doppler. The differing light emanating from the echo display provided a warm glow to the darkened room. The echo room would always be darkened for the examination. In preparation of baby or child for an echo much time would be spent quieting the infant or child and applying a jelly on the skin before positioning the probe to start the examination. In Dr Kwunn's hands, echo examinations were akin to a gala theatre performance. His opinion was good and always highly sought after by the surgeons.

The other cardiology consultant and senior clinician, Dr Wynn, was a plump, blazer-clad man with a keen interest in the finer things in life such as opera, sailing and expensive watches. He was less hands-on than Dr Kwunn but very supportive to juniors. I got to know him reasonably well while spending a day with him helping with an outreach clinic. A highlight was being transported to the clinic in his silver Mercedes. He encouraged me to do a research project reviewing the department's experience of treating arrhythmias. This project was stimulating, and I devoted many hours to reviewing patient records. The results of my research were interesting with several infants presenting in utero (before they were born) with tachycardias treated with maternal antiarrhythmic drugs. The project led to a presentation of the results at an international meeting in Thailand. Dr Wynn of course attended, presenting the findings. The work was also published in the conference's proceedings. I felt very satisfied that at last my name was in print.

The two cardiothoracic surgeons were very different to the cardiologists. The senior surgeon was a tall, well-spoken gentleman whose manner was exacting and stern but consistently polite when away from theatre – there he appeared to undergo a transformation of character, an angry man who often resorted to ranting with high-volume expletives if he experienced any difficulties with the operation. When he was in this mood his insults were largely aimed at fellow theatre staff. I attended theatre once to witness this behaviour and, from then on, decided to keep my interactions with him strictly out of theatre!

Also present was a younger surgeon who on initial encounter, seemed down to earth and friendly, however, he was a fair-weather individual. When things were going well, he maintained his nice persona, but if there were problems with his patients, he would reveal his vindictive side. He most often exhibited this side of his character at the 7.30 am Monday morning X-ray meetings. Following the presentation of the weekend progress of the paediatric patients, if any patients were ill in any way the blame would be aimed at ourselves. His main complaint was that his patient had received too much intravenous fluid. The exchanges often got very aggressive, and his bullying rhetoric upset my colleagues, both female. Dr Kwunn, when present, countered this verbal aggression, providing a calm voice of reason. He would regularly back us up, much to his annoyance of the surgeon.

Today the behaviour of both surgeons would be challenged. We know unfortunately bullying, racism and sexism is a major problem still in the NHS. I know women and ethic minorities in the NHS they have to deal with a lot of prejudice from a male dominated hierarchy which can be very undermining of their health well-being and career progression.

Halfway through the post it was announced that a number of children from an African country were to come for assessment and possibly surgery. They were funded via the African country's government and the operations were to be done via the private hospital adjacent to the NHS Hospital. These children, eight in number, arrived with just two carers; the parents were not funded to attend. An African cardiologist accompanied the children and they were all accommodated in two two-bedroomed flats. Our cardiologists and surgeons on the children's arrival set to work assessing the children over the following week. The children attended the NHS hospital for history-taking, physical examinations, ECGs, echos and in a few catheter studies. Clearly, the aim was to identify those children with cardiac abnormalities amenable to surgery and then carefully consider whether long-term benefits of surgery outweighed the risks. Unfortunately, a few of the children had advanced heart disease putting them in the high-risk category to undergo surgery.

One eleven-year-old boy, David, fell into this high-risk category. He was a pleasant, smiling boy but breathless at rest. His case was presented to the cardiothoracic surgeons. He was high-risk for surgery but if not operated on was likely to have only a few months to live. He was discussed at the meeting, and it was felt his only chance of survival was surgery. This was true but the option of doing nothing was not explored any further. The discussion did not consider the vulnerability of a child a long way away from his parents. No one seemed comfortable with saying that surgery was *not* appropriate, not because it was not possible but that the risks were too high. There were no parents to discuss matters with; the children had arrived with pre-signed consent forms. The operation went ahead in the private hospital.

The next time I saw David was when I attended his post-mortem. The cheery pathologist was extracting his heart from his lifeless body when I entered the viewing area of the post-mortem room. There was a stench of formalin that accompanied the view. The room contained three slabs, one for David and the others for two adults in various forms of pathologist's 'undress'; their heads were open with the skin of the scalp rolled back like a garment and abdomens open revealing the inner organs. David lay in a state of pathologist's undress, his body still but, to my mind, now violated. The pathologist showed us his heart, discussed the structural abnormalities and then placed it into a jar.

The carers took him back to Africa without his heart, along with the other children who survived. Talking with them it was certain that there was regret among the carers about him dying so far from his parents.

The case was discussed technically at the mortality meeting but there was no discussion of the ethics of carrying out such operations. I felt repulsed by what I had witnessed and been party to, not by what had been done but the way in which it had been approached. The approach did not stand up to scrutiny and was based on assumptions about consent not acceptable in our culture. With such a high-risk operation, parental informed consent is vital, albeit difficult in this case.

What did David feel? Clearly it being carried out through the private sector, whatever the result, the surgeons got well rewarded. David was from a different culture where child mortality was high and advanced disease, unfortunately, was common. For every high-risk patient there are many with better chances of benefit from surgical intervention, nevertheless, for David the dice was cast. Once he left Africa there was no looking back. He was entering a different culture, supposedly an advanced culture but, in my opinion, had been fatally let down. The retention of his heart without parental consent is contentious, but at the time this retention of organs was not considered wrong. This issue came to prominence with the Alder Hey organs scandal. This led to stricter governance around retention of any tissue from patients including getting informed consent without exception.

At this point, my free time focused on studying for the paediatric postgraduate examinations. These exams in my era were essential for progression. The exam was divided into two parts; Part One, a multiple-choice paper with a negative marking scheme (a loss of one mark for an incorrect answer), Part Two consisting of a written and clinical exam. This exam was set to dominate my life for the next two years. The majority of Part One at that time was based on adult medicine and so studying for it was slightly abstract to my daily working in paediatrics. I attempted it twice while doing my cardiology job, both unsuccessfully. One attempt, in my defence, was after a night on-call. My third unsuccessful attempt, took place at the beginning of my next post, missing the pass mark by just 0.1%.

My final attempt was during my next post. I prepared by attending a revision course in Manchester on three separate weekends. This was great fun as it involved taking an aircraft, a prop plane, from the Channel Islands where my next post was based, to Manchester. At the cruising height of ten thousand feet, it allowed me breathtaking views of the UK. I attended the course whose emphasis was on exam technique rather than knowledge. I stayed with two friends from medical school while at the course, allowing some sampling of Manchester nightlife.

This time I realised it was my last attempt at passing the exam and thus it was make or break. If I failed, I had agreed to go along with friends on an overland trip to Africa. If I passed, I decided I would continue in paediatrics. This was a crossroads and I sometimes wonder what would have occurred if I had failed. I passed, however, and this meant I could move onto study for the second part of the exam, which was wholly paediatric based. This was a seminal moment in my life as passing the exam meant I continued paediatric training and due to this I was destined to meet Claire, the love of my life! Failing the exam would have meant a change in direction and, like many things in life, would have opened other opportunities and different horizons.

I enjoyed the cardiology post very much but, socially, remained lonely. I did socialise but this was always with work colleagues. On a night out with the ward the two senior sisters attended; the older sister was a chain-smoker and had a very regal air. She was a stickler for things to be done correctly. I respected her and she always looked out for me.

"Harry, Dr Wynn will expect the echocardiogram results," she would warn me and so I was ready for the answer on the ward rounds. Her only vice was smoking and this was a true addiction – she had to depart the ward every hour for a 'top-up', as she put it.

The other sister was a wily complex character with a youthful demeanor but parchment skin gave away her age. She tended to get intoxicated on nights out. On one particular night I ended up in a taxi going back to the hospital, in her company.

"Enjoy the night, Harry?" she snorted, stretching out towards me on the backseat.

"Yes, great," I muttered and felt a hand on my knee.

"You're very attractive; don't you have a girlfriend?" her grip tightened. I looked at her and could see that at one time she'd been attractive, but now she looked worn and old.

"I'm okay," I replied firmly.

"Quite right; I'm old enough to be your mother. You know, Dr Rob and me used to do it on his echo machine. You all want the same thing."

With that she recoiled back to her side of the taxi.

The vision of the sister draped over the echo machine making love to a cardiologist filled me with terror and I quickly made my exit back to the residences – alone!

This recollection wakes me again. The consultant in my bay was reviews patients. I prepare for my turn. The entourage moves slowly, patient by patient, toward me.

I reach for my glasses on my locker and inadvertently knocks over the cardboard bottle of Chardonnay-looking liquid onto the floor.

The consultant speaks briefly with me, avoiding the spillage around the bed.

"You have had a significant accident and head injury, you must stay in another night to be monitored."

"Are you sure?" I plead. "Yes, I am," he insists.

I start to explain about the urinating patient and he outlines that he will try and move me. Interestingly, there was no discussion with the nurses about the incident. The medical team spends less than ten minutes on the admissions ward and they were gone.

The senior nurse approaches me and said,

"See? They don't care. We will try and move you."

I thank her and promise to try and help. I begin to realise that the lack of input of senior medical staff and managers in addressing the issues on this busy clinical ward make it a place of slow torture for many staff and an environment to endure for patients. Humanity and the human touch so badly needed by vulnerable patients was being lost among the task-driven culture (of bureaucracy) and understaffing. This was further coupled with the difficult patients these admission wards dealt with, often with frailty and mental health issues such as dementia. I lie on my bed contemplating the lack of hope that flowed from the senior nurse and re-enter my dream world of training.

Chapter Fourteen:

ISLAND LIFE FOR A YEAR

The offer of a registrar post in an Island hospital just off the English coast came unexpectedly. My colleague, Anne, was my senior, an experienced paediatrician. She had just passed both parts of the exam. She was offered the registrar job on the Island and initially indicated she would go. However, just a few weeks prior to commencing the post, she pulled out and the post became vacant.

The consultant on the Island had a good reputation, being charismatic, knowledgeable, fair and clinically astute. The senior cardiologist was a good friend of the Island consultant and asked me whether I would consider the post. With no ongoing job to go to I said 'yes'.

I flew to the Island on a crystal-clear sunny morning for an interview. The flight from London was spectacular. The English coastline was laid out in intricate detail with tiny inlets and rivers and the sea was glistening with boats of all sizes dotted majestically on the ocean canvas. The aircraft descended toward the Island revealing a vista of rugged coastline giving way to a patchwork of green fields and large houses with swimming pools.

Dr Paisley met me at the airport. He was a tall, well-dressed man with a reddened apple-like head crowned thick silvery hair. He wore a smile that revealed his prominent golden capped teeth. He moved with bustling intent and spoke with a hued Scottish accent.

"Welcome to the Island, the sunniest part of the UK," he boomed, and shook my hand ferociously.

I was conveyed to the hospital with reverence in his silver Mercedes. There I met most of the consultants in the hospital and visited the children's ward.

The hospital was set in the main town, a short walk from the town centre and the seafront. It looked inviting with well tended flowerbeds adorning the entrance. The hospital was modern, with impressive carpeted floors, which included the postnatal wards! The consultants all took time to talk to me. For the first time as a doctor I felt prized and valued by fellow professionals. Following the comprehensive visit, Dr Paisley drove me to his golf club.

He ordered two beers, turned to me and asked, "Do you want the job?"

I had been considering this since I had first heard about the job. The big disadvantage of the post was its heavy rota. It was a one-night-in-two rota, that is, every other weekend, working Thursday, Friday, Saturday, Sunday and Monday. The registrar in post, whom I met during the visit, had played down the excessive hours you were expected to work saying it was often not very busy. I felt that I could cope with the post although it appeared demanding. I looked at the sun shimmering on the golf course with the ocean in the background; it was idyllic.

I sipped the cold lager and further pondered the question. I had no job lined up and had not passed any exams. The lure of living in such a beautiful island was an opportunity not to be missed and I decided it trumped the long hours.

"Yes," I replied, "I would like the job."

"It's yours," confirmed Dr Paisley, beaming, and he shook my hand vigorously.

The post of paediatric registrar on the island certainly came with significant responsibility and challenges. The team covering the Island service consisted of myself, Dr Paisley and a SHO from the south coast GP training scheme. Although still relatively inexperienced I enjoyed the responsibility and respect from other clinicians in the hospital that went with the position.

On the day I arrived in the Island to take up the post, Dr Paisley picked me up from the airport. He then took me to his house for dinner. As I moved to get out of the car, he turned to me and said, "I have just two rules, Harry: First, never send a child with croup for a lateral X-ray of the neck and, second, I like to see my patients before they die." I adhered to the first rule. This was an understandable rule as children with croup, which causes upper airway obstruction, can completely obstruct their airway if laid flat or by being upset in positioning for such an investigation. The second rule, which seemed obvious, I adhered to except for one occasion that I will explain later.

The highlights during this post were the dealing with emergencies and subsequent transfer by plane of sick children and babies to specialist centres in the UK. For many cases this involved the transfer of premature babies. This was where my advanced skills in neonatology became essential. I became very proactive in stabilising premature babies in emergency situations, especially inserting lines and attaching a baby if necessary to a ventilator. Dr Paisley trusted my clinical judgement and had confidence in my clinical skills. My assertive approach seemed to engender a good working relationship. Dr Paisley was a lone consultant and available out-of-hours. The inexperience of the SHO meant he would attend in person for all emergency calls when the SHO was covering the service. This was challenging as he was called reasonably frequently. His respite and recovery from this close supervision of the SHO was when covering me out-of-hours. He relied on me to deal with most of the neonatal emergencies but I knew I could ask him to attend anytime. I therefore honed a proactive approach to the stabilisation of sick patients. Dr Paisley's dedication to his patients as well as providing a twenty-four-hour, seven-days-a-week availability was remarkable albeit incredibly tiring! He was one of the most committed, intriguing and caring doctors I have met. He taught me about integrity, honesty and the importance of putting your patients first.

My experience of transferring ventilated babies to neonatal units on the south coast was challenging to say the least. I had no specific training in the actual transfer hospital to hospital, of a sick child or neonate.

This is a far cry from what is expected nowadays. Today, specialist teams with specific training carry out hospital transfers.

These trips to paediatric units in the UK were always nerve-gangling, however, during my time they were all thankfully successful. The return trips to the Island were always fun, in contrast to the concentration and adrenaline buzz associated with the outward trip. Having a precious cargo on board like a sick baby or child concentrated the mind. On the way back I relaxed, often getting the thrill of sitting alongside the pilot in the cockpit with a ringside view of the seascape below. The planes used for these transfers were mainly Cessna prop planes but on two occasions it was a luxury executive Learjet.

I remember one notable transfer. It was a baby with congenital heart disease I transferred to the south coast cardiology unit where I had worked previously. As usual, I was preparing the transfer equipment when I received a call from the sister I previously described as regal from the cardiology ward.

"Hi, Harry, how are you doing? Sister Welsh here." She sounded slightly muffled and was whispering.

"I'm OK, how are you?" I responded enthusiastically.

"Well, you know you're transferring the baby, I wondered if you could bring me four hundred Benson & Hedges Lights; I'll pay you?"

I dropped the phone in disbelief at the request and then struggled to retrieve it.

"What did you say?" I said, slowly trying to regain my composure.

"Four hundred B&H. You can hide them in the drawer under the transport incubator,", she suggested in a matter-of-fact way.

"Are you sure?" I persisted.

"We've done it loads of times. Thanks, Harry, see you later," and she rang off.

So following the call, the transfer took on a new dimension. On arrival on the cardiac unit we transferred the baby into a bed and, seamlessly, a smiling cardiology sister slipped away with the incubator. After some time she returned, beaming, and announced the incubator was clean, her countenance a sign that she had relieved the incubator of its hidden extra cargo, securing Sister Welsh's 'top-ups' for the next few weeks.

I learnt a lot from Dr Paisley and his approach to practice on an island. I became aware of the importance of maintaining good relationships with your patients and their families. Clearly, a breakdown of a relationship presented great difficulties on an island. He was very conscious about his reputation, which I could see was important in gaining the trust of medical and nursing colleagues, as well as patients.

I had my own clinic and viewed a wide variety of rare conditions as the Island patients were captive and could not attend elsewhere. 'N = 1' became a very powerful learning tool in my clinic. I had many follow-up patient slots reserved for rare conditions. I saw the one child with *Christmas disease* on the Island, the one patient with a liver transplant and so on. It was a great experience and learning curve for me, consolidating my clinical knowledge.

When Dr Paisley went on holiday, consultants from the UK would cover him, coming to the Island as a consultant locum. Many would combine it with a family holiday. These visiting consultants became very reliant on me, as I knew the hospital system, and this engendered a close working relationship.

A visiting consultant who subsequently became a consultant colleague often came with his family. I remember having to call him urgently for an expected preterm delivery he had asked to attend. I observed him receiving the bleep from the 8th floor of the hospital; this floor looked out onto a magnificent bay whose main focal point was a medieval castle. The consultant with his family could be seen walking along a half-submerged causeway, none of them with shoes, and the consultant with his trousers rolled up. I felt a twinge of guilt as I put the phone down after paging him. I consoled myself that I was following his strict instructions to call him for an imminent delivery.

I watched the ensuing pandemonium as his bleep went off while he was shin-deep in seawater. He appeared just ten minutes later on Labour trying to look dignified with a damp ring encasing the lower aspect of his trousers.

On the day the consultant locum left the Island there was an hour or so before Dr Paisley arrived back from leave. It was an opportunity for Murphy's law to be proved, and so it was. A 16-year-old girl with learning difficulties was admitted to Labour in preterm labour at twenty-three weeks. Babies born less than twenty-four weeks were deemed not viable at that time. The midwives initially did not want anyone to attend but then, with the change in shift, I was called. I spoke with the girl and her mother and explained the poor outlook, as it was at that time. I explained that the outcome for babies born so prematurely wasn't good and that I would have to see the condition of the baby to decide if active treatment was appropriate. I had no consultant to call so attended the delivery alone. The baby was handed to me limp, wrapped in green drapes. I put the baby on the 'resusscitaire'. The baby gave a few gasps and I felt a very slow heart rate. It was a severely bruised baby; the eyelids were fused and it had a weight of 550g. I decided that the infant, which I felt looked like a baby of twenty-three weeks, despite taking some gasps, was not viable. I gave the baby to the mother telling her the infant was too weak and small to survive. She cradled the baby and after about ten minutes it died. Dr Paisley, midwifery staff, mother and family were supportive of my decision and the whole event seemed to have dignity for everyone.

Nevertheless, when I recounted this scenario to my consultant neonatologist in my next post, he took a very different view. A baby at twenty-three weeks, he felt, was viable and if the baby shows any signs of life it should be resuscitated.

Nowadays, a similar baby born in the UK with a few gasps and a slow heart rate would have been actively resuscitated, then, dependent on progress, active treatment would be continued. Withdrawal of intensive care would be considered if major complications occurred such as a brain haemorrhage. The outcome for babies born at twenty-three weeks is still poor with a 50% mortality rate and, even if they survive, over half will have major handicaps. In Holland this outcome data has recently led to a policy of not resuscitating babies less than twenty-six weeks. The pendulum in the UK has yet to swing in line with Holland. In fact, it has swung the other way with babies as premature as twenty-two weeks old being offered intensive care, despite very poor outcomes for the majority born at this gestation.

As I alluded to earlier, during my time in the Island I was fortunate to meet my future wife. The social life was hectic. All the junior doctors had to live in and socialise with each other. I swung along with the crowd, enjoying the parties, but also studying for my exams. The one-in-two rota did curtail my social interaction but allowed me to devote more time to study.

It was here that I fell in love with Claire, my wife of thirty years. Claire was a house officer in Surgery and her beauty struck me when I first saw her across the canteen. She was tanned with deep brown eyes, short hair, petite, and had a graceful manner. Encouraged by the heady party atmosphere among my fun-loving medical colleagues, I expressed my interest in her. I was too shy and pedestrian in approaching her myself. My neighbour, a doctor working in the emergency department whom I had known from my student days, heard about my interest and suggested he could help. He was tall, good looking with a deep northern accent. He was forever cracking jokes and loved to dance. A night out with him always finished in a nightclub. There he would show his dancing prowess. His body writhing rhythmically to the music, with his slick black hair oscillating form side to side while sweat poured from his brow and torso.

In the Emergency department where he worked, he was renowned as being outspoken. For example, he would treat an old lady for a leg wound calling her 'love' or 'lover'. When he had finished treating her and she was ready to discharge he often said, 'You are OK to go now, me love. Must do lunch sometime'.

The nurses were attracted by his flamboyant persona and he certainly lit up a routine day in the Minors area of casaulty.

"Harry, you like her; Claire, that is," he boomed.

"Yes, I do, but–"

"No buts, Harry, just positive vibes, please," he smiled and gesticulated. "Do you have a plan to take her out?"

"Well…" I mumbled. I had no plan. My adoration for Claire had been from afar. To ask Claire out directly seemed high stakes.

"I take that as a 'no' then," he whispered. "Man," he exclaimed, "you have to take a risk, ask her out. Life's too short."

"You're right, but I don't see her out, only in the canteen and last weekend with a boyfriend from medical school."

I can help, I have a plan," he smiled. " I will arrange us all to go out and I will get called away. That will leave things up to you." To my surprise, all went to plan and there began my infatuation with Claire.

Claire not only was, in my eyes, beautiful, but also great company, fun and positive. We both enjoyed sport, especially squash, and within a few months we were established as an item, both happy enjoying the social opportunities of the heady medical fraternity. We wined, dined and partied. A particular haunt was a club named the Blue Squirrel, which was popular due to its proximity to the hospital.

After six months things moved on, as always. Claire moved to London for her second house officer job. Her parting comments to me at the airport were 'Don't get too keen'.

I remained keen, visiting her in South London for weekends. Her room was small and situated in the usual tower block masquerading as hospital accommodation. The room was adjacent to the boiler house, which regularly let out billows of steam twenty-four hours a day. At night it sounded like the heavy breathing of the building lamenting its ugliness. We planned a trip to France from the Island.

Our trip to France was based in a gite among a plethora of cabbage fields. We spent an intense time in each other's company, surfacing for outside air on an intermittent basis. It was during this time we decided to marry. It was certainly one of the most intense feelings I have ever felt. My life now I felt had a focus, which felt exciting. The domination of work so far, my life was now challenged by something more ethereal and meaningful. We returned to the Island to convey the good news to our relatives. We celebrated by toasting champagne on our favourite beach before plunging ourselves naked into the sea (on a cold April day).

The next four months in the Island began to drag. The one-in-two rota became seemingly more onerous, especially with Claire in London. I became particularly friendly with Nick, a medical registrar. He was a red-faced slim man with an endearing but slightly offbeat manner. He analysed situations endlessly, which mainly involved other people's relationships.

His other great love was gambling. His weekend on-call would start with a thousand pounds and result in frequent trips to the bookies next to the hospital. On a Sunday evening his body language would reveal the outcome of these sojourns to the bookies.

The main organiser of the doctors' mess was a short, blond-haired, striking-looking doctor called James who had a love for parties (another one!), restaurants, fast cars, golf and women. He engineered a prolonged stay in the Island doing various posts and every six months would attract a posse of sycophants to entertain him. He became a good friend.

I passed my Part One exam and attempted the Part Two written exam. This involved a trip to Edinburgh and I went with Nick and another registrar, Sam. The trip was notable, not for the exam, which was held in the plush surroundings of the Royal College of Physicians and Surgeons of Glasgow, but for a night out in the city. Nick was the only one to pass and I began to dread the repetition of my failing the Part One exam. Dr Paisley was most concerned that his registrars went on to good posts. He suggested I apply for a further SHO job in neonatology in London at a renowned teaching hospital. I did and got the post. Claire got an A&E post a short commute away and we moved in together into a hospital flat.

Routines of the ward dominate the day. I lie on the bed and try to read but I can't concentrate because of the noise of alarms from unattended infusion pumps. I feel trapped in a system that had total control but is out of control. I become convinced no one knew my case and that you have to look after yourself. I stop telling the nurses about alarms sounding in the bay and keep rinsing my hands with hand gel, the fear of COVID at the forefront of my mind. I feel, although still unwell, that I have to escape this toxic environment as soon as possible. The senior nurse approaches at that point and says that they had another bed for me on the surgical ward. I am pleased and feel a wave of elation. The release from another night with the dementia patient and his minder, which has filled me with dread, is no longer be a reality. I smile, thank the sister again and return to my subconscious feeling reassured.

Chapter Fifteen:

London Experience – Senior SHO Neonatology

My previous extensive neonatal experience meant that, technically, I had no problems with practical procedures during my post in West London. I worked with a Spanish registrar, Alexis, who was in his forties, having spent many years working in South America. He was very softly spoken with a kindly but intense demeanour. He was a driven man who was passionate about neonatology, especially neonatal care in resource-poor countries. Alexis was particularly interested in the neurological adaptation of preterm babies and the benefit to all infants including preterm infants of skin-to-skin contact (SSC) of mothers and babies, called Kangaroo Mother Care (KMC).

My proficiency with routine neonatal care meant I had the time to learn new skills such as neonatal head ultrasound and Dubowitz Scoring to estimate age and neurological development of preterm infants. Overall, the post was extremely busy with eight ventilated intensive care cots, but somehow the unit maintained an academic interest that percolated throughout the department.

The two consultants running the department were opposing in character. The senior consultant, who became an esteemed Professor, was a well-travelled doctor involved in many government and charitable institutions. His ward rounds would often be attended by doctors working in different parts of the world such as Russia and

China. This always gave a zest to discussing routine neonatal care and relieved the monotony of many of the tasks in day-to-day work. The other consultant was new in the post and was previously trained up north; he was very uncompromising in style, keeping a distance between himself and his juniors. My recounting of the preterm infant of twenty-three weeks that I encountered on the Island brought a terse response:

"Here we would have resuscitated the baby."

This typified his sometimes unwitting and uncompromising style. I did not agree.

During my six months in post I witnessed the impact of research on clinical practice in the emotive arena of newborn babies. Firstly, was a research paper given prominence by the media written by a UK academic group (Golding et al)[9] on the universal use of vitamin K intramuscularly given soon after birth to prevent haemorrhagic disease of the newborn (HDN). The paper suggested an association of its use and subsequent childhood cancer. This association has now been refuted, but to the public these results were taken at the time as the 'truth'. The research quickly made headlines in the national press and ultimately led to women refusing vitamin K for their newborn babies.

As a junior doctor on the postnatal wards at that time, I found I had to spend onerous amounts of time counselling women about the limitations of the research and the potential hazards of a baby not receiving vitamin K. The postnatal round began to take twice as long. We produced an information leaflet that explained issues but despite this, many mothers refused vitamin K for their newborn babies.

In the U.K. the vitamin K scare led to an increase in babies with HDN. The refuting of the research findings took many years but did show intramuscular vitamin K was safe.[10] The impact of publicity of the initial research findings were profound with an increase in deaths of infants from HDN. This showed the responsibility researchers and editors have in publicising sound peer-reviewed research and the importance of commentaries contextualising research findings. It also proved the need for the NHS to take ownership of health scares with practical advice for frontline staff.

Later in my career I worked in Australia and asked about the vitamin K scare.

"We had no problem," responded a neonatologist. "We did not feel the research was robust enough to change practice so we carried on with intramuscular vitamin K. I couldn't understand the UK approach and shows the importance of good peer review of research especially in changing routine practice."

Toward the end of my post, my second interaction with the impact of research in clinical practice occurred when I was involved in the clinical care of several babies entered a clinical trial that the nurses termed the 'iron lung trial'. This was a trial of continuous negative extra-thoracic pressure in preterm infants with IRDS. Babies were randomised to conventional treatment or managed with the continuous extra-thoracic negative pressure tank (CNEP tank)[11].

To maintain negative pressure in the tank, the baby's body was placed in the sealed tank with a permanent seal around the neck. Any procedures had to be done through portholes with hand seals.

This turned out to be a trial that courted a lot of controversy and showed the great difficulties of carrying out research in babies and children. The professional approach of the research team was impressive but, unlike the surfactant trial where benefits of the intervention were immediate, judgements about the efficacy of the CNEP tank was less obvious – it required adjustments in accessing the baby to provide routine care. As mentioned, access to the babies was via portholes, which made practical procedures more challenging.

The research registrar running the trial was very enthusiastic, engaging and genuinely caring, speaking with the parents with great empathy. Watching him consent parents to enter the trial was challenging – he knew he had a recruitment time limit for the study if they agreed, although his approach emphasised there was no obligation. The parents at the stage they were approached about the trial were very vulnerable. They were, as parents, only just coming to terms with their baby born prematurely and with the added anxiety of their baby having breathing difficulties. In addition, they were adjusting to the realisation that, at just twenty-four to forty-eight hours old, their baby had a long and uncertain road ahead of them. The parents required support during this period and the added burden of making a major decision to enter a trial was difficult. I felt with such a bombardment of issues to contend with, parents may not have had the 'brain width' to weigh up the pros and cons of a clinical trial.

I was involved with just a few patients in the 'tank'.

The trial finished early and was closely analysed, looking specifically at issues around patient safety and recruitment in such a vulnerable group of preterm infants.[12,13,14] The analysis highlighted the difficulty of research in vulnerable, high-risk, critically unwell babies. It also emphasised the need for informed consent and long-term follow-up in this type of research. The trial led to much controversy among parents and doctors involved in it as well as the wider medical community. It reinforced, for me, the importance in medicine of informed consent; this means providing enough time for patient discussion and understanding of proposed interventions and emphasises both the importance and difficulties of trials that could be considered novel treatments in highly vulnerable groups such as preterm infants.

The registrars I met during this post were extremely focused and helpful. I studied for the paediatric written part of my Part Two exam and, with the aid of a correspondence course, passed! I was delighted, but I knew the next hurdle was to try and pass the clinical half of the paediatric Part Two exam. For this clinical exam, I was lucky enough to meet two registrars, both excellent, but with differing approaches to the exam. A research registrar, Jonathan, who had taken the clinical exam six times before passing, leant me a file with detailed notes of every encounter possible in the exam. The notes were excellent and showed me the application and persistence he had put in to pass the exam. The other registrar was Chinese, called Ben, and he had passed the exam on his first attempt. He outlined that pre-emptive strikes and positive body language were the way to pass the exam. Despite preparing solely on neonatology, a combination of tuition from these wise doctors, trailing the teaching rounds in different London teaching hospitals as well as working in the evening, allowed me to prepare for the clinical exams.

I took the clinical exam having just finished my post in West London. The exam went well; I met a wonderful adolescent girl with Down's syndrome whose sister gave a flawless history, providing me plenty of time to undertake a thorough examination including a developmental assessment. I presented her case using the advice given from my Chinese mentor and it went down well. One examiner turned up halfway through my presentation. He was a large, plump man who breathed heavily and smelt of the previous night's claret. He listened to the presentation and then, when prodded by his fellow examiner to ask a question, he leered over the table toward me, his stubby finger pulling down his lower eyelid.

"You mentioned Brushfield spots being a stigma of Down's syndrome. What are these?" he growled.

I remembered my advice about being pre-emptive and positive. Nervousness gave way to amusement at the ridiculous question, and posturing, as Jane Austen might have put it, this rather disagreeable gentleman.

"Brushfield spots," I said, noting the white spots encircling his iris.

"Do I have Down's syndrome?"

Before I could answer the bell went and I was ushered on to the next station, leaving the question floating in the ether.

I moved on to the short cases where two examiners waltzed me around a converted ward brimming with children and parents with a wide selection of physical abnormalities. I went through the drills of examination I had learnt, focusing on being positive. The examiners would often be quite dismissive or seem to have disdain for my answers, but this was all part of the game. I left the exam satisfied I had done enough, but inevitably focused on what I could have done better.

While living in West London our lives revolved around work and study. I discussed with Claire my desire to work abroad. I wanted to do something different and step off the treadmill of career progression. Together we explored the possibilities of a 'time out' in Africa. We first approached a charitable christian organisation that had projects in Tanzania. We were asked to meet with the project lead, a Kaftan clad middle aged woman who prattled on endlessly about needing experience of working in developing countries before working with her organisation. She then told us that working in challenging parts of the world could put a strain on a relationship and they would prefer it if we were married. I almost lost my cool over her rather patronising manner and rhetorical questioning. We both bit our tongues and maintained a subservient manner and were rejected for the posts.

After our rejection, Claire mentioned her consultant, Dr Ponchard, who she had worked for as a house officer, who had links with a hospital in South Africa. I immediately connected this with the account I had been given up north about working in South Africa. We made an appointment to meet with him. He was a silver-haired, short, slim and smartly-dressed man. He had just finished a clinic and, as we entered the room, he peered at us from behind a large pile of haphazardly placed notes on his desk.

"Come in, sit down." He waved us toward two chairs that brought him into full view.

"So you've come about a job in Boulder Rock Hospital." He lent back putting his hands behind his head and stretching out his legs.

"Wonderful place like nothing on Earth." His eyes seemed to glaze over.

"I can arrange it! Wonderful!"

He then began to enthuse about South Africa and the wonders of living and working there. It was like a switch had been flicked on, leading to an outpouring of radiance about a country far away, but in his soul. The deal was done and so we both accepted jobs as medical officers at Boulder Rock Hospital, South Africa.

I felt I had stepped off the treadmill of the UK system; my mind could be freed from the conveyor belt of heavy rotas and perceived success, which pervaded the medical world in the NHS. For once I was following my own deep desire, putting myself back in control. There were plenty of doctors who I discussed this move with, who disapproved, saying it would be wiser to wait for my exam result and get a registrar job. I approached my previous consultants about guaranteeing a job to return to in a year, but none were forthcoming. I later read a book by Maurice King that said, regarding working in a developing country, that there is no 'right' time to go; at some time you must just go. With Claire I decided to follow Nike's rebranding strapline advice 'Just Do It', and so we left the UK to return over a year later.

I had survived my experience of the Thatcher years in the NHS. I certainly had much experience but at the price of engrained, abusive working conditions that did not always consider a junior doctor as an asset. On reflection, the effect of long hours experienced in my first year was not the way to train a doctor and had a negative impact on patient safety.

At around 6.30 pm, the porters arrive to take me to the new surgical ward. I feel a twinge of sympathy for the patients in the bay who had to stay the night. I also feel a twinge of guilt as I am given special treatment in being moved. The perks of being a doctor in the system where most staff did try and do their best for you.

I lie on my bed awaiting the transfer and soon I am asleep, reliving recollections of my training, this time in South Africa.

STEPPING OFF THE NHS TREADMILL AND INTO THE RAINBOW NATION

"Travel doesn't merely broaden the mind. It makes the mind."

Bruce Chatwin

Chapter Sixteen:

STEPPING INTO A DIFFERENT WORLD – SOUTH AFRICA

We flew into Jan Smuts International Airport with an air of expectation. The flight had been bumpy, but we managed to get some sleep. The lack of passengers on the flight had meant we were able to have a row of seats each to stretch out on. The on-board television screen had meticulously traced our progress from Amsterdam Airport Schiphol to Johannesburg. It was unnerving to be eating our evening meal as we passed over Ethiopia and Sudan where millions were starving; just three thousand feet separated worlds that were poles apart – chilled Chardonnay and a three-course dinner versus dirty water and, if you're lucky, some mielie meal. Onward we flew, passing magnificent views of Mount Kilimanjaro, whose ice-covered top stood majestically above an encircling cloud mass toward Southern Africa.

Our baggage consisted of just two rucksacks crammed with what we deemed necessary items. However, the desire to take so many necessities meant we inevitably surpassed the airline passenger weight limit. This meant we had to part with several items at the ticket desk to get our baggage under the weight limit. Most of our larger possessions we had decided to send on by sea in a trunk with an estimated arrival time of six weeks.

Two major events had happened before we left for South Africa. Claire and I had married, and I had passed my Part Two exam!

Our wedding ceremony was on the Island, and our honeymoon in France, travelling by TGV trains to Paris and Biarritz. We did return to the UK for the Royal College of Physicians exam ceremony. We then headed to the Czech Republic staying in Prague, Český Krumlov and Karly Vavarye. Looking back at life during those few months I felt a great sense of achievement. At last life felt exciting and full of promise.

Having landed at Jan Smuts Airport in the early morning, Claire and I were soon reunited with our rucksacks. We then proceeded into the Arrivals Hall. Here we were confronted with a myriad of people clutching signs daubed with names of companies and people. Scanning the crowd, we saw a sign with our names written boldly in black felt-tip, 'Dr Stone and Mrs Stone'. The bearer of the sign was a melancholic-faced black South African.

"Hi, I'm Dr Stone and this is my wife." I blurted and thrust out my hand. His face imperceptibly creased, and he took my hand.

"Welcome," he said in a slow, deep, deliberate manner.

He ushered us across the concourse and into an awaiting Toyota Corolla. We were unable to put our rucksacks in the boot as it was full or on the unoccupied front seat as it had papers strewn across it. So, Claire and I had to squeeze into the backseat pinned in with our luggage. Then in silence we were driven deep into Johannesburg.

We were soon engulfed by high-rise gleaming office blocks rising majestically upwards, their geometric exactness a contrast from the chaotic city at street level. The streets had veranda-fronted shops resembling a bustling American Wild West town seen in cowboy movies. The most striking thing about the streets was the throngs of people young and old. Also noticeable was the lack of white faces. Those whites we did notice were large adult males, attired in shorts and boots, walking very purposely with stern and focused faces.

We soon pulled over down a side street and parked. Then, with an incomprehensible mutter, our driver indicated for us to wait in the car. Meanwhile he disappeared into a shop. We noticed later the shop was a pawnbroker. We waited for thirty minutes, viewing the passing parade of humanity on the street. The men were often shabbily dressed, loitering along the walkways. Interspersed among them were smart, suit-clad workers, weaving their way through the crowd. There were just a few women. They were all carrying an array of plastic carrier bags and infants secured on their backs by tight fitting shawls.

The driver on his return ignored us, just started up the engine and drove on in silence. After the third stop I enquired,

"Are we going to the hospital?"

"Just two more jobs…" he paused, "…this is for the hospital, you know."

He seemed preoccupied and hurried out of the car again. Claire and I began to feel anxious and vulnerable. After the third stop to fill up with petrol from a solitary pump in the middle of a backstreet motor yard, he announced much to our relief:

"We go to Boulder Rock Hospital now."

The porter transferring me was upbeat and expert at navigating me out of the ward and down corridors full of patients awaiting a bed. I saw the fear in the eyes of these unfortunate patients being housed in a corridor, as A&E was full. As became apparent to me earlier, 'corridor medicine' had become the norm despite its indignity and degrading situation.

"Terrible," the porter muttered. "Yes, awful," I splurged.

It felt like the corridor of shame. How can we accept this as the new norm? As I write, this corridor medicine seems to be commonplace around the country, a sad indictment of the depths of despair our NHS has been allowed to reach.

Chapter Seventeen:

FOLLOW THE DUSTY ORANGE ROAD TO BOULDER ROCK HOSPITAL

We were soon on a motorway heading out of Johannesburg. The tarmacked road was straight, framed on both sides with orange earth. The earth was a deep, strident orange due to the recent rainfall. Alongside the roads there were people walking with their backs to us. The procession of walkers were mainly women, laden with infants strapped to their backs, but also clinging onto large carrier bags.

The men tended to walk ahead of the women, clad in worn dusty jackets and a peaked cap. The cap often adorned a star symbol that was a sign of the Zionist Christian Church.

There was a striking contrast between these walkers and the pristine tarmacked freeway conveying sleek Mercedes and BMW cars. The walkers were a faceless line of humanity clinging to the orange earth. South Africa, to me, is a country of extremes where a burgeoning, needful humanity sits passively alongside the fast lane of modern life. I now understand that the issues faced by South Africa are a microcosm of the challenges that face all of us today. The difference compared to the UK and many European countries is that in South Africa you come face to face with the seemingly wanton wasteful First World, side by side with the have-nots. The South African tourist board had it right in describing South Africa as a 'world in one country'.

We turned off the freeway and after a few hours drove through a town deep in Afrikaner country. Pristinely white, wooden bungalows surrounded by green lawns doused by sprinklers, heralded the town. The green felt easy on the eye contrasting with the mile after mile of dusty orange earth sparsely covered in vegetation. The town centre was lined with veranda-fronted shops as in Jo'burg, but more striking was the *complete* lack of white faces. This was a white settlement, all the homes we had passed were for whites, mainly Afrikaners, but they themselves were not visible. As we pulled out of town, I spotted one white face riding a backie or pick-up truck. He pulled up resplendent in his shorts and long white socks and was met by a posse of men who loaded his vehicle with boxes of shopping. Two minutes later he was gone.

We drove out of town past the tobacco fields, lush and green and, again, being doused with water. We turned off the main road and began to climb; the landscape changed. The dry, dusty orange earth that hugged the wide straight tarmacked road extending to the horizon now framed a flat plain scattered with boulders. Among the boulders was sparse vegetation and shack-like buildings. The panorama gave a sense of freedom, the open space framed with a magnificent huge sky that gave the vista an ethereal feel. The buildings clinging to the boulders were made of corrugated iron in differing forms of decay, with the occasional brick dwelling. Walkers who had been absent around town suburbs returned. Children in small groups were running alongside the road playing, young women carrying water containers on their head or in wheelbarrows. Goats ran randomly onto the road. The accompanying vehicles on the road changed from fast-moving sleek BMWs and Mercedes to slow, rusty, overcrowded forms of transport in varying forms of un-roadworthiness. The driving, therefore, became more intense as the driver had to weave around the growing number of obstacles. Despite this, our driver retained his mask of melancholy and continued his fast, unrelenting pace at 160 km/hr.

It was evening, and looking out of the car's back window the sun was setting with a deep orange hue. The silhouette of multiple tin huts with woodsmoke rising from them was laid out over a vast plain. The whole vista was of biblical proportions.

After several hours I suddenly noticed a sign to St Peter's and soon afterwards at a crossroads a sign to Boulder Rock Hospital. It was dark by now and at the crossroads we turned right off the tarmac and onto the bumpy, unmade road. We passed a series of both corrugated iron and brick dwellings before spotting the bottle store lit up with a neon light surrounded by a throng of young men in various forms of intoxication. Next to the store a large sign read 'Surf – Put some brightness back into your life'. This heralded the entrance to the Hospital and the all-important water tap next to the hospital's entrance that served most of the community of Boulder Rock.

We turned into the hospital, stopping at the large metal gates securing the entrance. A group of children next to us paid little notice to our arrival as they queued to fill their water containers from the solitary tap. Some were laughing and chatting while others were stern-eyed, fixed with determination on carrying their full containers without spilling its contents. They slowly disappeared into the night carrying the containers full of precious cargo on their heads.

A guard with a cap sat awkwardly on his head wandered over with a staggering gait and shouted at the driver as he opened the gate. We had arrived at the Hospital seven hours after leaving the airport.

We soon found ourselves stood with our rucksacks at our feet having been unceremoniously dispatched from the car with a swift parting handshake from our driver. Out of the gloom there appeared a white, wiry, dark-haired, rather drawn- and gaunt-faced man in his late thirties dressed in white shirt and cream trousers, both ingrained with orange dust.

"Welcome to Boulder Rock," came his voice with a dry Scottish accent, slightly muffled by the competing rhythmical sound of the cicadas.

"Dr Phillip McCloud is my name, I'm the acting Superintendent," he announced, eyeing us both up.

"Can either of you do a Caesarean section?" he asked, with slight despair.

"I'm a paediatrician and my wife has just done Accident and Emergency," I replied firmly.

"You need to be able to do one to be on-call," he muttered. "He never tells anyone before they come," he commented, referring to Dr Ponchard.

"We are tired after a long journey. Please could you show us to our accommodation?" I mustered with a demanding tone, feeling too tired to discuss the relevance of our clinical skills now.

"Oh yes, you're in temporary quarters at the moment, I'll show you them."

He led us through past the doctors' eating and sitting area, up a dimly lit path to a brick-built bungalow that consisted of a kitchen, sitting room, bedroom and bathroom. We dumped our rucksacks in the middle of the sitting area.

"How are you? Welcome to Boulder Rock," came a bright, friendly female voice and a short, tired-looking woman with shoulder-length blonde hair appeared in the doorway with a toddler gripped to her side.

"I'm Phillip's wife, Sonia."

"We're doing a section tonight if you want to attend," Phillip persisted.

Claire looked at me in disbelief.

I was just about to deliver a tirade in his direction when his wife said, "Don't be silly, Phillip, they have only just arrived."

Phillip glared in her direction.

"I've left some milk and tea for you. We can show you round tomorrow, can't we, Phillip."

Phillip bowed his head muttering, and soon we were left alone.

Chapter Eighteen:

Steep Learning Curve – Medical Officer, Rural Hospital – One Year

Boulder Rock Hospital was in a black South African homeland in the Transvaal. The homelands were a series of areas set up by the government of South Africa in the 1950's. These areas were racially segregated, a cornerstone policy of apartheid. Prior to the homelands formation there was no government education or healthcare for blacks in the rural areas apart from that provided by mission schools and hospitals. Boulder Rock was one such mission hospital, which had in recent times been taken over by the homeland government.

Boulder Rock as a mission hospital was run by white male superintendents with the medical staff mainly consisting of many visiting doctors from abroad. It was during this time that Dr Ponchard had come to the hospital.

The secretary of Boulder Rock Hospital at that time was Mr Bill McBride, an Irishman with whom we were to get to know well during our stay. He knew the history of the hospital inside out and, crucially, knew all about the relationships between the differing South Africans running the hospital.

The formation of the black South African homeland governments meant that all mission hospitals eventually became government run. The result of this was a crisis in recruitment of doctors. The doctors from overseas stopped coming and locally trained South African doctors did not want to work in the rural hospitals. The reason for the reticence to work in rural hospitals was the huge workloads for minimal financial reward. South African-trained doctors understandably preferred the more lucrative remuneration found in the city hospitals and private practice.

In desperation the senior nurses at Boulder Rock approached Dr Ponchard and asked him to try and recruit for the hospital. The drive behind this desperate plea was the nursing school. The school was recognised by the National South African Nursing Association for training. This, however, was contingent on there being doctors in the hospital. Boulder Rock at one stage was tittering on the edge of having to close it's nursing school when it had only one doctor!

Much to his credit, Dr Ponchard managed over several years to sustain a doctor workforce by recruiting doctors like us from the UK. Bill McBride was his contact who, with his influence, dealt with the off-putting bureaucracy that accompanied any appointment. This had worked well until Bill had retired from his post after twenty-five years' service. He remained in the hospital having been provided a house in the hospital grounds courtesy of the government for service to the community. This was quite an achievement being white and showed the esteem in which the local people held him. During his time, he had paid for the education of two local boys who in return helped him with domestic duties. Bill's longevity and knowledge of the history of the hospital and community gave some seeming sense and security in what initially was a daunting complex situation. This especially applied to his knowledge of the relationships between staff in the hospital; we soon began to realise getting things done was dependent on being aware of who knows who.

Bill had seen a major change in the hospital, the new secretary, Homan Mamane, now had ten or so clerks working with him, previously there were none. The working relationships between the nurses and doctors, often white and foreign, had become more difficult. The African National Congress (ANC) was gaining more credence nationally and Nelson Mandela was soon to be released with the apartheid regime crumbling. In the Transvaal, a very conservative Afrikaner part of the country, the hard-liner Afrikaners were preaching their uncompromising racial hatred. Locally, nurses told me how they were afraid to go out alone at night in neighbouring white towns for fear of being attacked by white vigilante groups of Afrikaner men. In Boulder Rock this led to an increased radicalisation among the younger nurses, which manifested itself in militancy. Strikes in the hospital had, in recent years, become more frequent, often over seemingly trivial issues such as the allocation of breaktimes. This low threshold to take strike action was passionately supported by the younger nurses but criticised by the older nurses. It laid bare the divide between the matrons representing the old school 'mission hospital era' and the younger nurses, the new generation movement for change. The older generation matrons tended to be more eloquent in their expression of injustices whereas the younger nurses expressed themselves through raw passion and action.

This issue of disharmony among black South Africans was rooted in apartheid and it seeped in every part of life. The strikes represented an increasing resentment by many black South Africans of apartheid's obvious injustices. The more we noticed the resentment, the more it made me wonder whether, rather than being the solution to the hospital's staffing problems, we ourselves were the problem, being white and foreign. Dr Ponchard seemed oblivious to these undercurrents when he reminisced about his time at Boulder Rock. He seemed to recall his experience during the mission hospital era where racial compliance with apartheid was tightly controlled and at its most repressive. This was often a topic of conversation among the doctors at Boulder Rock.

The hospital itself was set on a campus, which included a school and a charitable organisation that was involved in helping families with malnutrition, called Stop Famine. Around this campus a community had grown, extending up to the crossroads. The crossroads was a hubbub of activity, and the main focus was a market that ran most days. It was a drop-off point for the overburdened black taxis. The taxis were people carriers bursting with people and booming out local music. I remember driving past this area one morning and witnessing an ambulance up on bricks having its tyres, which were new, being exchanged for older versions. The post office was also adjacent to the hospital. During our first weeks we were alarmed to be awoken by gunfire. The post office had become the site of a gun battle. It sounded dangerous and lawless but in truth it was just young men letting off steam, treating their weapons as fashion accessories. They were not trained in gunmanship and, thankfully in this case as in many cases, nothing was stolen, no one was injured, the police had responded, and no one was caught.

The hospital campus consisted of white walled single-storey corrugated iron-covered buildings lining a main drive. Jacaranda trees towered over the building resplendent with springtime purple blossom, which, when fallen, produced gorgeous purple circles of blossom that carpeted the orange earth – it gave the hospital thoroughfare a breathtaking Van Gogh colour swirl effect.

The hospital served a population of several hundred thousand people. This mass of humanity was spread over the entire area of the huge plains we had seen during our drive to Boulder Rock. The tarmacked road linking the white towns of the South and North were just one hour's travel time. In contrast to the tarmacked roads, the roads between the villages were poor. The history of the road was interesting, however, being related to an incident a few years earlier where there had been unrest in the area. The army, to have ready access to their base, had built a wide tarmacked road. This made for fast roads cutting through the homeland.

There were no major sources of employment in the area so most of the able-bodied men worked far from their families. The mines were the biggest employers of these men. There was an asbestos mine situated a few hours' drive away, but many worked further afield in the mines surrounding Johannesburg. The consequence of these absent men was that the homelands' population consisted of mothers, children, the elderly and the physically sick, disabled or mentally ill. Families were fragmented with parents often separated from each other most of the year. The result was profound in undermining the normal strength of family life.

This fragmentation could have dire consequences, which was exemplified by a child I saw early in our stay at Boulder Rock. The child had severe malnutrition and attended the hospital, brought incongruously by her well-dressed mother, a teacher. The mother sat very impassively holding tightly onto a child wrapped in a brightly-coloured towel. On my request she unwrapped her closely guarded package and pulled back the towel. This revealed a gaunt child with a wizened face. The child had a severe form of malnutrition known as marasmus. The story of how this child became so unwell was sad. The mother had returned to work just a few months after the child's birth.

Her work was many hours' drive away and she left the child with the grandmother. The grandmother had unsuccessfully tried to breastfeed the child and since it was still too young to wean, the result had been starvation. The poor infant died soon after I saw him, a victim of the fragmentation of families and poverty that was commonplace in rural South Africa.

This situation of impossible choices for families pervaded all strata of society in the homelands. Nurses, who in terms of the area had good jobs, were not immune from the realities of life. One nurse described to me that her two children lived with their grandmother in Swaziland, while her husband worked two hours north of Boulder Rock. They met up twice a year. The income they generated was all sent back to fund their children.

Many fathers and husbands would only return to their families once a year, usually over Christmas; this resulted in a peak in the delivery rate nine months later. The fathers often had two families, a family in the homeland through work relationships and another family *near* to their work. For women, fecundity was important and would often lead to a woman having several partners. This tendency would lead in some cases to a long-term relationship that would establish the partner contributing the income for the family.

This culture of multiple partners had arisen from traditional beliefs but also the social engineering of apartheid. It provided a fertile ground for the rampant spread of HIV today, which was a threat but not yet visible at the time we worked at Boulder Rock. Antenatal testing showed the prevalence of HIV to be one percent; a decade on its forty to fifty percent.

Communication is key to nearly all aspects of life and its control was another part of the apartheid legacy. The older nurses, especially the matrons of the hospital, spoke excellent English as well as the local language Northern Sotho, the mission schools having taught them all. The younger nurses had a much more fragmented English language, which, at that time, made it difficult for them to adequately express themselves. They had been taught in government schools that only used their own local language or Afrikaans. This had a major effect on education as books and materials in the local language were very limited. English was the preferred universal language in the hospital. None of the staff wanted to speak Afrikaans as they felt it represented the oppressor and was the language spoken by the whites in the Northern Transvaal territory. This illustrated the divide between fellow South Africans. Despite living in the same region, they had been institutionally divided by language through the Education Acts implemented by the apartheid regime.

Our arrival at Boulder Rock increased the number of doctors in the hospital to seven. They included Phillip, the acting Superintendent. He was Scottish and a rather dour individual but a jack-of-all-trades. Tina, the only South African doctor, a lady in her late thirties, trained as an anaesthetist, she was very committed but wore the guilt of apartheid on her sleeve; Sarah, a bright young Englishwoman who was pleasant but quite intense and driven to uphold best standards of care: an obstetrician; Gail, an ex-community medical officer who had an interest in community health and there was Aung Thakin, a charismatic and smiling Burmese ophthalmologist: hardworking with an entrepreneurial spirit.

The relationships between such a small group of doctors were understandably intense. This gradually lessened as the social circle of doctors increased with the recruitment of further doctors during our first few months at Boulder Rock. This rise in recruitment as well as coming from recruits directly found by Dr Ponchard, also came from an active campaign to employ doctors by the homeland government. This government had begun to aggressively take on doctors from abroad to fill posts in the rural hospitals. Cynically, this was said to be because they wanted to avoid an influx of ANC doctors. This was a time when the ANC was recognised as a legitimate political force and the homeland government – known for its corruption – would be threatened by ANC-affiliated doctors returning to rural hospitals.

Boulder Rock *did* benefit as a result of this recruitment drive. The input of Aung was important in liaising with the homeland government to recruit Burmese doctors fleeing from persecution in their own country. The Burmese doctors were diverse in their medical experience; they ranged from very junior house officers to seasoned pathologists and toxicologists. Many did not have the skill set required for the medical officer posts they were to fill. It had some parallels with our skill set on arrival which was lacking in training to carry out Caesarean sections or minor surgery. The expectation that they could all be working unsupervised in a few weeks certainly presented challenges. We did our best to aid their training to function safely in a rural hospital.

Two Zaïrian doctors joined the medical staff and, in contrast to the Burmese doctors, they were seasoned professionals. They were black, spoke fluent French, local Zaïrian languages and some English. Their skin colour, an obsession in South Africa, unsettled the perceived order of things, especially among the nursing staff.

Other additions to our staff included a male surgeon, Harran, from the UK who joined us with his wife. In addition, there was a UK doctor, Colin, who, like Claire, was still relatively junior and inexperienced. A Dutch doctor, Chloe, joined us, also recently qualified. Neil was another surgeon who returned to Boulder Rock every year for six-month surgery stints. He spent the other six months of the year sailing. Neil was in his seventies, wore shorts and had a vast experience of practicing general surgery in the developing world. He had trained as a TB surgeon in the UK in the fifties when, unfortunately for him, as he qualified, TB surgery became obsolete with the introduction of effective antibiotic treatment for TB. In view of this, Neil left the UK to practice abroad in developing countries. His motto for operating in the developing world was 'Only do operations that require the minimum of postoperative care'. Wise words.

As you can see, the hospital expanded markedly with medical doctors during our year at Boulder Rock. It became a 'melting pot of cultures' with doctors from differing backgrounds having differing aspirations and expectations. The backdrop for us all was the dystopianworld of the fragmenting South African apartheid that affected all aspects of life at Boulder Rock.

Arriving on the surgical ward I felt a release of tension that had built up following the urination incident while on Admissions. I was settled into a bed next to a middle-aged patient who was asleep under the covers of his bed. Opposite me was a young man with his legs strapped up in a plaster cast.

"Hello, mate, how are you doing?" he asked.

"OK; had a crash, just need to stay tonight," I answered.

I felt in control and that things could not possibly get any worse than they had been on the previous ward. This was wishful thinking… I had some sandwiches for dinner and settled down for further sleep. My South African dream continues.

Chapter Nineteen:
Getting up to speed

After our long journey to Boulder Rock, we both slept well. Breakfast was served in a building at the centre of the hospital. Here we met and chatted with some of the other doctors. After breakfast there was a short clinical meeting. It consisted of the doctor on-call recounting cases and events encountered during the night shift. During the meeting Phillip was slightly more positive towards us. Sarah the obstetrician was extremely welcoming. Clearly, the issue of doing Caesarean sections had to be resolved and so we were attached to Sarah for training.

"It takes years in the UK to train to do this, but we must do it in the next two weeks," she said thoughtfully. My heart started to jump out of my chest in panic – two weeks to learn obstetrics? This seemed an impossible challenge!

We set about learning about labour ward management and the technicalities of operating. The key to assessing labour was the partogram. This was used to assess the patient and helped drive management. The partogram is a chart tracking progression of labour over a set period. Deviation from the progression indicated a need for intervention of either a stimulation of contractions using a drug called syntocinon or an assisted delivery using a ventouse (rubber cap extraction) or, if neither of these were appropriate, we would take the patient to theatre for delivery of the baby by Caesarean section. The partogram chart assumed that the woman had started labour at a known point in time. We soon found out that that knowing this was often difficult. Many women were transferred in from outlying clinics having spent many hours in labour. This meant although they were started on the partogram on arrival we did not know how long they had been truly in labour. Many women went on to deliver healthy babies but, many did not. Asphyxiation of babies due to prolonged labour was common with many dying or left brain damaged.

The labour ward had three delivery beds for over three thousand five hundred deliveries per year and no antenatal ward. The women in the first stages of labour would wander around in a courtyard, pacing up and down like racehorses in a paddock prior to a race. Assessing these riders and racers was inevitably chaotic. The haphazard interaction between midwifery staff and the mothers meant the partogram accuracy was poor, even in the hospital. During the latter stage of labour, the women would enter the delivery room and, with no privacy or pain relief deliver their baby. Midwives encouraged the mothers often shouting " Tiisetsa" " Kookamush" , meaning keep going and push!

One midwife stood out head and shoulders above the others as a true professional. Her name was Cynthia; she was an excellent clinician and had a passion for her work. In full flow she was awesome. Her small stocky frame would manage a difficult delivery such as a Ventouse extraction with great skill. Despite her obvious aptitude and expertise for obstetrics Cynthia, like all nurses, were rotated to other wards every few months. This meant the Labour ward would regularly lose the benefit of her skills. I asked why she put up with this and wasn't allowed to stay where she was most effective.

"This is South Africa, I can't upset anyone; my family depend on me. You can leave at any time. You might say you're going to stay but you all leave. I must stay."

Claire and I began to do Caesarean sections having been taught by Sarah. Our simplistic approach was to assess the woman in labour ward if asked and decide if she needed a Caesarean section. We were reliant on midwives to make the decision. If all parties agreed, the midwives would consent and prepare the women for theatre. The expectant mothers would then be transferred from the maternity at one end of the hospital, to the operating theatre at the other, along an open-sided walkway.

On arrival in theatre, my routine was to insert a ventflon and preload the woman with two to three litres of intravenous fluid. I would then insert a needle into the woman's back to do a spinal anaesthetic block. We often ran out of spinal needles and had to use green ventflons instead, something unheard of in the UK. Once the anaesthetic block was working, I would then scrub, gown up and operate, only calling another doctor if the baby was compromised. I would be the anaesthetist, surgeon and paediatrician.

During my first solo section the theatre sister assisting me was Gladys. She was a tall, elegant woman who had a very calm and reassuring manner. When I had finished the caesarean section I felt elated. Despite my 'head in the wound' style of operating, which was associated with copious amounts of sweat pouring from my head – I had been successful.

"Well done, Doctor" Gladys said in her soft voice,

"What did you do when you had just one doctor here?" I asked.

"We did them ourselves. The Superintendent would prescribe a caesarean section and we would do them," she simply replied.

"How many have you done, Gladys?"

"Two hundred."

"Why don't you do them now?" I asked, exasperated.

"Because we have doctors…"

"But I've only done one–"

"But you're the doctor," she interrupted before I could say anything else.

I completed around fifty-five caesarean sections during my time at Boulder Rock. All the women survived and there were no immediate complications or postoperative infections. I realised you can learn a lot in two weeks, but having Gladys there was certainly reassuring. Working as a paediatrician now I look back at my obstetric career with some pride, thankful that I did not encounter any major perioperative or postoperative complications or deaths.

My duties day-to-day consisted of running three wards. The paediatric ward for children aged three–fourteen years; the baby unit attached to the labour ward; and the children's infectious diseases ward. Each day I would do a round on each of the wards sorting out problems.

At around 11.30 am, all the doctors were meant to attend what was known as the outpatient unit (OPD). This was, in fact, an admissions unit where, daily, around one hundred people would attend to be seen. The people attending the OPD had to pay the hospital a fee based on a crude means test. If the patient required hospitalisation, further payment for treatment would be required prior to discharge. Inevitability this meant many patients were unable to pay and so remained in hospital while hopefully the relatives could raise enough cash to pay for treatment!

At around 1 pm we would break for lunch and then finish OPD and ward work in the afternoon. The OPD work would often result in booking patients for minor procedures such as incision and drainage of an abscess or manipulation of a fracture. These would be carried out in the operating theatre corridor in the early afternoon. The main anaesthetic drug used for these minor procedures was ketamine. It is a short-acting, effective anaesthetic facilitating patients recovering within a few hours and going home the same evening.

Among the children attending OPD, infections were common and wide ranging. Respiratory infections, superficial abscesses, osteomyelitis, meningitis, rheumatic fever, TB and typhoid occurred regularly. Most children had some degree of malnutrition ranging from growth stunting with iron deficiency and rickets, to full-blown marasmus and kwashiorkor. The latter malnutrition states were managed on a specific ward with a programme of treatments including vitamin A, antibiotics, TB treatment and tube feeding.

Typhoid was a particularly distressing condition I saw on the ward. It was related to drinking contaminated water. This was a common issue among children due to the lack of safe drinking water in the area. The lack of water in Boulder Rock contrasted to the abundant water lavished on the nearby lawns of the neighbouring white town and the tobacco fields. The patients with typhoid would develop high swinging fevers with severe abdominal pain and often become delirious and obtundent. A truly awful condition.

Burns were also common, since most homes relied on open fires to cook and heat their homes. One patient, Precious, had extensive burns to her body and hands. She was treated by Neil the surgeon, and after multiple procedures recovered reasonable function of her hands due to successful skin grafts. The overall outcome was good, a testament to Neil's great skill and experience as a surgeon and Precious's positive outlook - a Boulder Rock success!

CHAPTER TWENTY:

EDUCATION, EDUCATION, EDUCATION

Although on arrival at Boulder Rock Despite I had good knowledge and experience of many clinical conditions , I however lacked experience in specific areas such as malnutrition, typhoid and tuberculosis. I was therefore particularly fortunate to meet and be taught by a world-renowned Emeritus Professor of Paediatrics from Johannesburg, John Hansen, who visited Boulder Rock monthly. He was a short man with parchment-like skin who wore hearing aids and dark glasses. He regularly drove himself from Jo'berg to Boulder Rock alone, conveyed by his old Mercedes. He was an incredibly generous man who I felt understood the legacy of apartheid. His support of the hospital was his way to help heal the wounds of apartheid that ran so deep among black South Africans. He provided the hospital with his experience and expertise in paediatrics. I especially benefitted from his teaching. Once a month he would arrive in the early evening, stay overnight and leave later the next day. He would teach all the doctors in the evening and then do a teaching round on our paediatric wards the next day. He was world renowned for carrying out the early seminal work on malnutrition. He taught me about treating the malnourished child with almost evangelical fervour. He regularly promoted the use of UNICEF's aide-memoire for keeping children healthy in resource-stretched settings – GOBI-FFF. This important set of letters outlined an ABC-like approach for sick children for newborn babies and I instituted it in the special care baby unit. All mothers attending the unit were taught this and it quickly became the focus of the discharge policy, which I outline below: G stood for Growth; O for Oral rehydration solution; B for Breast-feeding; I for Immunisation; F for Family spacing; F for Food supplements and F for Family education.

The visiting professor saw beauty in unusual places. He would often recite that among the chaos of a refugee camp the sight among the squalor of a mother breast-feeding, giving her infant something sterile and pure, was magical and without parallel.

Sadly, while writing this story I came across his obituary in the *South African Medical Journal* (27/12/1920–10/04/2011). It was profound and I realised I had been very privileged to have met him. The obituary read:

'While a gentle and respectful man, John confronted the inequity of apartheid early in his career and was a champion of a free and an equitable South Africa for his entire life. Before he passed away he shared his suggestions for a good life.'

His advice about life included the following:

'Value yourselves – body, mind and spirit.

Value your partners and be faithful to them.

Be friends with your children.

Be compassionate towards others.

Give positive affirmation to colleagues, friends and family.'

I am woken by a commotion in the bed next to me. The middle-aged man under the covers emerged like a slug sliding out from under a piece of vegetation.

He has a very ruddy complexion, was overweight and, as I am to experience, had the most disagreeable demeanour one could imagine.

"Nurse!" he bawls, "I wanna shit and I want it now!"

"Would you like to use the bedpan or go to the toilet yourself?" the nurse enquired.

"I wanna shit, I want it now and I wanna do it here!" he bellows.

The nurse continues, "It'll be good if you were able to go to the toilet and I could help you walk there."

"Nurse, I wanna shit, I'm doing a shit and I wanna do it now; get me the commode!" he demands.

The nurse calls for a colleague who gets the commode and manages to manoeuvre this hunk of abusive flesh and hatred onto the toilet to offload his excrement.

He gives the nurses no thanks for this. I begin to realise that nurses were having to put up with intolerable abuse and rudeness from patients. These were junior nurses being abused and the senior nurses, as I learn from the previous ward, are burnt out leaving junior nurses to deal with the abuse themselves.

"You don't have to put up with this," I say to the junior nurse dealing with my foul neighbour.

"It happens all the time, there is nothing we can do."

I realise nursing is also in crisis as they are abused, undervalued, poorly supported and their seniors are often burnt out – all familiar themes amongst present-day healthcare workers.

I return to my dream.

Chapter Twenty-One:

DILEMMAS AND MISUNDERSTANDINGS

One child exemplified many of the difficulties in managing sick patients at Boulder Rock. Her name was Blessing, and she was three years old. She had asthma, a relatively rare condition in rural South Africa. She presented to the hospital breathless and lethargic. I treated her with the usual medications including oxygen, steroids and salbutamol nebulisers. However, despite this she got steadily worse. Eventually, after a few hours Blessing had deteriorated and required urgent help with her breathing. Blessing was in respiratory failure and needed ventilating.

I presumed we could ventilate her in the hospital by anaesthetizing her and then placing her on a breathing machine. I therefore took Blessing to theatre and intubated her.

"Could you get the ventilator ?" I asked the nurse in theatre.

"We don't have a ventilator," came the nurse's response as I hand-ventilated the child.

"Oh dear," I mumbled, regretting my decision to ventilate her.

I urgently discussed the child with Tina, the new superintendent. We both felt there were two choices; firstly, to hand-ventilate her overnight in theatre or, secondly, to transfer her to Pretoria.

We chose the latter and I was tasked to ring switchboard to sort out an ambulance and driver for the proposed transfer. This proved not to be easy. The male telephone operator covering out of hours was on duty. He was key to liaising with Pretoria and organising transportation. The switchboard was based at the centre of the hospital, a room off the main corridor. The operator was a young blind man who had braided shoulder-length hair giving him a similar appearance to Stevie Wonder. The telephone exchange was old and consisted of a board covered in cords with attached jacks. This blind man was a deft hand at moving his hands up and down the exchange to identify the call. He was not, however, very reliable in his answering of calls, much to our annoyance. Visiting him at night you would often find him curled up in front of a-two barred electric fire enjoying a few beers. My urgent request regards Blessing took time. However finally after several reminders he identified the ambulance was broken and the driver was at a party. He promised to try and locate him.

At around 11 pm the driver appeared. I soon found myself travelling at 160 km/hr in a Toyota Corolla hand-ventilating Blessing on the backseat with the oxygen cylinder laid at my feet. I had an accompanying nurse. We were both exasperated when the driver had to stop for a smoke after several hours of driving. Five hours later we finally arrived at our destination, Maintown Hospital, Pretoria.

The hospital took referrals from no less than sixty hospitals, just like Boulder Rock. The receiving doctors and nurses helped us move Blessing from the car to ITU. None of the medical staff showed any surprise or shock at the way Blessing had been transferred.

The mother who arrived soon after us was understandably distraught. The nurses immediately sorted out the payment for Blessing's care. The mother had to pay before she could accompany her daughter to ITU. In South Africa the user pays healthcare system has no qualms about bringing up the issue of money even in a distressing or life-threatening situation.

Blessing returned to us a week later having been treated successfully at Maintown. She was soon discharged home on inhalers. At the end of my year at Boulder Rock I saw the father of Blessing and enquired how she was.

"She's late," he sighed. 'Late' was a term used to describe dying or being dead. This term was often used quite impassively as death was common and just accepted.

"Late?" I asked.

"Yes, she became poorly and we took her to the traditional doctors; her mother was scared of bringing her here as she thought Blessing would be put to sleep."

I realised that the mother never really understood that her daughter being anaesthetised had saved her life. This profound misunderstanding had led to tragic consequences.

Traditional healers were often more trusted in the community than the hospital. The reasons for this were manyfold. Culturally, there was a common belief among the community that spirits were primarily responsible for illness. Traditional healers used this belief to explain the treatments they offered. This approach was in tune with the deep-set belief system that had great capital among the population whereas the hospital had no such cultural terms of reference. The community saw the hospital as a place where you were at high risk of dying. This was partly true, as many patients often presented to the hospital late – often in the terminal stages of disease – and did die. Ironically, the late presentation was largely due to delays while trying to seek cures from traditional healers.

The 'cures' on offer from traditional healers were variable but were limited by the resources available. The lack of vegetation, associated with the overcrowding of the area and severe droughts, meant many of the medicinal cures included potentially toxic substances such as petrol and paraffin. It was not uncommon for children to be admitted with severe breathing difficulties caused by the aspiration of paraffin contained in some of these cures.

I witnessed myself a more disturbing method when visiting a traditional healer with a TB nurse, Blix, to try and find a boy with TB meningitis who had been removed from the hospital by his mother. The healer's house was set down a dusty track, a mile or so from the nearest village. A wailing noise emitted from the dark interior. Inside, his mother, who was stripped naked, was holding the boy with meningitis. She was daubed in white paint and was rhythmically swaying back and forth chanting. Her son laid limp in her arms. The healer also half naked and daubed in white paint sat impassively opposite the mother hands together in a trance. Blix managed to talk with the mother but could not persuade her to continue with the conventional TB treatment. Her belief in the healer and his traditional cures was unshakable.

"I told her about TB and the treatment but she's so simple," Blix told me despairingly. "She believes her son is possessed with evil spirits; she won't come. She says that only her healer can get rid of the spirit."

The mother disappeared back into the house.

"What's happening to those poor souls?" I asked, pointing to a courtyard behind the house where two men and a woman were chained by their hands and feet.

"They have mental illness," replied Blix. "They spend a week chained up and given medicine. We try and work with the healers to refer us patients we can help, but only a few will."

This emphasised to me the central role of the human and spiritual aspects of medicine and the importance of checking the patient's understanding. Listening to patients and being non-judgemental, combined with good communication skills, are key to practicing good medicine. Miscommunication, as you can see, can have devastating consequences.

Overnight the ward fills up, eight patients sharing one toilet with the added CoVid issues. A man with diarrhoea fills the last bed. I question the nurse whether this is appropriate on an open ward and she says the bed manager insists.

I go into survival mode; I don't want to get CoVid. I plan my escape from what seems like 'Hotel California' – you can check in any time but you cannot leave!

I ask my Foundation doctor to do my discharge letter for tomorrow and also asked the pharmacist, Bella, to have my drugs ready at the same time.

CHAPTER TWENTY-TWO:

BEING LATE

Sadly, death at Boulder Rock was an everyday event. It visited the young and old alike. In the maternity unit the perinatal mortality rate was more than eighty per thousand births; in the UK at that time, it was five to six per thousand. So, death or being 'late' was common, something I found difficult to accept. Nurses would often call to say a patient was 'gasping' and that meant the patient was moribund. There was no alarm, urgency or panic – ever! There seemed a calm acceptance of death.

I remember once being called at 6 am to see a man in the OPD with haemoptysis (coughing up blood). I saw him, diagnosed lung TB and started him on treatment. I went home for breakfast and returned at about 7.30 am to see him on the ward. I couldn't find him, so I asked the sister his whereabouts.

"He's late, Doctor."

Clearly, the nurses had to adapt to witnessing so many of their patients dying; the adaptation seemingly to be impassive and accept death – this was not an attitude that seemed to sit well in our more privileged western societies and could be misinterpreted as if the nurses didn't care, which was far from the truth. Funerals, for example, were taken very seriously with much emotion being displayed and were often lavish occasions.

One weekend I was grabbed by Harran who was in a panic. I knew it was serious as Harran was usually so calm and assured.

"We've got a problem," he said. In retrospect, I note how the word 'we' was used to immediately share ownership of what was an ethical dilemma.

"There's a funeral party who want to bury the mother and the baby." I had heard that a week ago a mother-to-be had died while eight months pregnant.

"They want us to deliver the baby before they can bury them."

I looked at him and then heard the wailing of the funeral party reverberating around the hospital. We made our way to the mortuary and, with the funeral party just outside the door, we extracted the body of the woman onto the slab. Harran assembled the instruments and then set about cutting into the flesh with my assistance to 'deliver' the baby. There was no joviality I associated with mortuaries, just a feeling of nausea and almost disgust at the mutilation we were involved in. We said little to each other and soon released the bodies to their fervent mourners.

The reality of working in resource-stretched settings was brought home to me when dealing with an emergency and assuming fellow staff would be available. We had access to a limited laboratory service and X-ray imaging and you will already know that we were without a ventilator. One soon learnt to take nothing for granted with these services. One such evening on-call I saw a young man who had been stabbed in the chest. Clinically, I picked up that he had a collapsed lung on the side of the wound. I called a radiographer, one of two in the hospital, but there was no answer. I put in a chest drain, which drained five hundred millilitres of blood, and started a transfusion. Clearly, he was bleeding in his chest so I called the radiographer again but he was still nowhere to be found. The patient needed a cardiothoracic opinion and so I sent the patient without a chest X-ray on the four-hour journey to our referral hospital, Maintown. I was just leaving OPD when I spotted the radiographer, worse for wear, staggering through the hospital gates. The next day I approached him, asking why he hadn't been available.

"For two years we have done on-call without being paid so now we don't do it".

CHAPTER TWENTY-THREE:
SURGICAL CHALLENGES ON-CALL

At weekends, two doctors remained at the hospital to cover emergencies. It was extremely challenging and tiring, physically and emotionally. The cover was from Friday lunchtime to Monday morning. After four weeks, Claire and I embarked on our first weekend on-call. Claire was on the first night and was soon called to spend the evening seeing patients in OPD. After dark you would be telephoned or if, as frequently was the case, the switchboard operator was incapacitated, a nurse would come and knock on your door – you didn't get bleeped. Claire rang me for advice about a man who had been hit by a car and had eviscerated his bowel out through an abdominal wound. I immediately consulted the oracle, a book called *Primary Surgery* whose first words are 'Don't panic'.

"It says here to 'extend the wound to make sure there is no bowel compromised by the wound, wrap it up in clingfilm or towels and send to a bowel surgeon'."

"Thanks, Harry, I'll give it a go." Claire returned several hours later.

"It went OK, but I'm knackered," she whispered and then collapsed next to me entering an uneasy slumber.

The next night I was on-call. The day had been busy with a steady flow of patients with problems. A significant number of these patients needed admission to the wards. In the evening I got a call to OPD. I arrived to find a young man sweating and moaning, holding a blood-soaked towel to the side of his chest. I pulled back the towel to reveal wounds severe enough to display the musculature of his chest wall. A spurt of blood gushed rhythmically from the wound. He had apparently been attacked with a machete. I booked theatre to suture his wound and as an interim measure clamped the spurting vessel. Just as I had finished with him there was a commotion and a six- year-old boy was rushed in. He was lethargic and very pale and, once again, was wrapped over his lower half with a blood-soaked towel. His companion an anxious, middle-aged man was clutching some bloodied flesh in a plastic bag. He had been at Koma School and was undergoing his initiation into manhood. He had unfortunately undergone a 'botched circumcision and half his penis had been severed and was residing in the plastic bag. The circumcision had occurred the previous evening and, clearly, the boy had lost a significant amount of blood. I resuscitated him and ordered a transfusion. His haemoglobin was two g/dl (normal 12 g/dl) and I booked him urgently for theatre. Meanwhile, I was rung by labour ward to be told there was a lady in obstructed labour with the baby's hand presenting from the birth canal. I said that she had to be prepared for theatre and rang Claire for support. Claire agreed to check the woman in labour ward and I headed to theatre. On the way I met Phillip who gently enquired how the weekend was going. I blurted out the dilemmas of the cases so far.

"You don't need to do a caesarean section for hand presentation, we can deliver it through the birth canal," he smiled. "Ever heard of an evisceration? Call me when she is ready and I'll help you."

I got to work. I sutured the man with the machete wounds. My mind was so preoccupied during the procedure that I forgot initially to inject any local anaesthetic. The man did not flinch but kept repeating the name of his assailant. I then inspected the boy from the Koma School, the severed flesh was not viable, and I elected to catheterise him and suture parts of the wound that I could. I rang Phillip as the woman with the obstructed labour arrived in theatre. Phillip arrived clutching a copy of *Primary Surgery* marked at the page *Evisceration for obstructed labour*. I stayed and assisted as we made an incision below the armpit of the baby that was dead and began to extract its lung, heart and bowel. It was a deeply shocking procedure, the only salvation being that it was in the best interests of the mother to avoid a caesarean section. Once the baby had been eviscerated, the baby was pushed back up the birth canal and then the head reengaged to deliver. The procedure worked and a limp, crumpled torso was delivered.

During the delivery, Claire had been called to the ward to review a man with a head injury who had been admitted earlier that day. He had deteriorated and had a poor conscious level with a right-sided fixed dilated pupil; this indicated that he had an intracranial bleed with blood pressing on the right-hand side of the brain. When Phillip heard this, he felt we should try and relieve the pressure by carrying out a burr hole, i.e. drilling a hole into the right-hand side of the skull to hopefully remove the blood and relieve the pressure.

Already exhausted from the weekend's work, I once again assisted Phillip, with Claire reading the *Primary Surgery* book for instructions as we operated. We did extract some blood, but it made little difference to the man's condition; he therefore joined several other patients due to go to Maintown that evening by ambulance. At the end of the weekend we were both physically and emotionally drained. Certainly, that first weekend was the worst we experienced. By the end of the post I had done fifty Caesareans, two ruptured ectopics and lots of suturing, drainage of abscesses and manipulation of fractures.

The contrast of the scope of work in Boulder Rock with my work in the UK was stark. The baby unit at Boulder Rock had one incubator with an oxygen cylinder, a far cry from neonatal intensive care unit in the UK. Premature babies could be nursed in an incubator only if there was enough room. It opened my eyes to the use of Kangaroo Mother Care (KMC), something I had heard about from the Spanish registrar in London. The use of Kangaroo Mother Care with mothers being skin-to-skin with their baby was very effective in keeping babies warm and it worked well. Oxygen could be provided into the incubator but there was no other breathing support so many babies therefore died – in the UK, even with fairly basic technology, they would have survived. The hospitals in Pretoria that had breathing support capabilities had strict criteria for ventilation of babies and would not ventilate any baby weighing less than two-and-a-half kilograms. The reality was, and still is, the lottery of where you live that counts and often determines your fate.

Chapter Twenty-Four:

Reality – Exotic Medicine and Administrative Necessities

Snakebites were something that I learnt to take very seriously. One morning during our first week at Boulder Rock, I opened the the door of our bungalow and was confronted with a hooded cobra. My initial instinct was to marvel at its magnificence. I quickly shut the door and grabbed my camera. I then proceeded to capture what I saw as it's majestic upright pose on film. My South African neighbours were appalled by my reverence towards the snake and immediately started beating the snake away with sticks and brooms.

"They're dangerous, you must chase them away. They can kill, especially the black mambas. At night, remember to make plenty of noise when walking to scare them away," they told me.

It was certainly true that snakebites were dangerous as I was to find out. On the ward several months later I saw two children with serious consequences from snake bites. A boy who died from haemotoxic shock as result of a snake bite and another boy who required lifesaving fasciotomies from tissue swelling due to cytotoxic venom.

At night, especially on call, I was often called to the OPD to see patients in the early hours. The path from the bungalow to the OPD was dimly lit. I developed a habit of a stuttering walk in order to make enough noise to scare away any snakes. I almost felt a surge of relief as I reached the quiet, well-lit corridors of the hospital. One night when returning from seeing a patient at the OPD, I started on the path to the bungalow. I was stuttering along thinking about snakes when I felt something grip my lower leg with a seemingly with a two-pronged grip. I was seized with panic and started to hurtle towards the bungalow. Once in the light of my abode, I peered anxiously toward the thing that still gripped my lower leg. Much to my relief, it was my stethoscope that had migrated from my trouser pocket and the earpieces were gripped around my lower calf.

An even greater threat to my life than risk of snakebites were, bizarrely, manhole covers or more specifically the lack of them. Once again, I was on- call and had a nearly catastrophic experience. The episode coincided with a night when there was a torrential rainstorm; the noise of the rain on the hospital corrugated roofs was absolutely deafening. I was walking back from OPD through the open hospital corridor, when suddenly I was plunged up to my neck in water, having stepped into an uncovered open drain. I managed to stop my descent by instinctively using my hands to grip either side of the drain. I felt I had almost succumbed to oblivion in an abyss and felt a surge of panic rip through my consciousness. The drain usually covered by a manhole cover was full and overflowing in the hospital corridor. Someone had obviously decided to remove the manhole cover. I slowly extracted myself from my sarcophagus, losing my shoes and grazing my elbows in the process. I returned home sodden, shaken and definitely stirred.

During our stay at Boulder Rock I soon learned that the priorities of the administrative aspects of the hospital were often in conflict with the medical priorities. This is similar to the complaints you hear today about the style of management in the NHS.

This was first exemplified when Phillip, after our first week at the hospital, said, "Would you and Claire go and visit Mkebune hospital? It has no doctors, and we visit once a week. The priority is to get around the wards and if you feel there are any patients that would benefit from coming here, you tell the nurses, and they will arrange a transfer."

We agreed to go.

We left in the morning with our driver who was a short, plump man with a very happy disposition.

"I'm Sukuli. You like our country? I will show it to you."

We sat next to him in the cab of his van and were soon heading back down the tarmacked road. After about two minutes we turned off the road and down a dusty, orange, earthen track. The track was initially flat and true, but soon the track surface began to deteriorate with the van being swung from side to side to avoid the potholes. Our driver whistled to himself all the way through the journey. Having lost sight of any habitation for an hour, with our only sighting of life being a baboon. We finally sighted a series of whitewashed buildings, Mkebune hospital.

On arrival the matron greeted us announcing it was time for lunch. We sat down to a carefully prepared meal of rice, mielie meal and chicken; our driver tucked in with gusto. After we had finished, we were directed to the matron's office where we were faced with forms to sign ranging from requisitions to sick leave requests. After an hour of form-signing, I addressed the matron.

"Matron, we need to see the patients before we go. Perhaps we can go now and finish the forms later?"

"No," said the matron firmly, "this hospital won't run unless all the forms are in order."

At around 3 pm we were allowed to visit the wards with a departure time of 4 pm to return to Boulder Rock. We split up – I visited the children's and infectious diseases wards while Claire headed for the medical wards.

As I mentioned, on each ward my priority was to identify patients that would benefit from transfer to Boulder Rock. The nurses, however, had a differing priority that was to show how capable they were in looking after their patients. I was impressed, given the responsibility; the nurses, at least superficially, seemed to be doing rather well. They knew their patients well and were following appropriate protocols. The assumption, however, being that the correct condition had been diagnosed in the first place.

Claire identified a young woman, pregnant and in heart failure with rheumatic mitral valve disease, who was suitable for transfer. She subsequently underwent cardiac surgery in Pretoria and did very well. It was frightening to think that her fate was down to a lightning visit by us. We both identified several patients for transfer and left the hospital around 5 pm. The journey back took half the time of the outward leg. The happy disposition of our driver replaced with determination to get home as quickly as possible.

Chapter Twenty-Five:

RECOGNITION BY THE SOUTH AFRICAN NURSING COUNCIL AND GREEN PAINT

The annual inspection of the nursing school was like a royal occasion. The first inkling that it was happening was when several painters appeared in the corridors and began to daub fluorescent green paint on the walls. The children's wards had, in previous months, been transformed by Harran's wife who had painted murals on the walls and got a painting programme going for the patients. This had transformed the atmosphere of the ward into a welcoming, friendly and child-orientated space and the ward staff appeared to be pleased. At our weekly meeting with the matrons I enquired about the painters and was told they were preparing for the nursing inspection. Several days before the visit, despite the protestations from the doctors, the matrons banned doctors from the wards. Our return after the banishment was to find many of the sick patients had been discharged and the walls of every ward, including the children's ward, were covered with green paint.

The sister on the children's ward, whom I thought I knew well, greeted me in an excited mood.

"We passed, they nearly found the dirty clothes I left under a bed but I managed to sit on the bed and disguise it!" and all the nurses around her giggled.

"But what about the walls, the pictures?" I asked.

"They were untidy and would not have passed the inspection."

I felt angry with the nursing inspectors who were white and had come from a university hospital in Johannesburg to judge Boulder Rock. The priority of the matrons was to pass the inspection to sustain their nursing school. The price was to present to the inspectors what they thought they wanted them to see, even if it meant sanitising the wards with green paint and discharging difficult patients. Who was right?

This has parallels with the present day attitude of NHS trusts to CQC visits. Announced visits result in staff being coached by managers to say the right things to pass the inspection, even if they contradict the reality on the ground.

The student nurses would often come and ask me for answers to questions that they were to be examined on by the South African Nursing Council (SANC). Questions such as, 'How do you care for a child after they have had a tonsillectomy?' When I was first asked this question, it was after a student nurse had been helping me with a twin boy with episodes of not breathing (apnoeic spells) whose twin had died that morning on the way to Boulder Rock. The story was tragic; the woman had been worried about her twins and taken them to a private doctor in a neighboring town. He had identified one twin as having episodes of his breathing stopping and had told the mother to bring the child to Boulder Rock. The mother had to catch a taxi and, on arrival, the twin was dead. I was angry at the lack of care that had been shown by the doctor, so when the student nurse asked the question I rather rudely replied:

"That's totally irrelevant, we don't do tonsillectomies; you should be learning about malnutrition and tuberculosis!"

She looked sheepishly downwards and wandered away. Reflecting on this sometime later I began to realise that getting a nursing qualification put these nurses on a par with any nurse in South Africa. It was important to them that they passed, even if the questions were esoteric for Boulder Rock. In a country with such a history of inequality this was a chance for them to have some equality. I could not change the Nursing Board's credentials and certifications and so, my compliance with the matrons in answering the student nurses' questions became my contribution, with their desire for parity with all nurses in South Africa.

After the consultant ward round I am discharged and I tell the nurses I will call my wife to pick me up.

"Oh no," the senior nurse begins, "it may take four or five hours to get your medication from pharmacy. You may have to wait till this evening."

"Well," I say, "could you just check?"

The nurse disappears and within a minute returned with a slightly bemused look on her face.

"The drugs are all here," she says, clasping the medication. "Thank you, Bella," I mutter under my breath.

I quickly take them and with that I leave the ward. My haste means I wait one hour on a winter's afternoon at the hospital entrance before being taken home.

Chapter Twenty-Six:
Strange Requests

My compliance with the matrons was tested to the hilt when one Friday I was asked by one of them to see a particularly troubled patient. I pulled back the curtain of the cubicle in OPD to be confronted by a huge, muscular man dressed in a sand-coloured police uniform towering over a hunched figure cowering below him.

"Hello Doctor, could you look at him?" he asked, thrusting a piece of paper into my hand. I read the paper; it was from the court saying the hunched figure had been found guilty of stealing and the punishment of the court was ten lashes.

"You need to let me know if it's OK to go ahead," the policeman said enthusiastically, his chest now pumped out asserting his bristling physique.

I turned to the matron.

"This is not ethical, I can't do this," I pleaded.

"You must, it's the law. If you don't he will spend more time in jail and he will receive a heavy fine," the matron said sternly. "The man wants you to allow the punishment to go ahead so he can get back to his family."

"I can't," I muttered.

"You must," pressed the matron and then, after a silence, she added, "You could reduce the punishment if you think he cannot take ten lashes."

Reluctantly, I examined the hunched figure and explained that I thought he was fit for six rather than ten lashes. The policeman and matron smiled. I had conformed and the system could dish out its punishment with my approval.

"I'll get it done right away," the policeman announced and dragged the figure away.

Nearly every doctor had his or her own philosophy about the situation in Boulder Rock, it ranged from the empathetic thoughts for the plight of the population to frustration with the nurses for incompetence and the management for putting their own self-interest over care for their patients. Harran, the young surgeon, soon learnt that doing complex operations, which needed good postoperative care, was difficult to achieve. Nasogastric tubes would come out, drains would dislodge and observations were variable. Having had several postoperative deaths due to these problems, despite doing late-night ward rounds, Harran soon adopted Neil's attitude (the veteran surgeon) of not attempting anything that was reliant on postoperative care.

In the baby unit I experienced difficult nursing issues. A nurse starting in the unit recorded that a bedside measurement of a sugar level was dangerously low. However, instead of treating the baby with a sugary feed, the nurse would just write the nursing record outlining that the mother and baby are bonding and that feeding was trying to be established. The nurse appeared not to see that the priority for action. I managed over a few weeks to change this response and the nurse involved began to take great pride in her work. However, after six weeks she announced she was being moved, as was the matron's policy of rotation. This meant that things took a backward step with the new incumbent, which became frustrating.

This has parallels with every system in today's NHS where all our new junior doctors start on the same day every year. It is known as Black Wednesday in August because, inevitably, patient deaths and medical errors increase during this period.[8]

Chapter Twenty-Seven:

South Africa – A World in One Country

Life outside work, during the week, was limited by the fact that we tended to remain on the hospital campus. This meant socialisation was mainly with our fellow doctors. The pressure of work was intense and if not controlled could be all-consuming.

As before, with our life in the UK, it became paramount to have some downtime to offload troubles from work, to relax, recharge and recover our brain width. We visited each other's accommodation to play cards, talk, share a drink and an occasional evening meal. A sundowner drink at around 6.00 pm became a regular routine. The consequence of this socialising was good camaraderie among the doctors but also caused intense relationships.

Among the doctors, the motives to practice medicine, apart from it being a vocation, varied markedly. The Burmese doctors had very compelling reasons to be in Boulder Rock, they were fleeing persecution in their own country. It was humbling and upsetting to hear some of their stories and experiences, witnessing fellow doctors and family members being tortured and even killed for being part of the intellectual elite in Burma.

Many of these doctors fled from Burma initially to the UK, hoping to work. To work in the UK they had to pass an entrance exam called the PLAB (Professional and Linguistic Assessments Board – an exam that had a very dubious reputation and was felt by many UK doctors as being unfair, with a low pass rate). Many doctors from overseas failed the exam and these Burmese doctors were in that category. They were stuck in the UK and, in desperation, moved to South Africa.

The medical students who came for their six- to eight-week elective attachments from medical school were always welcome. Their presence broke up the intensity of interactions among the staff and did provide some light relief from the often very strong opinions expressed by some of the doctors.

One young student doctor arrived full of enthusiasm but a naïvety that was heart-warming. He was a short, thin and wiry man with glasses and a honed English public-school accent. His suitcase contained just a few clothes but was otherwise stuffed full of rubber gloves.

"I was told by my consultant in England that I should take as many as I could, as you may not have any," he said solemnly. "What is the HIV rate here?"

I explained the situation. HIV rates were, during our stay, low among the population based on antenatal screening studies. I was touched by his sacrifice of luggage space to help us keep in gloves. Luckily, we of course had plenty of gloves. By the time he left, his luggage load of rubber gloves had been replaced by African curios, which he couldn't resist buying whenever he saw them on sale.

At weekends all the doctors, except those on-call, would travel away from the hospital. The bridge that linked the homeland with the main highway was like a time warp. Crossing the bridge you left the people walking by the roadside, wandering goats, worn-out cars and corrugated iron shacks and entered the First World of fast highways and sleek automobiles.

On our downtimes we often visited the nearby game reserve, the Kruger National Park, which lay on the lowveld. The journey to the Kruger from Boulder Rock, which was on the highveld, was spectacular, descending through the Rift Valley. The views during the descent were timeless, with the rocky cliffs of the Rift Valley plunging toward an ever-extending expanse of flat, parched land as far as the horizon. God's Window, the Three Rondavels and Blyde River Canyon Nature Reserve became familiar landmarks on our weekend sorties and were always exhilarating.

We stayed in hotels, holiday parks and lodges. This was a 'white world' in contrast to the hospital. The holiday parks were certainly a throwback to the apartheid era; this part of the Transvaal remained the domain of the white Afrikaner. The Afrikaner religion, the Dutch Reformed Church, preached the superiority of their culture over the black South Africans. The issue of their perceived inferiority of black South Africans came into most conversations with Afrikaners and was continually justified. They certainly could not understand our motives to work in Boulder Rock.

The Afrikaner culture was very male dominated with recreation based around driving large four-wheel drives, drinking beer (usually Castle) and a passion for watching national sport, especially rugby and cricket. Downtime was also associated with having a barbecue or, as Afrikaners called it, a *braai*. The holiday parks were geared up for these pleasures; one in particular named Merry Pebbles had the largest barbecues I have ever seen, supported by an endless supply of free, cut wood. At night, from each of the forty or so holiday bungalows, flames extended ten feet in the air, lighting up the night sky. This incongruous situation of extremes between the haves and have-nots was a common dilemma we encountered on these weekend trips. We enjoyed the stunning views and a spectacular barbecue and fire while, just a few hours away, people were living in poverty with lack of basic resources in the homeland.

The game parks were fascinating for both the panorama of the landscape and of course the wildlife. We saw many wild animals during our year in South Africa, either solitary or more than one: lion, elephants, impala, kudu, wart hogs, snakes, rhino and giraffes, to name a few. There is something raw and exciting about seeing wild animals in their natural habitat. Perhaps one of the most adrenaline- pumping moments was during a walking safari during a week's leave. It was in a game park called Mkuze in Natal.

We were among a group of eight holiday-makers walking with a guide early one morning in the park, when we came across a female rhino with her calf. The guide, the leader of the expedition, had explained to us that if we were charged at by a rhino, not to panic but to move quickly to the nearest tree, hide behind it and remain still. The reasoning behind this was that the rhino's eyesight is so poor that if you stand still they will not detect you. That morning this advice was tested. The female rhino, a hundred yards from the group, suddenly charged at us. Panic seared through the group and I soon found six of us, myself included, crouched behind a mere stick of a tree. One man in the group was running away leaving his girlfriend lolloping thirty yards behind him. Certainly, the adrenaline rush we all experienced in that moment sorted out where some of the group's priorities lay, i.e. 'look after number one'. Thankfully, the rhino, after several more mock charges, backed off. Once we got back to camp the man who had fled, leaving his girlfriend in his wake, had a lot of explaining to do!

One of the most striking things about South Africa was the variety and sheer beauty of the bird life. I remember the first time I saw the lilac-breasted roller, a magnificent-coloured bird. I spotted it on a telegraph pole on the way back from Nystroom where I had just bought a car. When I got back to the hospital I waxed lyrical to Claire about my sighting; the next weekend on a visit to the Kruger National Park I managed to impale a bird on my car. I was mortified to find the remains of a lilac-breasted roller on the car's grille. By the end of our year I realised it was a common bird but remained in awe of its colouring.

On the weekends that we did *not* go away and stayed on the hospital campus; we played tennis. There were two tennis courts, one overgrown that we cleared to practise on: the other, playable. Every Sunday the court became a focus for a social tennis game. The participants included Blix the TB nurse, two Indians who owned the petrol stations on either border of the homeland, the vicar of a nearby church, an Irishman, Claire and me. We had very competitive matches, everyone playing with good nature but with a desire to win.

An old water tank in the hospital grounds came to the attention of a few of the doctors who decided to convert it into a plunge pool. The water in it was not drinkable and agreement was sought from the hospital administration to use it. Chemicals were added to the water and a secure fence placed around the tank. A swim every morning in the tank was extremely pleasurable and for some weeks became a regular occurrence after a run. Nevertheless, one morning a body was found at the bottom of the tank. It was a child from the village who had broken through the fence and drowned while playing in the tank. The tank was drained and abandoned. A catastrophe.

I had survived the admission and plotted an escape route bypassing the usual engrained pharmacy delays. It felt like the hospital never wanted you to escape, akin to 'NHS Hotel California'. My main aim throughout my time in hospital was not to have contracted CoVid. 'No time to die'.

The NHS has much to learn about patient-centred care but also staff well-being and care. Acute arenas are scary places. Nursing staff and allied professionals in these areas are subject to the reality of verbal and physical abuse from patients, many with mental health issues. Staff from my observations got little visible senior support. Some studies indicate ninety percent of nurses suffer abuse but it goes under-reported as many nurses think it is just part of the job.[7] Senior staff are burnt out, have lost their empathy and are accepting poor working conditions and abuse. Managers spend the majority of their time in meetings and in front of computer screens with the focus often on rearranging the dwindling personnel on NHS Titanic. They are devoid of real-life experience on the wards or A&E. We seriously need to improve working conditions and rewards for staff in the acute clinical arenas. Senior input is required to actually work in the clinical arena – on the 'shop floor'. At present, the highest paid nurses are those that do the least frontline clinical work. Senior nurses should be omnipresent on acute wards and rewarded well for frontline work. Their presence is crucial to stop patients abusing nurses, i.e. enforcing a zero tolerance of such behaviour and empowering their junior nurses. Doctors and nurses, at present, act like two different tribes in these difficult high turnover acute wards. Establishing a clear, visible and approachable senior medical and nursing leadership team is needed to improve the working conditions in these difficult wards and to combat the issues of abuse that are prevalent and disturbing.

I went home feeling tired yet relieved, returning again to my dream.

CHAPTER TWENTY-EIGHT:

REALITY OF LIFE IN SOUTH AFRICA

Scarpa and his partner, Brigette, ran Stop Famine, a charitable operation that took referrals from the malnutrition ward. The families would be assessed, and then sustainable interventions would be sought for their problems such as siting a borehole to overcome a water shortage, supplying indigenous seeds to grow vegetables or developing an income such as weaving plastic bags together to make mats that could be sold.

Some women from the Boulder Rock were given an area of land on the Stop Famine site to cultivate, to show how productive this could be in providing food to sustain a family.

Scarpa, an Afrikaaner, was passionate about his work, but despite the compassionate aspects of it, he was seemingly very hard on his workers.

"They need to know whose boss," he would say. "Give them any leeway and you're lost."

This type of talk seemed draconian and fitted with the stereotype of the domineering Boer Afrikaner. He had an insight into our thoughts and would often explain at length that, to run a business or even a charitable enterprise in South Africa, you had to live in the real world. That meant being tough, running a tight disciplinary ship and not accepting laziness. This was something we heard again when we faced the reality of the unwritten rules in South Africa.

On one of our weekends off we decided to visit Johannesburg. Sarah had told us about a flea market she had been to, so we set off for the big smoke. We stayed in a hotel in Hillbrow, an area that borders the city centre. The next day we travelled into the city centre to find the flea market. We parked the car and started to walk to the market, passing a bus station. I became aware that we were the only white faces among a sea of black faces. I saw a fight occurring a little way ahead. I felt a wave of apprehension rise in my throat.

"I think we had better go back," I whispered to Claire.

We turned and, as we crossed back across the road, suddenly four young men sprung into our path and quickly encircled us. Claire screamed, a deep-seated scream that seemed to echo and linger. The men flashed knives at us, and Claire threw her handbag toward them. The bag lay between them and us; next to them were the car keys. Claire grabbed the keys and the men took the handbag and fled. We turned back toward the main street; plenty of people had stopped and watched and no one had helped. My trousers felt odd and as I looked down I realised they had been slashed, with my back pocket having been neatly excised. We moved quickly back to the car and two stocky men with light-skinned faces stood, arms folded, on the corner next to the car.

"We've been mugged," I exclaimed.

They remained unmoved. "You shouldn't be walking around here."

"We've lost all our cards and passports," I blurted out.

"You can drive around the block, and they might throw them away," they suggested.

We jumped into the car like startled rabbits, locked the doors and drove back to the hotel. We had no money. We asked to speak to the owner of the hotel, and she agreed to see us.

We were directed into a room darkened by the partially drawn curtains. A woman neatly attired in a light jacket and skirt with a beehive hairdo sat behind a desk and gesticulated to us to sit down on two chairs facing her.

"You wanted to speak to me," she said slowly in a clipped Afrikaner accent.

I recounted our experience, pouring out the emotion that had now caught up with me.

When I had finished, she sat impassively and then, with deliberate solemnity, said:

"This is South Africa, you have to obey the rules. You have been naïve and lucky,", she paused and continued. "You do not walk around the city centre at weekends. That's the rule. That's the reality. You English cite all your liberal attitudes but put you in *my* position running this hotel and you would be out of business in a month. I must obey the rules and be tough to run this hotel; I have staff from Natal, Transvaal, Swaziland and the Cape. They need rules and need to know that disobeying them will not be tolerated. That may seem unfair, in English eyes racist, but this is the reality. I respect them if they need to go to a funeral and they go for I know how important funerals are to my staff. You need to understand the rules and obey them; this is the reality of South Africa. You don't go into the city centre at weekends or at night, you don't stop at red lights after dark and you protect yourself."

We sat digesting her lecture.

"I'm going to help you. You can give me a cheque and I will take that as payment for the hotel and give you one-hundred-rand cash. Remember what I have said."

I wrote out a cheque and she ceremoniously handed over the hundred rand.

We rang Sarah at the hospital who, on hearing our plight, rang a friend who lived in a Jo'burg suburb who agreed to put us up. We arrived at Sarah's friend's house; the couple, Helen and Michael, with their four-year-old son, welcomed us and listened to our tale. Michael took us down to the local police station. A gruff, unshaven police officer listened to our story and then gave us a reference number, saying,

"We're to contact you if your passports turn up." That was it.

That evening, Helen and Michael outlined their philosophy of living in Jo'Berg. Michael was a lecturer at the University and Helen an HIV counsellor.

"Walk around here and all the houses have high walls and big dogs. Most people have guns to protect their property and armed response security systems. We have decided to have none of these. Most robberies are armed robberies, a self-fulfilling prophecy. You have a gun so they will have a gun. We accept the risks of not having security but that's the way we see it. You were unlucky, you could have been mugged in London."

That night the reality of South Africa hit home; you had to make choices, neither without a risk. You could try and live without the confines of security, theorising that this made you less of a target or follow the mass of white South Africans and get the trappings of security.

The next day, we nervously made our way to the British Consulate in Jo'Berg to get new passports issued. We darted like rabbits from building to building, the words of the hotel owner echoing in our heads. The local radio station that morning had a story of a woman being hijacked at a petrol station and then a story about a man returning from holiday and forgetting to turn off his armed response alarm before he entered his house. The security armed response team were duly dispatched and the man was killed. These stories fueled the perception of fear and need for security that pervaded White South Africa. The longer we stayed in South Africa the more conscious we became of this issue.

The next day, armed with reissued passports, we returned to Boulder Rock. The experience had changed our attitude, being much more aware of personal security. This contrasted with our fellow doctors. Locally there was a 'taxi war' going on that consisted of rival taxi companies shooting at each other. There were occasional fatalities but was considered by the local community as nuisance akin to antisocial behaviour but with AK-47s. On occasion, when driving to Boulder Rock, one would come across roadblocks with a gathering of taxis. Prior to the mugging I would drive through at speed but now I turned around and drove an alternative route even though it added an extra hour to the journey.

We did return to Jo'Berg to see a distant family cousin on my side, Debbie. She worked at a local brewery and lived on her own in one of the suburbs. Her bungalow plot was surrounded by a high fence and housed a pool but also the mandatory Dobermann dog. She had a tough attitude to black South Africans and certainly could not understand why we should be working in a homeland. She, and the friends we met through her, felt where we were living was dangerous and would not consider visiting us. One evening while we stayed with her, several of her friends came for dinner. They greeted us enthusiastically while depositing their firearms on the hall table with the same routine as hanging up a coat in a hall cupboard. They were all interested in our perceptions, but soon began to relay their own views on life in South Africa, with it not taking long for security to raise its head as the dominant topic of conversation.

A young man, loud-mouthed and daubed in khaki shorts boasted he always carried a gun strapped to his shin. He enthused about his time in the South African Defence Force (SADF). He described with enthusiasm a trip into Angola where his platoon machine-gunned the jungle while watching wildlife falling around them. He laughed and then started expressing derogatory opinions about Black South Africans; he came across as a very angry, scary man. A couple also present were, to the contrary, great company. The husband worked with our cousin, enjoyed running and had just completed the Comrades Marathon from Pietermaritzburg to Durban, an ultramarathon event. His wife was a diminutive figure with a mild countenance and nature; she enjoyed the wildlife, fauna and flora of South Africa and worked for a bank in central Jo'berg. Every day she drove in from the suburbs, apprehensive about carjacking, avoided stopping at traffic lights and carried a handgun in her glove compartment.

I asked her if she would use it and her face hardened. "Yes, of course, I have been trained."

This was the raw and frightening certainty of living in South Africa. There would always be hard choices and constant fear.

Staying with my cousin allowed me to crystallise my thoughts on living in White South Africa. Living here was living in constant perceived fear. Black South Africans cleaned the pool, ironed the clothes and tended the garden but were also the enemy to be feared. They were invisible, just exchanging pleasantries, appearing from nowhere every day and disappearing to shanty towns, a passive sea of humanity seemingly wedded to inferiority.

As previously mentioned, South Africa is, in the main, predominantly populated by Black South Africans and apartheid has dehumanised this group and entrenched fear on both sides of the Black and White divide. It lingers and infuses every aspect of life. To stay in South Africa you have to obey the rules and accept being a target for the legacy of the human misery of apartheid.

In a tent with Claire on a holiday camp in Bloemfontein, we considered our options looking forward. I had applied and been offered a registrar post in paediatrics in Durban, a great post but meant living in White South Africa. This would come with the constant perceived fear of security issues and we both felt that this was not a battle we wanted to fight. We decided then, with our tent leaking in a rainstorm, that we would leave South Africa. So, with our decision to leave South Africa made, we planned an exit trip travelling across South Africa from Kruger to Cape Town in our Mazda 323 and a trip overland to Victoria Falls, Chobe & Savuti game reserves, into Botswana and Okavango Delta.

Before we left Boulder Rock we had a party attended by many of the nurses we had met and it was the first time they seemed genuinely relaxed. Soweto sounds boomed into the night air as the energetic dancing became frenetic. Many told us that night that they wanted electricity, water in their homes, education and good housing. Their wants were normal and genuine, but among the White fraternity they seemingly went unheard. Nelson Mandela was released during the latter part of our stay. He energised the nurses at Boulder Rock, their demeanour had more agency and they all believed things could change. The yes/no vote occurred at the end of our stay, a vote to decide about free and fair elections for all South Africans. We met some Afrikaner farmers while travelling who told us:

"I vote yes with my head and no with my heart."

The legacy of apartheid runs deep in the psyche of South Africa. Mandela's rainbow nation will take generations to achieve. It was not our battle, I finally decided, and soon we were returning to the NHS and back to Thatcher's legacy.

At home I take to my bed, sleeping for up to twelve hours a day – plenty of time to recall my return to the UK from South Africa.

RETURNING TO NHS REALITY

"It's a funny thing coming home. Nothing changes. Everything looks the same, feels the same, even smells the same. You realise what's changed is you."

Scott Fitzgerald

CHAPTER TWENTY-NINE:

BACK TO THE FUTURE – AWAKENING

On my return to the UK I applied for registrar rotations. Following my first application I was shortlisted and called to interview. My South African experience generated much interest among the interview panel. I was offered the post a two year rotation between a district hospital and an inner city London children's hospital. I accepted the offer. Much to my satisfaction I had within a few weeks got back on the treadmill of a career in paediatrics.

The children's hospital had many similar challenges to that I had encountered in South Africa. The hospital served a diverse community, with families from all over the world. Communication issues were centre stage, as most parents had English as a second language. South Africa was a world in one country and London a world in one post code.

Consultations were conducted using the army of interpreters that inhabited the hospital. After hours the hospital provided an emergency service only. However, many children with non- urgent problems were brought to the hospital in the evening. This way of accessing care, centred around communication issues. Families not proficient in English, would often wait for a relative proficient in English to return from work. They will then ask or pay the relative to bring the child up to the hospital. This was challenging as these non-urgent cases competed for attention with emergency cases. It was frustrating but I learnt to be patient and non-judgmental regards these families.

The clinical work was varied and challenging. I gained experience in children with sickle cell disease (SCD), malaria, TB, bacterial infections, rare metabolic disease, cystic fibrosis (CF), eczema and so on.

I worked for an extremely progressive consultant who always challenged the status quo. She started at 8 am and would complete ward rounds quickly, so by 9 am we were often finished and having tea in the Mess. She challenged any investigations carried out on children.

"Why did you do a blood test?" "Why did you do an EEG?" "Why did you give antibiotics?" "What's the evidence for that treatment?"

The consultant was combative on the rounds, always talking with passion from the heart. Rounds became a series of justifications and reflections, which my team, my SHO and me, enjoyed. My SHOs were very motivated and one, Patrick from South Africa, was particularly talented. We both helped set up an Education Programme for the hospital and embarked on writing guidelines for juniors.

An event during my time in the inner city, however, exemplified the importance of patient safety and its link to staff wellbeing. Patrick, who had been on-call for forty-eight hours had, through tiredness, drawn up ten times the dose of morphine for a child with sickle cell to control pain. He and a nurse had opened ten vials, miscalculating the dose. Exhaustion and the pressure to control pain within fifteen minutes of presentation had led to this drug error. The child, following the administration of the morphine, had a respiratory arrest. Patrick was mortified and the incident was discussed but no formal investigation was forthcoming. The transparency about medical errors in the present day NHS contrasted with those days when the culture was to cover your tracks. I realised then that this was a systems error and, as Mess President, lobbied consultants for a reduction of SHO on-call hours. My consultant taught me to have agency, i.e. get involved and change things. She challenged management with variable success, but had a broad outlook working with deaneries and the British Council while completing a PhD as a consultant. She was a great role model and made medicine meaningful.

CHAPTER THIRTY:
NORTH OF THE WATFORD GAP

Following my two-year registrar rotation, I decided to fully train as a general paediatrician with a respiratory interest. However, there were few training posts at senior registrar (SR) level in respiratory medicine. I applied for several posts, in London and Oxford, but was unsuccessful. I decided to look further afield applying to rotations North of the Watford Gap. I was surprised when I was offered an interview. The interview went well. Once again, I found my experiences in South Africa became the centre of interest among the interview panel. I was offered the post and accepted it.

The relocation up north meant another move for me and Claire. She was working in south London in anaesthetics. She started to apply for anaesthetic training posts up north. We had to live apart for many months while she applied for jobs and finished her anaesthetic post.

This uncertainty about whether Claire could get a post in the same region made me feel guilty about applying to and then taking a post-up north. I had initially applied for job speculatively and only informed Claire when I was offered an interview. This in retrospect had been selfish on my part. Following the visit to the hospitals up north we both agreed the medical and life style opportunities in the region were worth the upheaval of moving away from London. After six months Claire was successful in securing a post on the up north on an anaesthetic training scheme- no mean feat!

Arguably today, transferring training schemes between regions is even more difficult than it was for Claire. This makes doctor-doctor relationships with both partners training very difficult to sustain. More flexibility is needed to allow transfer between training regions for personal reasons. However, this is extremely difficult to achieve in today's era of very regimented training programmes. This issue has added further fuel to the fire of dissatisfaction with the profession felt by many doctors.

Up north I was thrust into a busy clinical life. I initially worked in the paediatric neurology department for four months. The consultant who led the department was a great neurologist but kept himself somewhat aloof. He treated me with respect, but it took several months for him to trust me with cases. This initially frustrated me, but I soon realised this was the way he treated all trainees. He was the sole neurologist and kept clinical issues close to his chest. He was very careful and meticulous with all his patients. This meant he found delegating tasks to trainees difficult. I found neurology both challenging and interesting. The exposure to children with neurological problems I had, has been invaluable to me as a general paediatrician.

The relationship you have with your consultant is a key component of professional development. Nowadays providing feedback on a trainee's clinical progress is mainstream. However, in that era you often had to motivate yourself and look for avenues to progress your interest.

I enjoyed teaching and so while doing neurology I decided to set up an MRCP clinical revision course. The course was a resounding success and helped me network with fellow trainees and a range of consultants. I started to enjoy my role as a senior trainee.

Being an SR in neurology meant my opinion was frequently requested by other departments. This was most often from the oncologists asking for a review of children with brain tumours.

These consultations were always challenging. I found the tension that accompanied these encounters emotionally exhausting. I got drawn into assessing patients holistically rather than just focusing on their neurological issues. This was in part because there were few senior oncology doctors available on the neuro-oncology unit during the day. Being the only senior around I was often approached for general clinical advice e.g. on pain relief, antibiotic use and or fluids. My neurologist felt strongly I should just stick to advising on just the neurological aspects of cases. This was difficult to do in practice and of course the oncologists seemed to welcome and encourage my input into their patient's care.

However, one evening things changed. I had stayed late, on the request of an oncologist, to supervise the admission of a child for brain surgery scheduled for the next day. During the review I noted the blood tests had shown very abnormal salt levels. This raised the issue of whether the tumour had caused a hormone deficiency, which would explain the abnormal results. This in my mind needed sorting out before the child had an anaesthetic and surgery. I rang the oncologist who agreed. I explained the issue to the family and provisionally cancelled the surgery. The oncologist told me she would contact the neurosurgeon. However, unknown to me she was unsuccessful.

On the ward round the next morning, I was emergency bleeped to go to theatre. I entered the operating room to come face to face with the neurosurgeon. He was standing on a rostrum holding a hacksaw and was in the process of opening the child's skull.

"You're a bloody idiot Dr Stone. No one cancels my patients. Who do you think you are? "he shouted. He lifted his microscope operating glasses and glanced briefly at me with real hatred in his eyes.

" I was concerned about a hormone deficiency and …" I began to mumble. His ferocity had shaken me to the core.

"Don't you ever do this again. Don't you ever talk to the family without talking with me first. I could have you fired. Now p*** off".

I was shocked. I felt violated and publicly humiliated. I felt angry at his arrogance. I told the oncologist about his outburst. She was sympathetic to me but said she felt he was under a lot of stress and she had not managed to inform him about the concerns regarding the blood results last night. She told me rather apologetically that I could report him. I was surprised by her luke-warm response and concluded she did not want to get involved. I spent the rest of the day very angry and ruminating about events. I felt used by the oncologist. After much deliberation I decided not to report him. However, from then on, I vowed to follow my neurologist's advice, "stick to the neurology". Post operatively the child was indeed started on hormone therapy.

The behaviour of the neurosurgeon was not acceptable.

In today's NHS, bullying and abusive behaviour is still a major issue and remains under reported.

After four months of neurology, I moved to the paediatric infectious disease unit. The atmosphere on this unit was intense and demanding. The department nutured a real "team" feel about every aspect of the care of the children. The consultants were knowledgeable, friendly, enthusiastic and positive. My eight months working on the unit markedly improved my clinical skills and clinical decision making. I was encouraged to be proactive in writing up clinical cases which resulted in publications and presentations at international meetings. Delegation of clinical and academic tasks to trainees from consultants was constant and encouraged a collegiate feel to the team. Every Friday the whole team would meet up in the canteen at lunchtime for fish and chips!

Sharing a team meal together has been lost in the present-day time pressured NHS but for team bonding and morale it pays good dividends.

The unit was led by a very high octane, "can do" consultant whose positive influence percolated throughout the department. In retrospect he was one of the most impressive clinicians I've ever met. He had an ability to take a forensic history and silky examination skills. He always documented his findings in the patients notes with great care and precision. His proposed diagnosis was justified in beautiful, crafted summaries, including a long list of differential diagnoses. This approach to clinical work was inspiring and I soon became acquainted with a myriad of unusual diagnosis ranging from T cell activation defects eg ZAP kinase deficiency to chronic granulomatous disease. By the end of my eight months on the unit I was well versed in a wide range of rare conditions.

After one year I moved to a regional neonatal unit. Here I met further enthusiastic consultants who treated me as a senior trainee. This felt good and empowering. However, the reality of the NHS was never far away.

During the first week it became apparent there was no on call room allocated for senior trainees. The consultants and managers in desperation offered the use of a day bed overnight on a busy gynaecology ward. This felt very uncomfortable as accessing the bed meant walking through a busy female ward at night. In addition, the bed had to be vacated by 7 am ready for the day admissions. After a few nights trying this arrangement my colleague and I decided to take things into our own hands. We obtained a mattress and used it to sleep on the floor of our office. This is an example of the fallible underbelly of the NHS. The NHS expects highly professional standards from senior trainees with resident out of hours working but negates responsibility of providing suitable on call accommodation and rest rooms.

I remember vividly my last on-call before becoming a consultant. I slept in an on-call room which was in a building undergoing refurbishment works. To get to my room I had to negotiate scaffolding, loose floorboards, dusty corridors and holes in the floor to access an overheated room. Once in the room I had to sleep on a soiled soggy mattress draped in starched sheets branded with the logo NHS property. I then heard the familiar bleeping sound of an ambulance reversing and peered out of the window. The room overlooked the admitting ambulance bay. This room was not a lot different from my first on call room as a medical house officer. Doctors' well-being throughout my training had seemed to be bottom of the hospital priorities. I remember feeling let down and angry as I finished my final on call.

During the neonatology post I applied for fellowships in respiratory medicine. I had already decided that this was the speciality area I wanted to focus on. My interest had stemmed mainly from working with my consultant at the children's hospital in London. I wrote letters asking about respiratory fellowships to hospitals in America, Canada and Australia. The programme director of my SR rotation was supportive about me having time away to get experience which I could not get in the region.

One night at home, at the unearthly hour of 2:00 am, the phone rang. I answered it rather bleary eyed and sleepy.

"Hi this is Professor Wolfson from Australia are you interested in a job?"

I met Professor Wolfson the following week in London, taking him out to my favourite restaurant in Primrose Hill. He was very enthusiastic about the restaurant and this I hoped also extended to my application. At the end of the meal, he not only paid the bill but he also offered me a fellowship in respiratory medicine. I decided at that moment I must leave the north and head Down Under!

I had been close to staying as a consultant in the region while doing neonatology. During the neonatal post I had worked with perhaps the kindest consultant I have ever met. He was intense, honest, and likeable. He however often had self-doubt about his practice despite his extensive knowledge and experience. He was aware of my interest in respiratory medicine and so kindly set up a project for me assessing severe asthma patients under his care. The results of the project were interesting and were accepted as a presentation at the national annual meeting of UK Paediatricians!

During my time working with this consultant, he talked about devising a consultant post in respiratory medicine within the department. He asked me to draw up a job description for such a post which I did. He initially agreed to advertise the post when I was back from my fellowship in Australia. However, he suddenly changed his mind. The job was advertised. I felt obliged to apply despite the fact I was not fully trained in paediatric respiratory medicine. There were strong candidates for the post all fully respiratory trained. Being the local applicant, I was of course shortlisted and interviewed despite my shortcomings. (i.e. my incomplete training).

During the interview I explained my position regards my need to complete my training but to my amazement I was offered the post. My response was to negotiate for a delay in starting the post in view of the fact I was not fully trained. I asked for an extra few months' training after a year in Australia which I felt I would need to fully complete my training. This did not go down well and clearly my request was a bridge too far. The professor on the interview panel, in my opinion was livid with me, and perhaps rightly so. The offer of the post was withdrawn, and the post was then offered to a candidate who was fully respiratory trained with consultant experience. He accepted the post.

Reflecting now, I was naive to expect such a long delay before starting the post. I should not have gone to the interview without being clear what the department would accept. The consultants I'd got to know so well there, were understandably disappointed. I felt deflated and knew I had in their eyes 'let them down'.

The feeling of deflation and constant rumination about "what if I had taken the post" stayed with me for many months. I think looking back on the episode it sealed my fate never to work in the region as a consultant. My doubts about my training credentials meant I probably should not have applied for the post despite the upset this would have caused among the consultants. This was a lesson to me, that you cannot please everyone, but importantly you must be true to yourself.

ESCAPE TO THE "RIP SNORTER" DOWN UNDER

"Fail"Failure is the opportunity to start again, only more intelligently."

Henry Ford

CHAPTER THIRTY-ONE:

ESCAPE DOWN UNDER

We arrived in Australia incredibly jet lagged! It was a wet, cold and windy Monday morning. A taxi transported us towards the city, windscreen wipers on full to combat the driving torrential rain. We had pre-booked into a motel and around 9:00 am struggled into our room. We both collapsed with exhaustion and descended into a heavy daytime slumber.

I awoke suddenly, aware of a buzzing noise penetrating my consciousness. It was my alarm saying 3 pm I fought my desire to turn over and continue sleeping and slowly regained consciousness. In a zombie like state on that drizzly and windswept afternoon I made my way to the Children's Hospital. I had an appointment to meet the team in the paediatric respiratory medicine department.

"Hi welcome to Australia. My name is Derek, this is Brian Paul and Sarah ". A short pleasant slightly balding figure smiled holding out his hand. I grasped it and shook it vigorously. I suddenly felt a wave of excitement about the year ahead.

During the sixteen months I spent in the department I came to know the consultants extremely well. They treated with you with respect and as a junior consultant. Their emphasis was on challenging your assumptions and improving your clinical decision making. The post involved doing around six weeks of a research project, which in my case was a study of childhood asthma, and two weeks on clinical service covering the Children's Hospital from a respiratory point of view. This was an extremely rich experience both clinically and research wise. On my service weeks I provided respiratory consults for the many wards and specialties within the hospital. This meant being available 24/7 for calls during the two service weeks.

During one of my early services weeks, I had an unusual call out of hours.

"Hello, is that the respiratory fellow?" a loud rich drawl of an Australian voice demanded.

"My name is Doctor Fox, you can call me Foxy, I'm ringing from Dry Horse Creek". He paused expecting a response. "Look to cut to the chase I've got a sick pup breathless and on oxygen".

"Sorry it's my first day today. I am Doctor Stone respiratory fellow" I replied. "How old is the child and what are your observations?".

"Well, he's eight months old and pretty crook. But you will never believe it, I licked him, and he tasted salty!".

I couldn't quite believe it, a practitioner licking his patient.

"You did what", I blurted.

"Look here mate, Foxy is always on the lookout for cystic fibrosis and this time I think I've nailed it. The pup's salty!".

The child was duly transferred to our unit with a lower respiratory tract infection. The child had a sweat test which was positive confirming cystic fibrosis. Foxy licking his patients became the talk of the department for many days to come.

When on call as the respiratory fellow I was the first port of call for children suspected of aspiration of a foreign body. My responsibility was to assess the children in casualty and then liaise with ENT surgeons about a possible bronchoscopy to examine the airway and if necessary, remove the foreign body.

Foreign body aspiration can have serious consequences. A child that exemplified these sticks in my memory. The child presented to the casualty department with a wheezy episode. The child's parents were Chinese and spoke little English. The admitting doctors did not use an interpreter and so got a very superficial account of the child's problems.

The result of the inadequate history meant the admitting doctors made assumptions about the child's condition. They labelled the child as having a viral induced wheeze episode (VAWE). This was a very common condition in the winter months. The child was treated with asthma therapy, observed and then discharged home.

This is a good example of cognitive bias in decision making. The doctors assumed a diagnosis of VAWE despite the lack of information from the caregiver because the condition was such a common diagnosis at that time. This assumption was made without considering alternatives diagnoses. This is known more specifically as availability bias and can have serious consequences.

The next day the child represented very unwell and extremely breathless with a life-threatening pneumothorax (collapsed lung causing it by air leaking around the lung). The child needed resuscitation and emergency drainage of the air around the lung with a needle aspiration and then a chest drain. Following stabilisation, the child underwent a bronchoscopy (examination of the airways with the special fiberoptic scope). A wheat inflorescence was seen deep in the airways which was not amenable to extraction. The surgeon was called and advised the child should be observed for twenty-four hours and then they would consider a thoracotomy to remove the foreign body.

The following day at thoracotomy the inflorescent was removed from the pleural cavity (area surrounding the outside of the lung). This was an unusual case and through a literature search I discovered that inflorescences as a foreign body can migrate quickly once in the airways. There were reports describing an inflorescent migrating all the way through to the chest wall forming an abscess.

During second admission we retook the history, this time with an interpreter. The parents recalled the child as having a choking episode and then an abrupt onset of wheeze. This was an important clue to a foreign body aspiration. If the admitting doctor had elicited this history on his first admission the doctor the child would have been referred for a bronchoscopy. It showed there are risks in taking short cuts in history taking. This is especially true for caregivers where English is not their first language.

When I arrived in Australia it was winter, and the respiratory wards were full of babies with a lower respiratory tract infection called bronchiolitis. This was very familiar to me as I had just left a winter in the UK where bronchiolitis also filled most wards.

The main virus causing this condition is the respiratory syncytial virus (RSV) which rotates regularly winter to winter from the southern to the northern hemisphere and back.

In the Children's Hospital, clinical guidelines were in place for all the common conditions including bronchiolitis. The guidelines were strictly adhered to and any deviation from them had to be justified. This meant unnecessary investigations and treatments were avoided. However, it did rely on an initial correct diagnosis. The clinical pathway after diagnosis had its own paperwork with integrated nursing and medical notes. It was impressive approach to clinical care, way more advanced than the NHS. However, I was very surprised to find one respiratory ward with fifteen babies admitted suffering from whooping cough. In the UK at that time whooping cough was an uncommon condition to see in hospital.

Vaccination rates in the UK against Bordetella Pertussis, the cause of whooping cough, were high greater than 95%. However, in this Australian city the uptakes rates were 66%. This explained the increased prevalence of whooping cough in the community and hence the increased hospitalisation of young infants contracted with the condition. The low vaccination uptake rates were mainly due to the influence of a vocal anti- vaccine lobby. In Australia the cost of this poor pertussis vaccine uptake was plain to see on this respiratory ward.

The babies displayed distressing coughing bouts, every few minutes, rendering them blue due to a lack of oxygen. A number of these babies developed serious complications. The most serious was an inflammation around the brain sadly causing a few babies to die.

My respiratory fellowship allowed me to train alongside several other respiratory fellows in the department. It was a multinational affair with doctors from Australia, England, Belgium, Colombia and Thailand. These doctors were at the same stage of seniority as me. The multinational nature of the group led to very interesting discussions on both clinical cases, healthcare and life in general. Claire and I enjoyed a good social life. As a group we arranged meet ups with partners for barbecues and trips around the city. Claire had secured an anesthetic training post in a city hospital, so we were both working and enjoying the change in culture from the NHS. I felt as if I was part of something important and that I had found a rite of passage for training in paediatric respiratory medicine. Many of the clinicians I admired back in the UK had worked at some point in this department and this I found this extremely affirming.

I worked closely with the lung function laboratory team. Dick the lung function senior manager was cricket mad and England's performances were a constant source of gentle leg pulling throughout my stay. Dick was a genuine and generous man. He was a fantastic reservoir of knowledge regards lung function testing.

The Children's Hospital attracted visitors from around the world who were often invited to present at the weekly hospital grand rounds. It was inspiring to hear these eminent speakers from across the globe. A professor of intensive care revealed he had global health interests and presented his work on studies of children and infections in resource stretched communities such as Papua New Guinea. A professor presented his work from Darwin about the high rates of group A streptococcal infection in Aboriginal children. Complications of this infection such as inflammation of the kidneys (nephritis) was health issue in that part of Australia, the Northern Territories. The visiting professors came from far and wide eg UK, Europe, America, India and South America.

One of the most important messages I took from these meetings came from a professor of ophthalmology. He presented a map of the world which detailed all the eye disease in the world. He then superimposed the location of ophthalmologists in the world. There was no correlation. This was an example of the inverse care law. Where there is the greatest need or disease burden there are the least number of doctors!

Each morning, after the weekend, we would have a meeting, which all the fellows attended, to discuss difficult cases. I soon became very adept at considering common and rare differential diagnoses as well as appropriate investigation and management of many respiratory conditions. These sessions were invaluable, and I now look back on them as perhaps one of the most important times of my life.

The sessions made me analyse my clinical decisions. It helped my understanding of cognitive bias and its role in senior clinical decision-making. In addition to these sessions, we had a weekly journal club, that was described as a "beer session". These occurred on a Thursday at 5:00 PM and we took it in turns to present journal articles over a cold beer that was kept in the fridge. Over the sixteen months attending these sessions I soon became up to date with most of the publications of paramount importance in paediatric respiratory medicine, as well as developing a taste for cold lager!

The informality of sessions took some time to get used to. Derek would often use terms that, initially, I did not understand. Following the meeting on Monday morning he would turn to me and say, "Let's go and look at the pups". I wondered what Pups meant and then recalled the doctor from Dry Horse Creek. Pups simply meant children.

In addition, Derek would poke fun at the sponsorship of the hospital. He outlined that the A&E department was sponsored by a company involved in gambling especially the one-armed bandits' machines called Pokies. On the ward rounds Derek would often ask parents what they thought about a gambling company sponsoring the A&E department.

The parents often smiled, and Derek would go on "I bet you thought when you arrived here that you get your child seen, have a cold beer, a good feed and have a go on the Pokies machine".

It seemed that Australia had completely embraced sponsorship of the private companies in the public sector. The priority was to provide enough income to run a state-of-the-art children's hospital. This way of raising income for healthcare did raise conflicts of interest. For example, McDonald's can be found as a popular eatery on the ground floor of the hospital.

Derek was very skilled at establishing rapport with families and patients. This was very important as many of his patients faced very serious, life-threatening conditions. Another consultant colleague Sarah was also particularly adept at communication. She ran the adolescent ward in the hospital, which I visited on several occasions. On the ward, unlike any in the UK at that time, nurses together with the patients ran the day-to-day timetable of ward activity. The nurses did not wear uniforms and the adolescent patients dictated when the ward rounds were carried out. The staff were only allowed into a patient's private space if invited. This patient autonomy led to a very different atmosphere on the ward which initially I found very intimidating. However, after a while it became apparent it was more about respecting the young people and paying attention to patient confidentiality and privacy. This approach to adolescent care was an eye opener to me and I realised that the UK once again lagged behind in this approach to care.

The consultants were friendly towards the respiratory fellows. We called each other by our first name including the professors Derek and Brian. This inclusive atmosphere worked extremely well in building a cohesive and forward-thinking attitude in the department. Derek had had experience in the UK and Canada and was more anglophile than his younger colleagues. They tended to be north American influenced in their approach to clinical problems. Derek understood the pressures in the NHS and often drew parallels between it and the Australian system. I noted Brian who would trained in Africa was a very clear decision maker who drew on his years of experience in approaching difficult clinical scenarios. Paul and Sarah who both trained in North America took a very modern approach to clinical problems with more emphasis on investigation than clinical acumen.

The main research project I was involved with was an asthma study involving research teams in all the major Australian cities. Early in the study I went on a trip to discuss the methodology of the study with the other teams. It was a study that involved assessing asthmatic children and young adults. The assessment involved histamine challenges to test the participant's airway responsiveness, skin prick testing to determine their allergic status, blood tests to assess their genetic make-up and an asthma questionnaire to determine their severity of asthma.

I found the whole experience fascinating and challenging. I was now working with research professionals who were very exacting in their approach to research. The discussion among the research teams about the study soon brought up some ethical issues. The main study coordinator wanted to put in questions into an asthma questionnaire related to conditions other than asthma. In my opinion these extra questions opened the door to other research opportunities on conditions other than asthma, without the participants consent. A senior researcher colleague agreed with me, and after a late-night discussion over a beer we elected to challenge the study coordinator about this issue. After much discussion the coordinator removed the extra questions from the questionnaire. I was pleased with the outcome, and it emphasised to me the importance of not being reticent in raising ethical issues.

During my time at the Children's Hospital two weeks of clinical activity as a junior consultant were my most enjoyable time and gave an almost immediate job satisfaction. Research on the other hand although very interesting did involve some repetitive aspects when testing participants. My research assistant was experienced and highly motivated. We made a good team setting up testing for many participants. In all we completed testing of seven hundred children and young adults in the city. Meeting these children was interesting, but the process of completing all the components of the study was quite monotonous. Despite the repetitiveness nature of this aspect of the research I realised the rich experience of the post, clinically and research wise had built up my credibility as a paediatric respiratory specialist.

Professor Wolfson who had offered me the job retired soon after I arrived in the city. He had a Festschrift, which involved a day of presentations from speakers who had worked with him. The speakers came from all around the world. Each presenter paid tribute to the professor and included an update of their most recent research work. Doctors came from Europe, America, South America, China, Thailand and of course Australia.

My clinical experience grew and grew during my time in the department. I learnt all about lung function testing, exercise testing, bronchoscopy, interpretation of computerised tomography scans and chest radiographs. I became more familiar with the treatment of common conditions such as difficult asthma and cystic fibrosis. By the end of my post, I felt I was now well trained in respiratory paediatrics.

I began to reflect towards the end of my time in Australia on the comparison of being a consultant in Australia and the UK. In Australia there is a public service, but a great number of people choose to use the private sector. The consultants I met mostly worked in both sectors. They would carry calling cards advertising their services. Financial rewards in the private sector and public sector were very good and lucrative. Consultants doing just a few clinics a week could earn as much as consultant starting in the NHS. However, the NHS was a busier clinical arena. For example, a consultant outpatient clinic in Australia might see six patients whereas a consultant in the NHS will be seeing eighteen to twenty patients per clinic. However, when one considered the effectiveness of sorting out the patients' problems this was much better done in Australia. So, seeing less patients allowed adequate consultation time and a better outcome for patients. The adage "Less is more ".

The end of my sixteen months in Australia despite the attractiveness working as a consultant in Australia I was ready to return to the NHS. The feeling had similarities to how I felt in South Africa. My battle and affinity lay with the NHS and not the attractive lifestyle of Australia.

Throughout my work in Australia, I met a lot of fantastic people. During one of my research projects I met a nurse who was a member of a bushwalking club. She invited me and Claire to a weekend walk. On a Friday evening we met up at around 7:00 pm in the evening and then drove for three or four hours out of the city and into the Bush.

We arrived at the campsite at around midnight. On the following morning we hiked up to the top of a limestone mountain. The views were spectacular. Here we had a celebration in honour of fellow bushwalker who had sadly recently died in a road traffic accident. It was an extremely emotive occasion. We toasted his memory with a glass of champagne while viewing an awesome sunset. During the day it had been hot, around 30 degrees. However, as the sun set, and day turned to night, the temperatures plummeted to just above freezing point. Both Claire and I slept fully clothed in sleeping bags, but still felt cold. The next day after our nightime refrigeration, we had a frugal breakfast and started the descent down through a limestone rock formation. This was exceedingly challenging. I was carrying a heavy backpack and had a fear of heights. During the descent I had to jump across a crevasse. I found this jump difficult to execute especially in view of my fear of heights. After much cajoling from fellow hikers, I discarded my rucksack and made a leap of faith across the crevasse. The sense of achievement at the end of that weekend was phenomenal. This trip showed the variety of experiences Australia has to offer.

We did of course spend a lot of time on the beaches enjoying surfing and scuba diving. We had dived initially locally, recertifying our diving qualifications that we had previously obtained in South Africa. Toward the end of our time in Australia we journeyed to the Great Barrier Reef. Here we joined a live aboard dive boat at Lizard Island and travelled along the Ribbon reefs to Cairns. We managed three dives a day and saw phenomenal coral reefs, large groupers, turtles, manta rays and it goes without saying sharks. Overall, a cornucopia of wildlife.

We lived in a flat near some exotic gardens close to the city centre. Getting to and from the hospital was a pleasant water-side bike ride. This city like all the cities in Australia was a great venue for sports whether a participant or a sports fan. Australians are obsessed with sport and the national teams are treated with reverence.

During our stay down under we participated in badminton, tennis, golf and swimming. We travelled to several cities as spectators to attend a few of the must-see national sporting events. These included the Rugby League final, Melbourne Cup horse race, Boxing Day cricket test and the Australian rules football semi-final. Tickets to all these events were readily available and not extravagantly expensive. The ease with which we were able to attend major sporting events in Australia was in stark contrast to experience in the UK, where seminal sporting events sell out quickly and are notoriously expensive.

Australian in summary was and still is, a great place to live and work. It's got a vibrancy and a "can do" attitude among the people. Outdoor living is part of an Australian's DNA. You can enjoy a surprising variety of terrains range from deserts, rivers, limestone mountains, beaches, coral reefs, lush rainforest and in the winter, snow fields with ski resorts!

The downside of these wonderful places to visit and enjoy, is the small risk of meeting a poisonous snake or spider, a hungry shark or snappy crocodile.

The cities are where most Australians live. They have a multicultural feel to them. Longstanding naturalised communities from Europe Asia and the Pacific provide modern Australia with a rich tapestry of food, arts and languages.

However, there is a major issue I should mention that infiltrates all aspects of Australian life including healthcare. It relates to the indigenous inhabitants of Australia, the Aboriginal people, who have not adapted well to modern multicultural Australia. Aboriginal communities continue to have the worst indices for mortality and mobility, addiction, unemployment anti-social behaviour when compared to the other Australian communities.

The historical legacy of the brutal treatment of Aboriginal communities by the early European settlers is well known. This legacy still dominates the socio- political discourse, with volatile contradictory views expressed about the Aboriginal rights to land ownership in the right to go "walkabout". The polarised views were exemplified in the recent Australian Indigenous Voice referendum 2023. This national vote rejected the proposal that Aboriginal people should be recognised by the constitution and a body established to advise parliament on Indigenous issues.

Successive Australian governments in recent years have committed significant number of resources and expenditure to try and redress Aboriginal inequality. Reserves have been set up outside cities for Aboriginal communities to reside in. The reserves themselves provide subsidised housing, healthcare facilities and employment opportunities. Despite these government initiatives, uptake by the Aboriginal community is variable. There is a deep resentment among Aboriginal community regards the way they've been treated by governments. This has led to mistrust of authority among the indigenous people mirroring what is seen in the First Nation people in other parts of the world e.g. Canada and America.

This lack of engagement of indigenous people with modern life, is often vilified by other Australian communities. The mistrust of authority by indigenous peoples perhaps has his roots in the way they view the world. They start from a spiritual view of the world in contrast to a European more evidence-based view of modern life. This has parallels with my experience in South Africa where peoples' spiritual beliefs meant they would seek help when unwell from traditional healers rather than attend hospital.

After sixteen months I was sad to leave Australia, we had made good friends and I had learnt a lot about respiratory medicine. However, I felt a sense of excitement about the prospect of returning to the NHS, despite it's faults. The political landscape had changed in the UK. Tony Blair had won a landslide general election with his soundtrack being the anthem "it can only get better". I felt enthused about the new political direction of the UK. The NHS principle of being free at the point of delivery irrespective of income, I realised was truly unique. Medicine in the UK was a social transformative movement and I wanted to be part of it. I wanted to help shape the future of our beloved NHS!

JOURNEY'S END IN SIGHT

"Failure is success in progress."

Albert Einstein

Chapter Thirty-Two:
Back to Reality

We returned to the UK earlier than planned; I had been shortlisted for a consultant job in the hospital where I was due to work. I was full of confidence and felt that now I had the credentials for practicing paediatrics with an interest in respiratory medicine.

I arranged to see the essential consultants related to the post prior to the interview. These meetings, rather than being affirmative, made me doubt my achievements. My Australian experience was, in my opinion, excellent, however, this was not an opinion shared by the homebred consultants. These doctors seemed to have a very narrow-minded attitude and were generally dismissive of the worth and experience gained elsewhere.

The mood music I began to hear was not good. My previous interview was a likely contributory cause. You may recall that at this interview I had been offered a post but at the time I felt I needed more training and so had turned it down. The Professor who had been at this interview agreed to meet me. He kept me waiting for an hour.

His greeting was very lukewarm.

"You still waiting to see me? I've got five minutes now. I suppose you can come in."

The body language was negative as he retreated into his office. He then listened to my pitch, avoiding eye contact. He showed no interest in my Australian experience. I felt deflated. The reality was that he had the power and influence, and I was therefore doomed not to be successful despite my credentials for the post. On reflection, the Professor was understandably still annoyed at my rejection of the previous consultant post in the region.

The incumbent consultant, retiring from the advertised post, was very blunt about his allegiances. There were two candidates, a doctor called Sam and me. Sam had trained solely in the region and had worked with this consultant for years.

"To be honest, Harry," he mused, "I want Sam to get this post." I looked at him in disbelief.

I met another consultant who would be a colleague if I was successful. He had been disparaging of previous specialist posts in the region and was also predictably dismissive of my training and experience. In desperation I approached my bow tied hero consultant who was upbeat as usual but outlined the reality of my situation.

"Harry," he began apologetically, "I know it looks tough but it's all about the interview – you are both good candidates. All you can do is perform well in the interview."

Despite his positive vibe, I saw a glimpse of despair deep in his eyes; I was a lost cause.

I toyed with the idea of not attending the interview. I stayed in a hotel the night before the interview. It was aptly named a Swallow Hotel. I unfortunately got little sleep as I was kept up all night by the grunts and expletives of a couple in the adjoining room.

The interview, predictably, did not go well. The Professor adopted an aggressive style of questioning, trying to portray me as incompetent.

"Tell me about your research proposals in detail if you got the post," was his opening gambit.

I started to outline my interests in improving patient communication in trying to achieve adherence to medications in severe asthma.

"That sounds very broad; I want detail," he interrupted my answer. "Dr Stone, do you have the research proposal ready to go?"

He knew I had plenty of ideas and had explained them to him prior to the interview.

"I have drawn up a broad proposal but it needs finalising," I said positively.

"So, you *don't* have a proposal fully worked out yet?" he asked slowly.

"No," I replied.

"So you don't have a research project ready to go?" He looked menacing and now maintained eye contact.

"Not straightaway," I blurted.

"Why not, Dr Stone?" he retorted. I felt anger welling up in my body.

"I have just come from Australia where I have been involved in research and have some great ideas, which I hope I can develop," I replied firmly. The silence that followed was filled with the Professor furrowing his eyebrows, ready for the kill.

"But no research proposal worked out,", he announced triumphantly.

"No," I conceded.

The next interviewer sat next to the Professor and continued the onslaught.

"Have you ever worked in a transplant unit?" The panel knew that I had not.

"Well, I have been involved in care of children with lung transplants on the children's ward in Australia." I did have some relevant experience.

"No, Dr Stone, you misheard me. Have you ever worked on a transplant unit?" His eyes deviated to take in the Professor looking smug. He continued.

"Dr Stone, is it right to say you have no experience of working on a transplant unit?"

"I have looked after children post-transplant—" I repeated my answer but was interrupted again.

"So, the answer to my question is 'no'," and he looked at me with disdain.

"No," I confirmed loudly.

The Professor smiled. I had been cornered.

The infectious disease consultant then took over the questioning, I think trying to help me.

"Dr Stone, tell us about your experience in Australia and what areas of respiratory medicine interest you."

This was an open canvas for me to outline my extensive experience to the interview panel. The Professor who sat back with eyes deviated upwards while I was speaking, however, had done the damage.

This whole process was upsetting, and I had been naïve not to have listened to the mood music pre-interview. I was never going to be successful without professorial support. I should never have gone to the interview!

Following the interview, I had to return to the region for a last stint as a senior registrar. This was unfortunately the most unsettled period of my life. The outcome of the interview meant I felt a failure and was depressed. I now had to work with two consultants. Firstly, the newly appointed consultant, who was courteous and respected my predicament. Secondly a consultant who was perhaps the most difficult character I have ever worked with. He was dismissive of all my experience, which he made no bones about letting me know whenever possible. He treated me like an incompetent doctor. He adopted a combative style of communication which I found it very undermining and upsetting. It made me more depressed and angrier. For the first time in my training, I couldn't wait to leave the post.

My general paediatrics fared no better; I fell out with a new and previously London-based consultant. He was outraged when I left a patient for him to review while I was busy putting a central line into a patient requiring a prolonged course of IV antibiotics. I was pulled in two directions and misread his likely reaction in my asking him to see this patient that I had been unable to see.

In short, the relationships with senior colleagues were difficult and perhaps some of this was coloured by my lack of success at the interview. On reflection, these senior consultant issues would have been an ongoing problem even if I had been successful in getting the consultant job. After much soul-searching I realised that not getting the consultant post was perhaps a blessing in disguise.

During my last series of on-calls I had to deal with four successive child deaths with little consultant support. On call at weekends, I also found challenging. The consultant on duty would pop in for a few minutes and initially talk with the nurses. He would then briefly ask me about the patients before leaving. His parting words were "Call me if you need me." This was code for 'don't call'.

On my last night on-call, my SHO went off sick and I had to cover the service alone. No locums were available, and the consultant kept a low profile. I was beyond having the energy to kick up a fuss. I was exhausted. That night I slept in an on-call room navigated through a building site next to the ambulance entrance. It reminded me of the General Hospital all those years ago.

I scoured the *The BMJ* for further consultant posts and applied for a post 'down south'. My consultant was predictably dismissive about the post whereas I saw it as an opportunity. It was a post in paediatric respiratory medicine at a district hospital linked to a tertiary hospital. I did the obligatory visits and attended the interview; there were four candidates for the post. The interview this time went well and I waited for a call.

JOURNEY'S END

"It is good to have an end to journey toward; but it is the journey that matters, in the end."

Ernest Hemingway

CHAPTER THIRTY-THREE:

END OF THE ROAD

The call came the next day relaying good news; I was finally successful in getting a consultant post in the southern region. We left life north of the Watford Gap and moved down south. The post I had been offered was a consultant post in General Paediatrics and Paediatric Respiratory Medicine in a district general hospital linked with a tertiary centre.

I have worked there now for twenty-three years. The link with the tertiary centre has worked well and enabled me to develop a comprehensive district paediatric respiratory service.

Life as a district paediatric consultant is hard work. I am lucky as my colleagues both medical and nursing are very supportive and a constant source of knowledgeable advice. I started on an on-call rota one in four nights spending most of the evening in the hospital and working three-day weekends. A throwback to my earlier years. This however is evolving and many departments now run a shift rota for consultants. An evening shift ensures consultant presence in the hospital til 10 pm recognizing 6-10 pm is the peak time for admissions. Close supervision of juniors is expected and so as a consultant nowadays you must be hands on.

Reflecting on my training, it would seem life as a trainee today is better in many ways. Many of the routine tasks for example blood-letting, siting venflons and ECGs, a bugbear for junior doctors, are now performed by advanced nurse practitioners and physicians assistants. Training is more organized with an induction week, statuary assessments, protected teaching and a mentorship scheme all now mandatory. Shiftwork has replaced on call nights with a cap on hours worked.

So why despite these improvements in the NHS is dissatisfaction among staff is at record levels with high dropout rates of doctors from medicine, high rates of stress and poor morale. [6] The reasons for this are multiple. Medicine is becoming more complex, treatments more intense and time critical. The man with the stroke who I saw as my first admission as a house officer had minimal treatment whereas today, he would have been worked up rapidly to assess whether treatment with thrombolysis was indicated. This puts pressure on doctors to meet deadlines and make complex clinical decisions within a short time frame. Patient expectation of the NHS is they will receive this state-of-the-art treatment. However, for doctors the reality on the ground is patient demand is outstripping resources. Doctors get frustrated and demoralized as they cannot provide optimal care. For patients seeking emergency care the NHS welcome too often long waits to be seen in overcrowded emergency departments. Chronic understaffing of doctors and nurses is endemic with pressure on existing staff to cover rota gaps. This is very demotivating and can lead to staff being burnout. CoVid has extenuated all these issues and many staff are still traumatized about what they saw and had to do during the pandemic.

The NHS management culture of targets has some merit but too often is non-aligned with clinical priorities. This can make the workplace toxic, where there is open disharmony among senior staff. The fragmentation of the firm structure has resulted in doctors feeling isolated and undervalued. Provision of out of hours food, rest areas and senior support is inadequate further fueling this feeling of "no-one cares".

The GMC has further impacted on doctors' morale by its role in striking off a junior doctor from the medical register unfairly for gross misconduct. The GMC's stance seemed to indicate that doctors, even at a junior level, are individually culpable for system failures in their working environment and their reflective notes used to develop their clinical decision-making are admissible as evidence in court.[14]

This case has made juniors, understandably, wary of being transparent when things go wrong. The ongoing shortages of staff also provide major concerns. Clinicians working to do their best to cover staff shortages can seemingly be accountable for this if things go wrong. Juniors have begun to fear reflecting on practice, an essential element of clinical learning, as it could be used in retribution against them. This is a worrying unsupportive backdrop against which to train as a doctor.[14]

The junior doctor strikes over pay are extremely worrying as this exemplifies the deep disenfranchisement of the next generation of doctors. The demand for more pay is justified but should be coupled with addressing issues of ensuring adequate staffing, reinvention of team working and providing well-being facilities on site in hospitals. CoVid revealed the deficiencies of NHS management in protecting their own staff with Protective Personal Equipment (PPE) and so trust in management is at a low ebb. Management needs to be more respectful to clinicians, working with staff to address the reality on the ground. NHS still has a long road to follow to make the standards of care across the service equitable, of high quality and sustainable. To achieve this inevitably means change, but this should be driven with the ethos of treating patients, doctors, nurses and all allied health professionals with respect and putting patient safety and patient-centred care at its heart. Staff well-being, zero tolerance of undermining behaviour and bullying, good supervision and training of doctors all need to be centre-stage. To do this the medical profession needs to seize back control of the well-being agenda, reinvent the team working and ensure doctors are not scapegoated when errors occur.

The title 'junior doctor' is a misnomer; these doctors in training are highly skilled individuals and perhaps the title 'junior' should be dropped and return to terms such as senior house officer, registrar and senior registrar. Junior doctor appears an inappropriate term for doctors who have entered the profession after five years at medical school and who will undertake ten years of training for hospital specialties' and take *six years to become a GP. 'Junior' implies the doctor is inexperienced and a novice which is a simplification and misleading. I know many doctors who are often seasoned, excellent clinicians, who find the term 'junior' demeaning. The use of the term 'junior' can lead to other allied health professionals undervaluing doctors.*

Healthcare is a twenty-four-hour service and there is an expectation that doctors will deliver care efficiently and equitably in- and out-of-hours. On-call or out-of-hours working in today's health service is now akin to normal hours working, often with greater intensity. The introduction of a skeleton team at night covering the hospital wards is in my opinion problematic. Patient care is compromised, as if you are sick, you will be seen by a junior doctor who may have minimal experience of your illness and not know your case. The result is the doctor may just fire fight problems feeling isolated and unsupported. This system of providing care out-of-hours needs a radical overhaul with the medical profession taking the lead.

Looking at my experience, I know juniors need to be valued and feel part of a cohesive team. We have allowed as a profession managers, lead clinicians and nursing matrons – all often distanced from the clinical arena – to dictate rotas, shift patterns and workplace conditions.

Doctors and nurses can make a formidable team in providing excellent clinical care. However, the reality is doctors and nurses too often act as two tribes inhabiting the same space. They do not co-ordinate well as a team. Consultant ward rounds often do not have an accompanying lead nurse or nurse at all. This contrasts with my training era where there was a definite hierarchy with lead nurses taking ownership of the ward round. Integration during medical school of doctors and nurses would be a way forward to promote better understanding each other's role in patient care. Patients often today too often see a lack of continuity and ownership of their care.

The era of poor supervision, long hours and sleep deprivation should be cast to the history books, but should be remembered as how not to train a doctor. The present training arena is no nirvana and there is a need to make training a nurturing, supportive, safe and fun endeavour. Our aim in training is to produce adaptable, knowledgeable, compassionate and valued professionals who have agency and can lead us into the future. Doctor well-being is inevitably linked to patient safety and outcomes. There is still a lot to do!

CHAPTER THIRTY-FOUR:
EPILOGUE – FIXING THE NHS

I stretch over for the cardboard urine bottle I keep as a memento from the hospital beside my bed at home. I manoeuvre myself under the top sheet and start to fill the container. The exercise of positioning the bottle and relaxing enough to allow a stream to rattle the bottom of the container, a major achievement. I, however, had not thought about how to ascertain whether it was full; I assume it could hold the contents of an average full bladder. I feel a warm, wet sensation move up my back; the bed was soaking. I lie for a while contemplating my predicament and then a doctor approaches as I now lie in a urine-soaked bed.

Medicine, at its core, is a human business with the expectation of patients that doctors will be safe, professional, well-trained, trustworthy, good communicators and that they are working in a caring, well-led cohesive team. The world over, the old adage of the Hippocratic oath, 'Do no harm' and Immanuel Kant's categorical imperative, 'Do unto others what you would want for yourself' still applies to the practice of medicine. Professionalism is doing the right thing even when no one is watching.

Medicine continues to be a noble human endeavour and at its core is about human interaction and the use of safe ethical systems in the care for patients. The era of training doctors with the 'see one, do one, teach one' approach to medicine has thankfully been relegated to the history books. Training is now scaffolded with a clear curriculum; work-based assessments, *clinical and educational supervision and patient safety at centre-stage. However, despite improvements in many aspects of training there is still much to do! There is an urgent need for a review of working conditions and the well-being agenda for doctors. This is a repeated issue highlighted throughout this memoir.*

The clinical arena remains a fascinating place to practice medicine. Reflecting on the past we, as a profession, know 'how not to train a doctor' and must use this knowledge to provide a supportive, caring, organised and high-quality training environment for doctors fit for the future. Consultants need to embrace the navigation of the clinical arena as a priority and take back control of work conditions in this challenging terrain.

"Hi Dr Stone, how are you this morning?" asks my GP on a home visit.

Where shall I start?

A beautiful Sunday when I drove out with my family on that fateful day, it had been a very intense and difficult week. This was not unusual and then, in an instant, life changed.

REFLECTION ON THE JOURNEY OF HUMANITY

"Life can only be understood backwards; but must be lived forwards."

Anonymous

Chapter Thirty-Five:

A Synopsis of Important Aspects of Medical Practice

To make sense of this memoir the following section will hopefully be very useful. While this section is not essential to accompany the memoir, if you have limited exposure to the medical world it will give you an understanding of the accompanying backdrop to my story. A story of relentless change management and regulation in the National Health Service (NHS).

The drivers for this lexicon of change management impacting working conditions for clinicians in the NHS needs to be understood. This will provide context for the many pressing issues affecting professional practice today.

Doctor-patient relationship and trust

The bedrock of medical practice is the unique doctor-patient relationship. This relationship is reliant on trust. Doctors are trusted to abide by a code of conduct, always putting the patient's best interests first. In return, doctors hear a patient's personal stories and innermost worries. They also, with consent, carry out a physical examination and clinical procedures. This trust is built through mutual respect, honesty and confidentiality. When these agreed values are not upheld by the medical profession, patients lose faith in their doctor and medicine becomes very difficult to practice.

Culture, regulation and medical errors

When I began training, senior doctors 'ruled the roost' and medical errors were frequently dismissed as 'that's just the way it is'. This was the era of patients accepting the mantra 'doctor knows best'. This is now outdated, and patients expect decisions about their care to be 'in partnership with doctors with sufficient understandable information'. In the past, patients with concerns about their care were often ignored and medical errors just accepted as inevitable. Today, staff are encouraged to report incidents or concerns about care. These incidents are then categorized and investigated in a NHS culture of fairness, transparency, learning and increased accountability. One such investigation into care at an NHS Trust (Francis Report 2013)[4] investigated public concerns about emergency care. It revealed breathtaking failings in patient safety and delivery of care. Shockingly inadequate care had led to increased patients' deaths! The response to these revelations was swift with implementation of endless regulation and monitoring to improve patient safety in the NHS. This has put patient safety centre-stage and led to formation of the inspection regulators such as the Care Quality Commission (CQC), who can inspect any hospital or general practice institution and rate the standard of care. The supposed culture of transparency and learning in the NHS still has some way to go. There is still a tendency to blame individuals when the system is at fault. This weaponization of incidents against individuals works against a culture of transparency and learning.

In the 1980s, the Thatcher government introduced Sainsbury-type hospital managers into the NHS.[1] This reform was initiated following the Griffiths report (1983). The report found senior clinicians who held managerial posts were in their opinion barriers to healthcare change. The managers, often with little clinical experience, quickly grew in importance, directly affecting the clinical arena. They began to challenge the status quo. This influence initially drove positive changes such as implementation of the limitation of working hours for junior doctors; medical error reporting systems; and more organised training programmes. Managers rose in importance, and this was reflected in their increased remuneration and power within the clinical arena. This influence nowadays surpasses senior doctors. This change in power locus has led to managers becoming much more autonomous, answering not to senior doctors but to the Department of Health and Social Care (DHSC). This managed system has allowed the government further central control of the clinical arena, which was previously the domain of senior clinicians. Worryingly, this new-found managerial confidence has encouraged inexperienced managers to take on huge clinical responsibility without the necessary accountability. This previously was a remit of senior clinicians who had the appropriate experience and clinical credentials.

The introduction by the Thatcher government in the 1980s of the marketplace into healthcare, changed the NHS. It meant NHS providers had to compete for contracts from fund holding GPs in primary care. This clear focus on budgets and efficiency was readily embraced by managers and shunned by many clinicians. This divide of us and them lingers even today among many medical staff. The more recent health and social reform bills (2012, 2022) have allowed private companies greater ability to tender for NHS contracts. This decision has undermined many NHS services not used to market forces. It has also driven a hardheaded financial and managerial attitude towards clinical care which now pervades the NHS. This can distort clinical priorities and has made the NHS a less joyful arena to work in.

This dominance of the manager has led to a wasteful bureaucracy that overloads clinicians with huge amounts of documents and emails daily. Many clinicians with management roles are expected to attend a plethora of meetings which are ineffectual. This has led to a disillusionment and disconnection between senior medical staff and managers. Unfortunately, this atmosphere of distrust pervades many NHS hospitals. Addressing this disconnect and recalibrating the power base in the clinical arena is key to fixing our broken NHS. Introduction of a regulatory body for senior managers seems inevitable now in view of fatal failings of senior management to listen to clinicians laid bare by the Lucy Letby case.[2]

So let's look at the clinical arena where medicine is practiced. This is a starting point in understanding the way forward to begin to fix our NHS.

Clinical swamplands and Greek philosophy

A term used to describe the clinical arena where medicine is practiced is the 'clinical swamplands', the real world of unpredictable human- to-human interaction. This term I derived from Schon,[19] a famous reflective practitioner, who described clinical practice as swampy lowlands' where life is indeterminate, complex and incomplete.

Similarly, the Greeks have a useful philosophical view of the world, which may aid in further understanding of the clinical arena.[20] At the centre of the application of knowledge in the clinical arena is Episteme that represents certainty – certain knowledge often associated with science and evidence-based medicine. Surrounding this is Gnosis that stands for *un*certainty. This is the domain of human-to-human interaction, relationships and behaviour. This is the clinical 'swampland' where medicine is practiced. Surrounding Gnosis is Zoe, the spiritual world that transcends Episteme and Gnosis.[19] Interestingly, Indigenous peoples (e.g., First Nations people and/or Aboriginal people) often see the world from a differing initial starting point to our western worldview. They start from Zoe the spiritual view rather than Episteme. This partly explains why traditional healers are the first port of call by Indigenous peoples when unwell. They may choose the healer in preference to modern doctors because healers share their spiritual view of the world. In this view, the healer and patient believe their illness is because a bad spirit or deity possesses them. Engaging this view mandates a spiritual issue is at the root of a person's illness. This can lead to ritualistic, sometimes barbaric and seemingly unjustified treatments to rid the person of the spirit.

Modern western medicine, in contrast, looks at the world starting with Episteme, that is, certain knowledge. This has been extremely successful in treating many illnesses. However, since Gnosis is where medicine practiced, doctors need to be aware that Episteme, despite its power, has limitations. An understanding of human–to-human interaction is fundamental to practicing modern medicine in the uncertainty of the clinical swamplands. You may have the best drug or facility in the world for an illness, but if the people don't have trust or faith in the practitioner or system the innovative advancement in care will falter.

Communication as a medical practitioner

Good communication skills are paramount in medical practice. A doctor in the modern clinical arena must be able to listen to patients and fully explain procedures and treatments in a language the patients can understand, without using medical jargon. As discussed earlier, the era of 'doctor knows best' has gone. Today, shared decision-making is best practice, with the doctor and patient working in partnership. This relatively recent change can prove a challenge for many doctors used to the more 'do what I say' approach. Rightly so, there is an expectation from patients that they will receive and be able to understand all the information required to consent to procedures. This is known as informed consent. In addition, patients expect that doctors will be honest, transparent and inform them if errors in their care have occurred. This is called duty of candour. Communication today means that a doctor needs to give patients their full attention, show they care and take ownership of the patient's needs. The Chinese put it well in highlighting key aspects of good communication: Listen with your ears, eyes, body and, most importantly, your heart.

Hinterland of getting into medical school

To study medicine, I had to choose my A levels, which I was told had to be the three sciences. I attended a comprehensive school in South London in the late seventies. My main academic advice came from a biology teacher. Her son had gone to medical school, the only pupil ever from our sixth form to do so; I felt compelled to follow the teacher's advice and chose biology, chemistry and physics A levels discarding, with some regret, humanities subjects. This binary choice between science and the humanities is now considered misguided; after all, medicine is a human endeavour with humanities at its core. Interestingly, the recently established medical schools are realising that students studying humanities subjects have useful skills for the study of medicine. Limiting entrants' requirements to mainly science subjects and mandating chemistry excludes many capable students from applying to study medicine. Chemistry, for example, is not offered and/or well taught in many state schools. This therefore limits those eligible to apply for medicine from the state sector. This may explain why our doctors come from a very narrow stratum of society with a high proportion of students being privately educated and from the white middle classes. The medical profession benefits from being representative of the society it serves and so change is needed to achieve this goal. A recent initiative of the government in creating four new medical schools in the UK has an agenda to widen participation in the medical admissions to train as a doctor. This has led to several schools adjusting their students' entry requirements to account for disadvantages of pupils from the state sector. This involves allowing entry to the course with widening A level subject choices, including humanities. It has also led to some medical schools no longer mandating chemistry A level.

For me, studying A levels in the sixth form was a time full of expectation and the realisation that good results were required to study medicine. I was very keen to leave home and study something I thought worthwhile and exciting. Our head teacher was ambitious for the school and took six pupils, including myself, to Oxford to inspire us to consider applying to Oxford University. On our return we were offered extra tuition to prepare for the Oxbridge entrance exams. I accepted and started having extra teaching sessions with my biology teacher. This expanded my knowledge and honed my exam technique. The school, however, forgot the Oxbridge project and no applications to Oxford or Cambridge were sent. I was disappointed. In our sixth form of two hundred, twelve went to university and no one to Oxbridge.

The months spent preparing for the Oxbridge exam were not in vain, however. When I sat the biology A level exam I 'smashed it' (I could recite the Krebs cycle with all the enzymes in my sleep). For chemistry A level I had a great teacher and performed well, but I found physics tedious. I am not sure if my struggles with it were due to the teacher or me. The teacher was well-meaning but straight out of college and came across as young, uninspiring and insecure. She spent much of her time writing copious neat notes on the blackboard. I would try and concentrate but often drift away, my mind drawn to the notion there had to be more to life than this. The teacher's name, ironically enough, was Miss Muddle and a muddle is how I would describe my understanding of physics and my performance in the A level exam.

My A level results were relayed to me whilst on an expedition with the Venture Scouts in Norway. I received a message from the tour leader, John, who thrust four cans of Tuborg lager into my hands and announced:

"Good news, you got into medical school with A, B, C; A in biology, B in chemistry and C in physics. Well done, mate."

I had offers to go to two medical schools. My preference was the school where I had attended an interview. To me, the face-to- face assessment and success at my interview trumped an offer, just on grades, from the other school.

Getting into medical school was a much easier path than it is today. Three B grade A levels were the usual offer a far cry from today's requirements three A star grades. There were no aptitude exams, no necessity for work experience, nor any cramming of courses to aid interviews. I had managed to experience the medical world by spending one single day with my mother's colleague, a general practitioner (GP), as my mother was a health visitor. This was interesting but the doctor was aloof and non-communicative. The school arranged a visit to the Maudsley in London, the psychiatric hospital. This was exhilarating. During the visit we were aware of danger in certain areas we were visiting. One area called the Villa, a secure mental health unit, seemed fraught with danger and intrigue, which made medicine seem exciting, and so at just eighteen years of age, I went to a Midlands medical school.

Are 18-year-olds too young to train as doctors?

At this point I must pose this question: Should medicine be a post-graduate subject? My belief is an emphatic 'yes'. If you review the desired outcomes for medical graduates produced by the General Medical Council (GMC) it describes an almost perfect human outlook. Many of these professional behaviours are about understanding life, human needs and moral codes.[6]

At eighteen years of age your frontal lobe is still developing. Neurological pathways are being formed that pertain to social interaction and revolve particularly around discovering your own personality and grappling with risk-taking. It is a time when you need to experiment, to explore your self-being, i.e. your place in the world, relationships, your self-belief, sexuality and personality. Many teenagers struggle to find themselves and this can be expressed in narcissistic behaviours and experimentation with risk. Peer group pressure at this age continues to be strong and I know myself that as a medical student I have, at times, exhibited unacceptable behaviour due to perceived pressure to please my peers.

My plea is that, at eighteen years old, you are too young and immature to understand or implement the GMC expectations of a doctor, especially in the uncertain and messy real world of the clinical swamplands.

Conceptually, medicine is the science of the uncertain and the art of the probable. This is a difficult concept for well-attuned clinicians with experience to understand, let alone a medical student just out of school exploring their own uncertainty about self-identity. This mismatch, of expectation versus self-development, may lead to students and young doctors getting disillusioned with medicine, expecting certainty and being faced with *un*certainty of real-life medical practice. This, in part, may explain the high dropout rate in medicine during the course and in the first few years after qualifying as a doctor.

At its core, medicine is a human-to- human interaction. A doctor must be competent with specialised medical and scientific knowledge but, importantly, be able to apply it in the clinical arena. A doctor must be able to listen to patients and families, show empathy and compassion, be non-judgmental, have agency and make decisions.

I spent five years at medical school in the Midlands, entering as a schoolboy with little life experience, qualifying in 1986 and then entering the NHS clinical swamplands.

Historical context

For those of you not familiar with the medical world you may find this next part of the introduction helpful in providing a historical context for my story. The period I describe and contrast with today's arena spans an era of immense challenges and changes. Some changes have been good, some bad and some ugly. To understand these changes, we need to consider a historical perspective. I hope you find it informative, as there is a lot to consider since medicine dates to antiquity.

Ancient world

We must thank the Greeks for a more systematic approach to medicine; a code of conduct and a contract between the patient and the doctor based on trust. Hippocrates developed the famous Hippocratic oath that laid down the conduct and moral code all practitioners of medicine would adhere to – the most important dictate in treating patients being, firstly, 'do no harm'.[21]

This code differs significantly from traditional healers who predate Hippocrates. They viewed disease in people as being a person possessed with a deity 'bad spirit' that needed to be eradicated by whatever means necessary. This, as we have discussed, can lead to subjecting patients to seemingly barbaric practices to drive away the spirits. This persists in many cultures today. I experienced it in my time in South Africa, as you will read, and comes from cultures that view the world initially from a spiritual point of view.

It is of note that the great medical thinkers in Ancient Greece, Aristotle, Hippocrates and Galen, had ideas about medicine that persisted till well after the fall of the Roman Empire and into medieval times. Advances in medicine during this period resided predominantly in Arabic countries and China.

The Ancient Greeks believed the body had four humors: blood, phlegm, yellow bile and black bile. It was understood that to be in good health, these four humors had to be in balance, i.e. equal. In illness, the humors were unequal, and treatments were about restoring the balance using opposites. Bloodletting, purging the bowel, reading urine and cold or hot exposure were all used with the aim of restoring balance.

Medieval times

Hospitals in medieval times were institutions for caring for people in a peaceful, clean environment where dying patients were not admitted. We certainly have something to learn from this as in our society most people die in hospital, despite the wish to be supported to die in their own home. Also, the thought of the restful, peaceful nature of those hospitals is in stark contrast to the modern wards of today, which run at 95% occupancy with a high turnover of patients in a noisy and often chaotic, understaffed hospital setting. The benefit of a peaceful environment in patient recovery is crucial. Our present-day hospitals need to relook at how they can reintroduce wards where patients are able to recover in peace rather than having to endure and survive, only to recover at home after discharge. Recent acceptance of 'corridor medicine' as the present norm is a very worrying trend in our system.

Medical practitioners in medieval times were mostly in religious institutions. Monks trained themselves in the Greek traditions. Doctors outside religious institutions were expensive and just advised on treatments. Apothecaries became popular, as they were cheaper and used herbal treatments, but some 'treatments' were poisonous. Surgery was carried out by barbers who had little book knowledge or training. Advances in surgery mainly came from the need to devise necessary treatments for warfare injuries.

The first medical schools were founded in the ninth century in Italy. The Ancient Greeks had a more apprenticeship/community-based training for their practitioners. Padua Medical School was founded in the thirteenth century[22]. William Harvey was perhaps the most famous practitioner attending Padua. He was born in Folkestone, schooled in Canterbury and then studied in Padua. Through careful research with dissection, he produced his seminal paper on the working of the heart and circulation *De Motu Cordis*. This finding was key in moving medicine on from the Greek foundation of medicine, built on the belief of the four humors, to our modern understanding of the heart as a pump and circulation consisting of arteries and veins. Interestingly, Galen's anatomy drawings stood the test of time, showing the expertise of those early ancient pioneers of medicine.

Enlightenment

The Enlightenment led to a much more scientific questioning approach to medicine. The discovery of the microscope and its use in medicine led to a revolution in the understanding of germs as causes of infection and disease.

Birth of modern medicine

Famous bacteriologists such as Koch and Pasteur discovered bacteria as the cause of common infections and diseases such as tuberculosis. Florence Nightingale and Mary Seacole highlighted the need for good, professional nursing care. Public health interventions became increasingly important in disease prevention with significant breakthroughs in the discovery and introduction of vaccination. Mortality and morbidity of populations improved with these advances in the early twentieth century.

It was still the pre-antibiotic era with the discovery of penicillin, the first antibiotic, being relatively late in 1928. Modern medicine was born in this scientific age with advances in anaesthesia paving the way for modern surgery. X-ray imaging discovered by Marie and Pierre Curie revolutionised investigation of the disease and led to deeper understanding of disease processes.

Medical education in the modern era.

In 1910, the *Flexner Report* was published in the United States (US), it reviewed the performance of US medical schools.[23] The report found them wanting, mediocre, profit seeking and unscientific It called for a revolution in medical education and outlined the need for a much more rigorous scientific approach to training. The German schools of medicine were cited as being the model to follow with their rigorous scientific training.So, medicine advanced scientifically but perhaps, in hindsight, lost sight of the human-to-human interaction essential to medical practice.

Our beloved NHS.

In 1948 the NHS was born. Its revolutionary basis was 'Healthcare for all free at the point of delivery, independent of income'[24]. This idea that all people are equal, and care is dictated by need, not income, is fundamental to the popularity of the NHS. This is truly a remarkable organisation and its pledge to be free at point of delivery is something admired worldwide. Across the political spectrum the NHS principles are revered, however, there are storm clouds gathering around the future of funding the NHS.

The recent advances in medicine, for example: sequencing of the human genome and development of monoclonal antibodies, are revolutionising treatment of many previously fatal conditions. The move is toward bespoke treatment regimes for individual patients. This is already a reality in treating many cancers. These advances are making modern medicine increasingly complex and expensive. This is a two-edged sword; on the one side there is increased survival for many conditions especially cancers and on the other, success in treating many conditions leads to an increase in the ageing population with chronic conditions and an increased health and social need. Sustaining adequate funding for a service dealing with this conundrum is problematic. The truth is the continuation of most of the care being free in the NHS is now untenable, especially if it aspires to provide state-of-the-art care in the future. User payment for care in some form seems inevitable. Presently it is painfully apparent that the NHS is struggling. Very sadly, emergency care in many of our hospitals are overrun, understaffed and failing; nurses, junior doctors and paramedics are striking; doctors and nurses are leaving in record numbers. The NHS is broken.

Since 1948 there has been an emphasis on the scientific rather than humanities approach to medicine. This has meant the NHS has not paid enough attention to the continuing need to establish trust between the doctor, patient and healthcare system and to improve the work conditions for health professionals. The influence of Big Pharma has at times, dominated the clinical arena with an unhealthy relationship with senior doctors. Many senior staff enjoyed a decadent lifestyle being wined and dined on exotic trips to far-flung destinations. This meant many senior staff who could have lobbied for improvements in the NHS spent their energy and expertise helping promote pharmaceutical companies and products. Indeed, much of the educational arena around medicine became entwined with promoting pharmaceuticals, losing its impartiality[14].

Revisiting of trust and regulation in medicine.

I feel as doctors during this post-war period that followed the formation of the NHS we have, over time, neglected the art of medicine. That is the human-to-human interaction required to be an effective practitioner in the current clinical swamplands. The bond of trust we have with patients, the bedrock on which we practice modern medicine, has become fragmented. Trust began to be undermined with scandals involving NHS institutions and practitioners, betraying the values and attitudes expected of the medical profession.[2,3,5,24] The profession itself, in my view, looked the other way as the fragmentation occurred, being obsessed with science, evidence and efficiency. Evidence-based medicine is powerful in arming the practitioner with knowledge to use in practice, but this must be implemented in the clinical swamplands, which are full of uncertainty. Without a secure trust between doctor and patient, application of some of the best evidence-based interventions will fall on barren land.

Regaining patient trust and importance putting humanity centre-stage.

Remembering medicine is a human-to-human interaction is key to improving trust in the future. The care and well-being of doctors, healthcare professionals and, most importantly, patients' needs to take centre-stage. The link between practitioner well-being and high-quality, safe, patient-centred care needs to be understood by the NHS hierarchy.[20] Systems in healthcare have been found lacking as medical errors became endemic. Shockingly, medical errors are the third leading cause of death in the US.[26] A new era of putting the human back into medicine is required. This includes championing patient and staff well-being, making our hospitals caring institutions, challenging undermining and bullying behaviours and embracing the fact that, as humans, we all make mistakes and are prone to cognitive bias.

Professional practice can be represented by an iceberg.[26] The activities of medicine such as consultations, procedures and treatments – visible everyday activities – are the part of the iceberg above the water, however, often hidden below the surface these activities are underpinned by experience, knowledge and feelings. In addition, further below the surface of the iceberg lie the practitioners' assumptions – attitudes and moral code the foundation of practice, i.e., beliefs and values.

When things ago amiss with medical practice, it is worth considering this metaphor of practice. For example, there was a famous liver surgeon who was found to be using the diathermy to imprint his initials on transplanted livers. He was a technically excellent surgeon, well-respected by colleagues and patients.[28] His behaviour showed a problem with his beliefs and values, and this is a fundamental foundation of practice.

Training doctors in today's NHS

Over time, trainees must become competent but, more than this, they must become confident professionals. To do this they must develop their complex clinical thinking; this involves understanding that there are multiple intelligences not just academic intelligence. For example, social and emotional intelligence are important intelligences needed by practitioners in healthcare.

Doctors with just academic intelligence may struggle in the swamplands. Doctors do need academic and textbook knowledge but also implicit and tacit knowledge. Additionally, they need to understand clinical decision-making and the tendency to bias. They need to be aware of human factors that affect their performance including anger, sleep deprivation, shift work, hunger, loneliness and tiredness. Understanding about working in teams, good communication and safe handover are also essential skills in addition to more obvious clinical activities such as managing emergencies. We know now that the well-being of healthcare staff is paramount in improving patient care.[18]

Miscommunication accounts for most medical errors. This emphasises the fact that future doctors need to be excellent communicators. Good communication skills can be taught and improved on during a career. Decision-making is a key aspect of being a doctor. Understanding the clinical decision process and tendency to cognitive bias is important for practitioners to recognise in their own practice. Better understanding of bias would encourage more participation of practitioners in the design of systems to mitigate tendency to error. Further training on reflective practice is needed to make practitioners aware of its pivotal role in revealing cognitive bias in the swamplands.

Appraisal of consultants: need to be meaningful

Knowing that communication is key to good medical practice, it is strange consultants do not have any direct assessment of their consultation skills in the annual appraisal. Many doctors, therefore, can spend their whole careers making the same consultation mistakes again and again. The way forward, in my opinion, is that all consultants should have regular direct observation of their clinical practice. This would help illuminate many important aspects communication not captured by the present appraisal process. This real time assessment in the clinical arena would be formative helping consultants further develop their communication skills.

Perhaps a department of behavioural science could be formed in each Trust with trained assessors providing high quality feedback on observed consultations especially as part of the consultant annual appraisal process.

Working 'til sixty-seven years

The retirement age is now sixty-seven years in the NHS. Most doctors retire, in the present era, at around sixty years of age. In many acute specialties this is driven by exhaustion, especially if still participating in out-of-hours cover. For all consultants pension issues have forced retirement decisions (the government has just announced adjustments to pensions to address this issue). The loss of this experience to the NHS on both counts is worrying. Senior doctors should have options at an agreed age (mid-fifties) to move away from out-of-hours working and encouraged to progress into managerial or educational roles. This arrangement does exist but needs to be formalised, especially if doctors are going to work until they are sixty-seven years old.

Call to arms

You can already see for this synopsis that we desperately need to address many issues to fix our broken NHS. This memoir will hopefully provide some learning of how *not* to train a doctor so we can improve doctor well-being and patient care. With many junior doctors and nurses wanting to leave the NHS action is urgently needed to improve working conditions for all staff in our clinical swamplands. So, let's learn from the past to make a better future for all, society, patients and medical staff.

Chapter Thirty-Six:

Postscript – Medical Stuff

Clinical reflections from the clinical swamplands, the power of N = 1

While writing this memoir, I have had the opportunity to reflect further on my clinical training. I now understand the term 'clinical swampland', which captures the real world of uncertainty in clinical practice. To operate as a clinician inhabiting the 'swampland' you need to be astute and pay attention to details.

Over the years I recall cases that stand out as memorable and highlighted to me the need for a clinician to be alert, listen to their inner mood music and keep up an inquisitive nature regards Medicine. Every consultation is a unique clinical human experience. Some consultations resonate as memorable, providing the clinician with important lessons for informing future practice. Reflecting on these interactions is important to contextualise the learning, knowing that N = 1 experiences can be very powerful in influencing practice. Incorporated appropriately into practice, these experiences can give the clinician a rich database of useful real-world 'pearls of wisdom'. However, uncritical acceptance of this data, although tempting, has significant limitations. Without reflection the data can just reinforce engrained cognitive bias or dogma. So it is important to use reflection methodology on the data before filing the experience as a pearl of wisdom.

Every clinician over time develops their individual pearls of wisdom. In my experience, they are very enthusiastic about passing on these to trainees. This communication of this type of learning however is often sporadic occurring in the heat of a clinical encounter. Since there is no formal capture of these pearls many are lost to future generations, remaining memories for an individual and if not written down. Looking to the future clinical decision-making needs to be discussed more openly. More formal capture and dissemination of pearls of wisdom will aid more understanding of cognitive bias in the decisions doctors make.

I have decided to end this memoir with a series of cases N = 1 that have, in my opinion, influenced my practice. My pearls of wisdom. This is likely to be biased but I would contest they still have some merit. I feel that they show that understanding your feelings and thoughts are important in being a state-of-the-art clinician.

'Pearls of wisdom' N = 1

1. Be thorough and in any sick child always measure the blood pressure

A case that immediately comes to mind occurred when I was a newly appointed registrar doing my first on call weekend. I was contacted by the surgical team to review a seven- year-old boy who they wished to take to theatre for an appendectomy. The surgeons were concerned solely about his routine blood results. His full blood count had shown an abnormality, his platelets were very low. They could not explain, this and so quite rightly asked for a paediatric opinion prior to surgery. I agreed to see the child and informed my consultant on-call. The consultant agreed to cover me as the child was at another hospital site.

The children's surgical ward was in a different hospital to the medical ward. Stand-alone children's surgical wards in district general hospitals (DGH) are now thankfully rare and it is agreed modern best practice is a single children's unit taking medical and surgical paediatric cases.

On arrival to this children's surgical ward I spoke with the nurses and was taken to the patient in a side room. I eyeballed the patient and immediately felt a wave of dread pass through me. The seven-year-old boy, was lying quietly in bed with his anxious mother beside him holding his hand. He looked unwell, pale and gaunt.

I took a history. He had been complaining of abdominal pain, headache and vomiting. As I talked with him, I became increasingly concerned about his symptoms of headache and vomiting.

Looking at the observation charts I noted the blood pressure had not been measured. Since this is one of the first measurements that should be carried out in any sick child, I asked the nurse accompanying me whether the blood pressure had been taken.

"We do not take blood pressures routinely on this ward," she replied in an irritated voice.

I was amazed and picked up on the somewhat defensive demeanor of the nurse. I knew I needed to be assertive.

"Well, we need to take blood pressure now,", I said firmly.

"We do not have any blood pressure machines," she announced curtly.

"Well, you will have to get one from a neighbouring ward. So please can you do this." It was an order, not a question.

The nurse mumbled her dissent and disappeared.

After some time, the nurse brought a sphygmomanometer, placing it ceremoniously on the bed and raising her eyebrows to show her disdain for having to search for the equipment.

I started to take the blood pressure. The cuff was the appropriate size, encircling two thirds of the upper arm, and as I pumped up the pressure in the cuff indicated by the mercury measurement, the pressure reading moved past 100 mmHg, past 140 mmHg, past 180 mmHg, to above 200 mmHg. A wave of shock and disbelief passed through me at such a high reading and I began to shake. I began to grip the pump tightly, fixating on the blood pressure cuff, avoiding eye contact with the boy or mother. The final measurement for the systolic blood pressure was 240 mmHg with a diastolic blood pressure of 160 mmHg. (Normal pressures for his age were 110 systolic and 60 diastolic).

The mother, an ex-nurse, started to become very agitated, realising the blood pressure was so high. In silence, and despite the tension now palpable in the room, I proceeded stoically with my physical examination.

The last part of the examination was looking at the back of the eye with an ophthalmoscope called a 'fundoscopy'. On viewing both sides I saw both optic nerves were swollen, he had bilateral florid papilloedema. This indicated raised intracranial pressure most likely due to the severe hypertension. I finished the examination and now had the full attention of the mother and nurse.

"He's got a very high blood pressure and signs of raised pressure in the head," I explained to the mother. "This needs investigation and urgent treatment and not surgery."

"Thank God you measured his blood pressure," the mother exclaimed looking at the nurse.

I rang my consultant on-call to outline my findings. We transferred the child to the paediatric medical site and commenced the child on a combination of antihypertensive medication, liaising with the tertiary nephrology team. We arranged an urgent ultrasound that afternoon which showed evidence of renal artery stenosis.

"Should we do blood pressures on all children on our ward?" the nurse on the surgical ward asked me.

"Yes, that would be advisable," I said assertively.

It is now of note that all children undergoing surgery at the hospital site have their blood pressure taken.

This case showed me the need to be thorough, take your responsibility to review a patient seriously and stick to your guns even when it can cause some irritation to others in the healthcare team. In doing this you must remain firm but courteous.

2. Listen to your gut feeling and reassess.

Understanding your gut feeling is important in any walk of life. The physical feelings represent compressed experiential experience and so should help in clinical practice. The case that follows exemplifies the need to listen to these feelings as they can aid your decision making.

A six-month-old was admitted with a history of fever, severe episodes of agitation, high-pitched screaming and some intermittent vomiting. I was a registrar supervising four SHOs who quickly alerted me to the infant's attendance and their concern that the infant was unwell. I attended swiftly, examined the infant and set about, with my team, a systematic investigation and active management of the infant. We took the appropriate blood tests, carried out a lumbar puncture that showed crystal clear cerebrospinal fluid and started the infant on the appropriate broad-spectrum antibiotic for suspected meningitis. This was done, all in record time. The examination of the infant seemed unremarkable, apart from some pallor and signs of an upper respiratory tract infection. I convinced myself we had done everything, but still there was a nagging doubt and gut feeling that I had not explained adequately the symptoms.

I admitted the child to a cubicle and around four hours later the nurse reported that the infant had passed a red currant-like jelly-type stool in his nappy. Reassessment of the infant revealed a sausage-shaped mass in the abdomen that indicated intussusception. This is a concertina of bowel which comes and goes but finally obstructs the bowel. The child had an attempted air enema to try and resolve the obstruction but this failed and the child required surgery in the end, making a good recovery.

The lesson for me from this case was always listen to your 'gut feeling' – share it with the team and always be prepared to reassess. A second examination is an important part of assessing children in acute paediatrics. Gut feelings have been described as evidence of compressed experiential knowledge and should always be a reason to review and reconsider the clinical situation.

3. Careful assessment – *The test feed for pyloric stenosis a 'gala performance'.*

Paying attention to details always pays dividends in medicine. It usually starts with taking a careful history and thorough examination.

This is always time well spent.

I recall three babies I saw as a registrar within 24 hours.

They all presented to the children's ward with vomiting. The first infant, just six weeks old, had a one-week history of progressive non-bilious vomiting suggestive of a condition called pyloric stenosis. This is an obstruction to the exit of the stomach to the small intestine (the exit known as the pylorus). I informed my consultant of my suspicions and arranged an ultrasound.

"Let's do a test feed first I'll be there in five minutes "he replied with an upbeat tone.

The consultant soon arrived buzzing and took great pleasure in showing me how to do a test feed to make a diagnosis of pyloric stenosis. I was to subsequently diagnose two more babies within the following 24 hours using his technique (a record !).

My consultant was always careful with any clinical encounter always introducing himself by his first name, surname and his position, consultant paediatrician. This introduction to parents and children is so key to building rapport and trust with patients, parents and families.

He initially retook the history. The mother now gave more detail about her baby, describing the vomiting as becoming more forceful over a week and then for the last two days being projectile. Between vomits the infant had been well but losing weight despite being ravenous for feeds. The infant's appearance was wizened; he had lost weight and had loose, prominent skin folds. The diagnosis from the history and examination we agreed was most likely to be pyloric stenosis.

My consultant then with the panache of a star theatre performer showed me his approach to a test feed.

"I've booked an ultrasound," I reminded him.

"Oh, you don't need that!" he exclaimed. "If the test feed is positive.

I am happy to send them for the operation. I am not convinced that an ultrasound being positive is enough if I have not felt the obstruction."

He then proceeded to his test feed, a gala performance.

He got the baby lying on the mum's lap and carefully positioned a towel on the mother. He then proceeded to distribute paper towels on the mother's legs and chest before lifting the infant and repositioning the infant back on the mother's lap. The infant was now cradled by a nest of strategically placed towels.

My consultant then ceremoniously undid the nappy to expose the abdomen. His party trick was to sprinkle talc on the abdomen to show up any peristalsis (movement of the abdomen wall caused by the underlying stomach contracting to try and push stomach contents through the pylorus).

On his instruction the mother started to feed the infant, with the consultant, bare-armed, clad in a plastic gown, exuding regal authority, sitting in a chair next to the mother. The infant guzzled the milk and soon a satisfying wave of peristalsis was visible, moving from left to right across the upper abdomen.

"See that?" he exclaimed as the mother held the baby forward as it started to wretch.

The infant was repositioned again and now he palpated the abdomen centrally, working his way toward the liver on the right. The palpation was deep, and his eye suddenly flashed with glory.

"I can feel this one. *You* have a feel."

He took my hands and carefully retraced his deep palpation with my hand. With two of my fingers, I suddenly felt an olive-type mass; I could get above and below, it was the thickened pylorus.

The diagnosis was confirmed, the infant producing a projectile vomit that covered the towels strategically positioned as the final proof.

Since then, I have always taken time with doing test feeds using this technique. An ultrasound is routinely done nowadays but I did observe one infant go to theatre for a pylorectomy with a positive ultrasound and no test feed who did not have a pyloric stenosis. My pearl of wisdom is, if you suspect pyloric stenosis always do a test feed. Pyloric stenosis is most common in first-born males and can run in families presenting at about six to eight weeks of age. Any infant presenting with projectile non-bilious vomiting needs careful assessment but if pyloric stenosis is suspected then do a test feed. It may occasionally be necessary to repeat test feeds over a few days if the infant is in the early stages of pyloric stenosis. These infants can get dehydrated over a period of days and weeks if undiagnosed. They can develop classical metabolic abnormalities due to the vomiting fluid and loss of ions.

Surgical treatment is not urgent in these infants and the initial management plan is focused on rehydration and correcting the metabolic abnormalities before operating. This rehydration can take forty-eight hours. The pylorectomy to relieve the obstruction is a straightforward operation, which is often done today with a laparoscope.

4. Use Airway, Breathing, Circulation, Disability, Exposure, Tummy, Temperature, ear, nose and Throat (ABCDE ttt) to approach the sick children even when uncertain about diagnosis.

Uncertainty is something in Medicine you must get used to. You may not immediately know the diagnosis but a structured approach especially when dealing with emergencies means you can live with uncertainty while knowing your assessing and treating important things that will save lives.

A 14-year-old boy with learning difficulties and autistic traits presented with loss of fluid causing shock and severe anaemia. He required resuscitation with fluids and a blood transfusion. We treated him without knowing the diagnosis, which is unsettling but by using the systematic ABCDE ttt approach I knew, despite the uncertainty, that I was prioritising important life-saving interventions. The approach does not require a definitive diagnosis, which in this case was a bleeding Meckel's diverticulum (a rare congenital abnormality in the intestine that can cause gastrointestinal bleeding) that required surgery. The boy's autistic traits and learning difficulties added complexity to the situation.

Dealing with uncertainty is a common dilemma in acute paediatrics. During my career I have seen the impact of the ABCDE ttt in effective resuscitation of sick children even without a diagnosis. This approach is now the bedrock of practice for all healthcare professionals in the team dealing with sick children. It means everyone knows the drill and can contribute. Prior to the ABCDE ttt approach becoming routine practice, resuscitation was haphazard and not systematic. In many cases this led to omissions in treatment causing poorer outcomes for sick children. The approach encourages leadership in these stressful situations and the importance of cohesive team-working. Remember the parents are part of that team and their concerns about their child should be taken seriously.

5. Question assumptions – craggy masses and constipation

A common clinical finding in childhood chronic constipation is the palpating of a craggy mass in the abdomen related to accumulation of faeces in the bowel, which becomes dried out and hardened. This can be alarming when first encountered and you initially think that this child has an abdominal tumour. Once you are familiar with this finding you relax and do not subject these children to investigations routinely. On my last consultation face to face consultation prior to lockdown, I examined the abdomen of a five-month-old presenting for a routine screening review and felt a craggy mass. The mother said the infant occasionally got constipated and in view of this part of me reasoned it was likely to be faeces. However, on questioning the mother more closely about the infant's constipation it did not seem severe but mild and intermittent. I started reasoning to myself, recalling in my experience. I had not felt this mass due to constipation in any infants less than a year of age. I therefore decided to investigate the mass further and arranged an ultrasound urgently. The ultrasonographer rang me and asked if this infant really warranted an urgent scan. I listened to my 'gut feeling', which was telling me a scan was indeed required urgently. I insisted on the scan as soon as possible. The ultrasound scan revealed a likely neuroblastoma (NB), which was subsequently confirmed. This case taught me that questioning your assumptions is an important part of complex clinical thinking.

6. Don't stop thinking and be willing to take time out to review the situation with the team.

Taking a time out to review the clinical situation always useful.

In a child presenting with a UTI it is critical to consider an underlying abnormality such as reflux (vesico ureteric reflux) but also the possibility of a neuropathic bladder. The assessment of the child should include asking about bowel movements and remembering to check lower limb sensation power and reflexes.

I saw a ten-month-old infant who presented with failure to thrive and recurrent UTIs. During a ward admission for investigation, he was noted to have a probable neuropathic bladder on renal ultrasound and had developed slight weakness in his lower limbs.

During the admission he spiked a temperature and was generally unwell. I assessed him, without knowledge of the ultrasound result, and was concerned that he may have a serious infection. I carried out blood investigations and attempted a lumbar puncture to exclude meningitis. Both my SHO and myself were unable to get cerebral spinal fluid despite several attempts. We took time out and considered the situation again; noting the ultrasound report was still awaited, we chased it up. The report indicated a large bladder and queried a neuropathic bladder. This finding made us consider spinal cord compression and we went on to get spinal imaging, a more appropriate approach to investigate him in view of his presentation and signs. He had a spinal dermoid cyst that was compressing his spinal cord causing his neuropathic bladder and lower limb weakness. He went on to have surgery.

In retrospect, we should have imaged first before the lumbar puncture, but I was so fixated on getting specimens I had multiple attempts, before reconsidering the situation. A 'time out' earlier would have been more prudent when unsuccessful on a couple of attempts to get the specimens. This would have allowed a review of the situation and an opportunity to discuss the issues fully with members of the team. This is a primary lesson to learn. It is crucial for patients and within teams to have a common language around raising concerns and making space for re-evaluation of a situation. CUS is an example of a tool used to raise safety concerns: C = I am Concerned, U = I am Uncomfortable and S = Stop – this is a patient safety issue.

7. Use mobile phone footage – seizures and non-epileptiform seizures and more!

Don't ignore mobile phone footage!

I have seen many children with signs and symptoms suggestive of seizures. In these cases, as always, it is important to carry out a thorough history and examination. However, with the advent of mobile phone video technology, parents can often capture episodes of the possible seizures and these if viewed can be very informative. Many of the referrals sent by GPs as possible seizures turn out *not* to be seizures but other non-epileptic phenomena.

A recent referral of a seven-month-old girl highlighted the use of video footage in an infant referred to the clinic as having possible seizures. The concern revolved around episodes of head-shaking and very rapid oscillations of the body that only occurred when she was sitting in her high chair. The history was otherwise unremarkable, revealing normal child development although it was worrying that these episodes were happening more frequently. My initial thoughts, in view of the age of the infant, was that we needed to be sure this was not a serious condition called infantile spasms (IS). IS is a serious seizure disorder that presents at around 5–8 months of age and can lead to developmental regression and delay. Early detection and treatment is important in getting the best developmental outcomes. In the clinic the infant looked well, and the neurological examination was normal. A video of the episode was very revealing, showing clearly that the child did not lose consciousness but did continually oscillate up and down on the straps of the highchair. The footage confirmed this was self-gratification behaviour related to the highchair straps. Having the mobile footage allowed confirmation with the neurologist and so rapid accurate feedback and reassurance was provided to parents without need for further investigation. Mobile phone footage has in the past enabled me quickly to diagnose petit mal epilepsy in children of various ages. These episodes show children with eye-fluttering and some impairment of consciousness (absences) and have been confirmed by an electroencephalography (EEG).

8. Early detection and treatment of Infantile Spasms (IS)

Certain conditions require urgent investigation and treatment.

IS is a particularly concerning form of seizure as I have mentioned. It has a typical picture of hypsarrhythmia (chaotic but pathognomonic pattern) on the EEG and, if not treated, can lead to significant developmental delay in children presenting with normal development, and in those with developmental issues can make their development significantly impaired. These children usually present at 5–8 months of age and typically have what we call 'Salaam attacks' where they throw their head forward with arms flung out, for just a few seconds. These episodes can repeat again and again with runs of attacks sometimes up to a hundred at a time, occurring intermittently throughout the day. The key thing is to recognise the possibility of IS in this age of the infant, and if IS *is* suspected, to diagnose and treat correctly as soon as possible.

I remember vividly a five-month-old twin who my staff grade doctor had seen urgently at my request. The infant had been initially referred routinely because the GP had noticed repetitive movements occurring many times during the day. I had seen this referral while triaging routine referrals from GPs; sending the referral to our department was a daily occurrence. I was concerned from the age of the infant and the repeated episodes that we had to exclude IS and so I fast-tracked a review of the infant the next day. My colleague, an experienced staff grade paediatrician, saw the child the next day and spoke to me about her findings. The child was well but the episodes were suspicious of IS and so we arranged an urgent EEG. Phoning the electrophysiologist directly and booking an emergency EEG the next day expedited this. I reviewed the infant the following day knowing an EEG was already booked. The EEG showed evidence of an early hypsarrhythmia, suggestive of IS. We liaised with a neurologist and the infant was started on ACTH injections, i.e. high-dose steroid-stimulating injections. The infant suffered significant side-effects from the treatment such as irritability, weight gain and increased appetite although the infant's spasms responded well and she is now—importantly – developmentally normal. Prompt treatment is so crucial in IS.

During my career I have seen quite a number of children with IS and in all cases it has reinforced to me the importance of taking a good history, looking at video clips of possible seizures and carefully examining the skin. Additional examination of the skin with a Wood's lamp (an ultraviolet light) usually done in a darkened room can help pick up allied neurocutaneous conditions such as tuberous sclerosis complex (TSC). Hypopigmented macules are particular in diagnosing TSC using a Wood's lamp examination. I have seen three children presenting with infantile spasms where we made an allied diagnosis of TSC. They were all started on vigabatrin rather than high-dose steroid therapy. These children had some developmental issues prior to their presentation, and this persisted but did not regress following treatment of the hypsarrhythmia.

9.Developmental regression (red flag) and seizures

Beware missing crucial clues to progressive brain disease.

It is noteworthy to take a good developmental history in any child presenting with seizures and recognise the red flag of associated developmental regression. I recall a case of a child who presented with what seemed initially to be simple febrile convulsions. Following up this child in clinic, the mother mentioned he had begun to cease walking and had become less talkative, a history of developmental regression. This child, unfortunately, had Batten disease and sadly died around eleven years of age due to this fatal degenerative neurological disease.

Another child presented with recurrent febrile convulsions, initially presenting in status epilepticus (SE – continual seizures for over thirty minutes). On close questioning of the parents the infant had also experienced several non-febrile seizures but also a plateauing in developmental progress. In view of this he was investigated further and, subsequently, on testing for sodium channel disorders, was diagnosed as having Dravet syndrome. This is a particularly severe malignant form of epilepsy where there is marked developmental delay associated with the seizures, which can be very difficult to control. I diagnosed three children with this condition, and they have all been very challenging to manage.

10. Headache and red flags

Pay attention to red flags.

Headache is another very common symptom in paediatrics. Once again, a careful history and examination is crucial, especially remembering the red flags for possible brain malignancy. I have, during my career, seen several children presenting with brain tumours – they can be difficult to pick up and differentiate from other types of headaches. I was always taught to see children with any concerning headache twice having initially excluded obvious red flags for malignancy such as occipital morning headaches or headaches that wake you at night. This meant seeing children in six to eight weeks with a headache diary following the initial consultation. The reasoning behind this review being that brain tumours can occasionally mimic other types of headaches early on in their evolution and a second examination can help exclude malignancy and clarify a more benign headache such as tension headache or migraine.

I have seen toddlers and young children on several occasions presenting just with morning vomiting as the only symptom. They each had very large brain tumours. I have seen children presenting with non-febrile and often focal seizures with underlying brain tumours. Equally, neurocutaneous conditions such as neurofibromatosis type 1 (NF-1) can make children prone to developing optic gliomas. I have had several children diagnosed with NF-1 and subsequently presented with optic gliomas. It is therefore paramount that children presenting with this condition are carefully monitored and if they have symptoms suggestive of central nervous system disease it must be investigated promptly.

11. Muscular disease and tremor

Careful neuro-muscular assessment is an important skill to perfect.

Another significant yet not uncommon symptom in acute paediatric practice is tremor. I saw a boy around ten months of age who presented with a tremor and slight ataxia (unsteady and wobbly sitting up). I carried out imaging, which was normal, and it subsequently transpired that the child had a form of spinal muscular atrophy (SMA) type 2.

Children with muscle disease are not uncommon in paediatric hospital practice. The children with SMA type 1 and 2 are of normal intelligence, but all have progressive significant weakness. SMA type 2-diagnosed children are less severely affected than type I, but are often wheelchair-bound in early childhood and remain very dependent as adults.

SMA 1 and 2 are now being treated more aggressively with the advent of gene therapy. When I started as a senior registrar in neurology the infants with SMA 1 were not offered any active treatment. Then, more recently, with the advancement in non-invasive respiratory support, palliative respiratory support was offered to patients. This was not without controversy, however, as many parents became aware of the difficulty of the dilemma of how far to go with respiratory support in a condition which progresses. The concerns were twofold: the child lives with a life of dependency on non-invasive ventilation or, in some, a tracheostomy for long-term ventilation with no prospect of any improvement in the condition. Recent developments in effective treatment with gene therapy are changing the balance in favour of fully active respiratory support.

12. Breathing disorders common but remember wide differential – key: take a good history

All that wheezes is not always asthma

Respiratory disease is very common in paediatrics and there is a vast range of conditions that can present with respiratory symptoms and signs. As with other conditions, it is paramount to take a thorough history and examination. Asking about common symptoms such as a cough; whether it is wet or dry, persistent or intermittent, whether there are associated breathing difficulties, breathing in or out and/ or has any particular precipitating factors, are all diagnostically important in guiding appropriate investigation.

During my many years of practice I have seen a wide variety of upper airway problems, some of which I'll outline below.

Foreign body ingestion and aspiration is not uncommon. I was part of the on-call rota for the ENT team in Australia and would clerk all the children presenting acutely, with possible foreign body aspiration. I saw children presenting who had aspirated foodstuffs, pen lids, Christmas decorations and, on one occasion, a seed inflorescence.

The clue to the possible foreign body aspiration is nearly always revealed in taking a thorough history. In ninety percent of cases there is a history of abrupt onset of symptoms and poor response to usual treatments trialled for respiratory distress such as asthma treatments. If a foreign body is suspected, then a bronchoscopy is required to examine the airway and remove any foreign body. This needs to be done in an expert centre as it can be quite a challenging procedure. In Australia, patients would be taken to theatre by the ENT team who would proceed with a rigid bronchoscopy and, if detected, attempt to remove the foreign body. Foodstuffs produce an intense reaction in the airway making extraction difficult, and from an anaesthetic point of view, many of these children would have periods of low saturations during the attempts to remove the foreign body, which made things challenging.

Breathing difficulties due to the upper airway are common problems in paediatrics. This is because the airway is narrow in an infant and a small amount of swelling in the airway can cause significant obstruction and therefore respiratory distress.

Children presenting acutely with stridor (inspiratory noise indicating upper airway obstruction) commonly have croup or laryngotracheobronchitis. This is a self-limiting viral infection, rarely leading to complete airway obstruction, but often needing hospitalisation for close monitoring. It responds well to steroid treatment. Infants who do not respond to treatment and have persistent stridor, biphasic signs (inspiratory and expiratory) or have history suggestive of another condition need to be investigated promptly, usually requiring at some stage an examination under anaesthetic with a bronchoscopy.

I have seen children presenting initially as possible croup who had other conditions. One child I cared for with persistent stridor had on investigation, haemangiomas in the airway. The clue to this was that the child had no evidence of airway obstruction at birth and then an onset at six weeks of increasing persistent stridor. This correlates with the natural history of haemangiomas, which can be very small at birth but through vasoactive growth factors grow rapidly over the first months of life before they start to regress at about a year. Treatment in such cases today, which is very effective, is low-dose beta-blocker treatment. The case I cared for had a tracheostomy and the lasering of haemangiomas.

The most common condition producing variable stridor from infancy is a floppy larynx or laryngotracheomalacia. These children account for most of the cases of chronic stridor but I have seen children who have had congenital vocal cord palsy and acquired vocal chord palsy after cardiac surgery. Children can present with stridor due to a vascular ring such as an aberrant subclavian artery or a double aortic arch (DAA) obstructing the airway. The clue to this diagnosis is persistent stridor or which, unlike laryngomalacia, does not tend to vary with position sleeping or feeding.

I have had a child presenting with acute or chronic stridor with tracheal stenosis and another with a lymphangioma.

I have learnt that children presenting with airway problems should be prioritised and, as always, it is crucial to take careful history; if the child is persisting with stridor then specialist input is required just to check that there is no underlying condition.

Tracheomalacia and bronchomalacia (easily collapsible walls of main airways) are important conditions to recognise. They can present with breathing difficulties and common signs such as cough and wheeze. Wheeze is a common presentation of asthma but, of course, can be caused by other conditions. In malacial airways there is often characteristic noisy breathing such as a barky cough with accompanying wheeze. The medication given in acute asthma to relax the smooth muscle, which is constricted in asthma (bronchoconstriction causing small airway obstruction is a cardinal feature of asthma), can make children with underlying malacial airways worse. This is because relaxing the smooth muscle, which in a malacial airway is helping keep the airway open, exacerbates the collapse of the airway, making breathing difficulty worse. So a poor response to treatment or deterioration when trialling asthma treatment for presumed acute asthma is a clue to malacial airways. Diagnosis is made on flexible bronchoscopy of the airways.

I have seen many children wrongly labelled as having severe asthma who have malacial airways. It is therefore an important diagnosis to make as it can avoid the tendency for clinicians to wrongly assume it is asthma and escalate inappropriate treatment with both bronchodilators and steroids in acute exacerbations of respiratory distress.

Bronchiolitis is a very common lower respiratory tract infection that affects the majority of infants. Each year, in the UK, ninety per cent of children meet the respiratory syncytial virus (RSV) in the first year of life. RSV is the main cause of bronchiolitis. Other viruses that can cause bronchiolitis include adenovirus, metapneumovirus influenza virus, *Para influenzae* virus and many more. Children usually make a good recovery from RSV bronchiolitis. However, those infants hospitalised having a slightly increased rate of developing subsequent asthma.

Common conditions like bronchiolitis account for much of acute hospital practice in the winter months but not uncommonly – uncommon conditions masquerade as bronchiolitis. Here are some of the rare conditions that I have encountered masquerading as bronchiolitis : disseminated tuberculosis (clue, rash; contact with smear positive TB, no crackles on auscultation of chest), *Pneumocystis carinii* pneumonitis (clue, severity of lung disease although RSV-positive looked for other organisms when ventilated by doing lung wash BAL), bronchiolitis obliterans (clue, persistence of oxygen requirement, persistent crackles and respiratory distress) and truncus arteriosus (clue, fast heart rate with gallop rhythm, murmur and large liver).

The above are rare diagnoses but show the importance of taking a good history and having a differential when seeing children with common symptoms. Your brain during bronchiolitis season is understandably prone to availability bias and rare conditions can be easily missed. It is said in paediatrics that 'rare conditions occur not uncommonly', therefore it is paramount during your training that you pick up knowledge about rarer conditions. Also, if you suspect a rare condition, liaise early with your seniors and discuss with a specialist.

13. Be aware and listen to others: we can all make mistakes.

We all make mistakes (6 per day), have humility and listen to others. As I have already touched upon as it is such an important message, you can be caught out in medicine by making assumptions that can mislead your diagnostic accuracy and so management of the patient.

I was a SHO in Casualty when I witnessed a famous professor who had been found after three days delirious and unable to walk, having fallen on the floor. I clerked him in and sent him for an X-ray of his hips as he had some signs of a possible hip fracture. The X-rays came back and I misinterpreted them as normal and referred him to the Medical Team.

In the coffee room I met the radiographer and on discussion she mentioned that there was a fracture on the right-hand side of the patient's hip. I subsequently rushed back to the A&E Department and made the appropriate referral to the orthopaedic team. It showed me that working with your colleagues and being approachable, friendly, accessible and being an excellent communicator can help you with medicine when you least expect it. It's like a 'Get out of jail free' card in *Monopoly*.

14. Clinical signs – always try and explain and, if difficult, review.

Always try and explain the clinical signs you elicit.

Paying attention to clinical signs can be far-reaching. I came across a strange sound when examining a teenage girl presenting with chest pain. The sound was only audible when listening to the lower left-hand chest in the cardiac area on lying down. The noise was Hamman's sign, which is squeakiness heard during the cardiac cycle due to air adjacent to the heart and can indicate a pneumothorax.

I initially misinterpreted the noise as being indicative of a likely cardiac problem such as pericarditis. A radiologist's opinion of the chest radiograph noted a small pneumothorax.

Fundoscopy (looking at the optic nerve at the back of the eye using an ophthalmoscope) can be challenging in young children but is an important skill to maintain. I examine fundus on many children in clinic to hone my skills. I do note that many trainees are not confident with fundoscopy, preferring to refer patients to Ophthalmology for

this examination.

I have found fundoscopy is a useful skill during my training, as exemplified by the case I recounted earlier with the child who had malignant hypertension. In this case the finding of papilloedema confirmed raised intracranial pressure and urgency for treatment. This was further reinforced as a useful skill when I reviewed a child who presented with a seizure and vomiting. I carried out fundoscopy and noted bilateral papilloedema. The child had a brain tumour and raised intracranial pressure. Papilloedema I have seen not uncommonly in my career in acute paediatrics and I would still recommend that fundoscopy is an important clinical skill to have.

Nowadays there is an issue with a condition called Drusen, which is benign, but the appearance of the optic nerve can masquerade as papilloedema. Increasingly, opticians are referring these children with Drusen because they are concerned about missing true papilloedema. These children are well and asymptomatic and do not have raised intracranial pressure. In these cases, before they are subjected to intense investigation, an ophthalmological opinion early is warranted as a definitive diagnosis and can avoid unnecessary tests and worry for families.

Benign intracranial hypertension is another not uncommon cause of papilloedema I have encountered, usually these are teenagers who complain of headaches and have a normal imaging (usually MRI of head).

Retinal haemorrhages related to shaken baby syndrome (SBS) and non-accidental injury (NAI) is another key finding on fundoscopy. I have seen children who had been subjected to NAI needing resuscitation and ventilation where the cause of NAI was only suspected after fundoscopy on a paediatric intensive care unit, many hours after the child presented.

15. Fever or rash?

Remember careful evaluation important for all.

Febrile children are very commonly brought in for assessment by worried caregivers, to primary care services and Casualty departments, usually out-of-hours. Distinguishing the few children with serious infections from the many mainly benign viral infections continues to be a major challenge for paediatricians. Most acute fevers and rashes are due to benign self-limiting viral infections. The dilemma is distinguishing benign infections from serious infection such as meningitis, pneumonia, UTI, septicaemia and septic arthritis.

During my career I have made many diagnoses of meningitis, some with significant complications such as raised intracranial pressure, seizures, brain abscess, hemiplegia and other neurological sequelae. In addition, having spent time working on the meningococcal disease regional retrieval team, I have seen many children presenting with meningococcal disease, either septicaemia or a combination of septicaemia and meningitis. The severest case I have seen was an infant with severe purpura fulminans, the infant developing gangrenous legs and hands. The infant eventually died after a period of intensive care; survival would have been at huge cost with all four limbs requiring amputation due to gangrene. This infant, forty-eight hours prior to death, had presented with a fast heart rate for her age and cold-like symptoms. The clue to her serious infection was the high heart rate. I therefore recommend before seeing any acutely unwell child you are always aware of the fundamental parameters for essential observations and so can flag up abnormal findings and consider serious infection early. If you suspect meningitis it's really important to treat children early to help prevent a sequela and to monitor them carefully.

16. Rashes can be important

Always take rashes seriously.

Rashes can be a clue to a clinical diagnosis; for example, causes of a petechial rash (non-blanching rash) include Henoch–Schönlein purpura, idiopathic thrombocytopenic purpura, leukaemia, chronic meningococcal disease and or NAI.

I remember a mother just mentioning about her son having a rash as she left the consulting room following consultation about another condition the boy had. I was running late and could have not paid attention, but I did, and noted a petechial rash that needed urgent evaluation. We checked a full blood count and later that afternoon the blood count came back showing acute lymphoblastic leukaemia (ALL). Once again, this emphasised giving your patients your full attention even if this causes some inconvenience to yourself.

17. Absent Femoral pulse – if in doubt, refer

If in doubt and it is important clinical finding, back your clinical suspicion and refer for another opinion.

I recall as a registrar admitting a 10-day old infant who presented in heart failure. The infant was nearly moribund and required extensive resuscitation. The infant had absent femoral pulses (pulses at the top of the leg) and in view of this finding, an intravenous prostaglandin infusion was started, which established an adequate circulation for the infant before it was transferred to a cardiothoracic surgery specialist unit. The infant had coarctation of the aorta (CoA – narrowing of the main blood vessel supplying oxygen to the body).

At birth, in all babies there is a *patent ductus arteriosis* (PDA), a communication between the pulmonary artery and the arch of the aorta. In utero the PDA helps blood bypass the lungs and can remain open for first few weeks of life. In coarctation the duct aids some circulation of oxygenated blood to the body by bypassing the obstruction in the aorta. When the PDA closes after ten days an infant with a coarctation will rapidly become unwell as the PDA closing means no blood can get to the body. A prostaglandin infusion can help open the PDA temporarily helping maintain some circulation until they can receive emergency surgery.

The clue to a diagnosis of coarctation (not easily picked up on antenatal scanning) is the infant has absent femoral pulses (as stated earlier, a pulse at the top of the leg). This was subsequently confirmed in the 10-day-old infant as it was successfully retrieved to a cardiac centre and had an emergency operation. The baby, although presenting near to death at the time, did very well.

My consultant knew the infant's family socially at the time.

He had arranged to do a postnatal examination of the infant as a favour and had checked the femoral pulses. My consultant at the time berated himself for missing the diagnosis, trying to recall if the femoral were easily felt when he saw the baby. Interestingly, he says in retrospect the femoral were difficult to feel, i.e. weak. This was something that I subsequently reflected on that if you have any suspicion of weak femorals then you must get it further evaluated rapidly.

This pearl of wisdom stood me in good stead when I was the consultant in charge one Saturday morning. A registrar approached me wanting to discharge a child home from the postnatal ward where there had been concerns about the infant's femoral pulses. The infant was kept on the ward for twenty-four hours just to be observed.

"We need a cardiology opinion and echocardiogram urgently!" I blurted. I then related my previous experience to the registrar: 'So if you think there is an issue with the femorals then the infant needs a cardiac review and an echocardiogram'.

Keeping the child on the ward did not seem logical to me, as we know that coarctation can progress rapidly, presenting with a life-threatening emergency. We therefore sent the child straight up to the cardiologist's and a diagnosis of coarctation was made. This showed me the value of reflecting on your experience; it helps your future practice.

18. Non-accidental injury: Always demanding.

Challenging situations require all your attention.

One of the saddest and most difficult issues paediatricians often deal with is NAI where a child has been injured on purpose. I have met many consultants who, in the past, have ignored it as a possible diagnosis and others who refer the possible cases immediately to another colleague without taking any ownership of the issue. The latter attitude was quite common; in my experience more prevalent among more specialist paediatricians, however, overall, most consultants embrace the notion that they must follow things through, putting the child's best interests first.

The reason for some clinicians to be reluctant about taking on these cases, in my experience, is that they take time, require you to listen, involve working within a team and are always intellectually and emotionally challenging.

In dealing with NAI cases I have found discussion with colleagues is worthwhile and you must be rigorous about assessment and documentation. I, sadly, have met cases of infants dying related to NAI.

One case I was involved with still resonates with me today. An abusive father on the postnatal ward was threatening to discharge his wife and newborn baby against medical advice. The parents were both heroin addicts, deemed by social services to be 'safe' and engaging in a methadone programme. I saw the father and then connected social services and explained the situation, especially the abusive father's behaviour. I felt the mother and infant should stay. Social services insisted the parents could cope at home, despite my concerns regarding the father. My gut feeling was the mother and infant should stay, but as soon as social services had given the green light, the nurses quickly relayed this to the parents who were delighted to leave. I informed my consultant of my concerns at the time who supported my efforts but felt social services had to take the responsibility.

Two weeks later the infant, just two weeks old, was brought in dead to A&E with a severe head injury inflicted by the parents. I realised then I should have listened to my gut feeling and insisted that social services see the family, especially the father, before discharge. Sometimes for decision makers to understand the gravity of the situation it is necessary for them to experience the encounter face to face.

This case an example of N= 1 did influence my practice. I am now always cautious in discharging children and babies home when social services are actively involved. This is especially true when drug abuse is a factor in the family.

I also note from the reviews of the regrettable NAI cases of Victoria Climbié and Baby P, both had seen paediatricians in their last weeks with undetected injuries.[28] The paediatricians missed the diagnoses because they did not examine these young children. One consultant I worked with said 'I examine all of my patients especially young ones' and this has stuck with me. Over the years I have picked up incidentally on examination, large livers related to metabolic disease, bruising and ligature marks related to NAI, imperforate anus, hip dysplasia, haemangioma, neuroblastoma (NB) and self-harm lacerations.

The importance of examining children was also brought home to me when I met a GP in the waiting area of the High Court in London. We were both there giving evidence in an NAI child case. The GP told me he was very concerned because he had seen the child involved on a home visit the night before the child was admitted to hospital with a fracture of the leg. He unfortunately at that home visit did not examine the abdomen or lower legs of the child and so missed the femoral fracture (femur is the thigh bone). He now regretted his mistake and told me he is now fastidious about always fully examining young children. On the home visit he explained he had been in a hurry and the home was dimly lit but berated himself for not being more thorough in his examination. This case (n= 1) was very powerful in highlighting the need to be thorough with examination even if there are difficulties making examination a challenge.

Child abuse can take many forms and unfortunately, you'll come across cases of neglect, emotional abuse, grooming, ritual abuse, factitious disorder and chronic sexual abuse. Today the reporting of proven or suspected child abuse is encouraged and all agencies dealing with children are now mandated to have training in detection of abuse and referral of children to safeguarding agencies.

Welfare of children is now centre-stage with improved safeguarding systems in place. However, despite this, there have still been recent revelations about grooming activities among gangs of men, usually, involving hundreds of victims in our cities.[29]

Clearly, during my era of training there were major scandals regarding chronic sexual abuse among paedophile rings. Shocking revelations over Jimmy Savile, who over decades, sexually abused probably four hundred victims aged five years to seventy-five years and yet was able to do this with impunity. He covered over his activities to such an extent that he was sadly able to maintain a persona of 'national treasure' among the public for charitable fund-raising and with many friends among the political, royal and celebrity elite.[30]

These cases highlight the need to listen to children and take seriously their disclosures. Recognition of high-risk behaviour patterns should not be accepted as the 'norm'. Looked after children are a particularly vulnerable group in our society. The damage child abuse has on victims is often profound and long-standing. Prevention of child abuse by investment in parenting support and education, early schooling provision and training in child abuse for all people dealing with children has to be a priority.

Power of N = 1 in medical practice

N=1 is so salient in medicine and influences practice, often in our subconscious. It can lead to cognitive bias, which can be irrational in some cases. For example, if following the NAI case I decided not to discharge infants of drug-using parents. To overcome this, reflection is so necessary; this is where you look at the experience through differing lenses to create new understandings. Our system of work- based assessments in training go some way in establishing good reflection habits, but this needs to be a feature of every practitioner's practice. Once again, looking to the future I feel consultants need to further engage in reflection, discussing N = 1 experiences, including errors. This can be done with groups of colleagues including nursing staff. This would help the consultants' practices, colleagues' practices and make discussion of errors and difficulties visible to encourage a transparent, non-hierarchical, open cultured way of working, which is so important in building a patient-centred safe healthcare service.

Chapter Thirty-Seven:

Final Salute

Life is fragile. It can be extinguished in an instant. We all walk this earth for such a short period of time and our experience of life is just a grain of sand in the desert of eternity. However, each grain of sand has a unique experience of life and a story to tell. Sadly, so many of these stories are lost, whisked away into the desert, unheard. They are forgotten and gone forever. Year by year, tales, once so vivid, become fragmented memories before they enter the oblivion of eternity.

My grain of sand with its story has now been told. Thank you for reading it. I now understand the value of walking in another person's shoes as I found being a patient. It highlighted to me the scary roller-coaster ride that is a patient's experience in today's under-resourced NHS. Corridor medicine, for example, is frightening but is now accepted as the norm in our local hospital. My experience of this environment is that it is inhumane, demeaning and dangerous for patients and staff. It should be relegated to the history books.

The NHS has deep-seated problems and to solve them we must heed the lessons from the past. Senior staff should be present on the frontline working alongside trainees and nurses, not attending pointless meetings and writing endless policies tucked away in offices behind computer screens. Seniors working on the frontline should be well-rewarded and this should be the main career progression. Staff well-being and teamwork is key to good patient care and must become a priority. In summary, a template for improvement despite the challenges is required but, importantly, it must put humanity centre-stage. The management style of endless meetings and obstruction of innovation needs to be challenged.

A good friend of mine, a running coach, told me of a pneumonic, which summarised his philosophy in building a good ethos in any institution, which I think is applicable as a broad template for improving the NHS. The pneumonic is the three As: Atmosphere, Attitude and Action. Provide a conducive Atmosphere where people feel valued; change the Attitude of management to be more compassionate and root out sexism, racism and bullying; and build a culture of quality improvement based on effective Action. This perhaps is a good way to start to fix the NHS. So, to all staff in the NHS, life is short so let's all seize the day and be an agent for change!

CHAPTER THIRTY-EIGHT
HELPFUL REFERENCES

1. Griffiths Report on NHS 1983 http://www.sochealth.co.uk/national-health-service/griffiths-reprot-oectober-1983/

2. Hospital bosses ignored months of doctors warnings about Lucy Letby 2023 https://www.bbc.co.uk/news/uk-66120934

3. Kennedy report, 2001. Public enquiry into children's heart surgery at Bristol Royal Infirmary 1984–1995. Learning from Bristol.
http://www.wales.nhs.uk/sites3/documents/441/The%20Kennedy%20Report.pdf

4. The Royal Liverpool Children's Inquiry. Alder Hey retention of organs, 2001
https://www.gov.uk/government/publications/the-royal-liverpool-childrens-inquiry-report

5. Francis enquiry. Report of the Mid Staffordshire NHS Foundation Trust Public Inquiry, 2013
https://www.gov.uk/government/ publications/report-of-the-mid-staffordshire-nhs-foundation-trust- public-inquiry

6. GMC Outcomes for Graduates, 2018. https://gmc-uk.org>education.

7. Work and wellbeing in the NHS, 2022. Royal College of Physicians access https://www.rcplondon.ac.uk/file/2025/download

8. Royal College of Emergency Medicine new campaign to end corridor care as data shows more then 100,000 patients waiting over 12hours in A &Es this winter. 03/03/2020

   http //as-data-shows-more-than -100,000-patients-waiting-over-12-hours- in-A&Es-this-winter

9. Golding J, Greenwood R, Birmingham K and Mott M, 1992. Childhood cancer, intramuscular vitamin K, and pethidine given during labour. BMJ; Aug 305(6849): 341–346.

10. Fear NT, Roman E, Ansell P, et al., 2003. Vitamin K and childhood cancer: a report from the United Kingdom Childhood Cancer Study. Br J Cancer; Oct 89(7): 1228–1231.

11. Samuels M, Raine J, Wright J, et al., 1996. Continuous negative extrathoracic pressure in neonatal respiratory failure. Pediatrics; Dec 98(6Pt1): 1154–1160.

12. Boseley S, 2000. NHS on trial over secret baby tests. https://www.theguardian.com/society/2000/may/09/futureofthenhs.health

13. Bossley M, et al., 2006. Southall's CNEP trial more than stands up to scrutiny. The Lancet; 367(9516): 1030.

14. Will patients really die this week because of new NHS hospital doctors? (Article on 'black Wednesday' and new NHS doctors, 2012 https://www.theguardian.com/politics/reality-check/2012/aug/01/ black-wednesday-new-nhs-hospital-doctors

15. Bawa-Garba: timeline of a case that has rocked medicine, 2019 https://www.pulsetoday.co.uk/analysis/regulation/bawa-garba-timeline-of-a-case-that-has-rocked-medicine/

16. Elliott C, 2014. Relationships between physicians and Pharma: Why physicians should not accept money from the pharmaceutical industry. Neurol Clin Pract; Apr 4(2): 164–167. doi: 10.1212/ CPJ012. PMID: 29443239; PMCID: PMC5765617.https://www.

ncbi.nlm.nih.gov/pmc/articles/PMC5765617/Gera R, 2020. Where I come from. Reflection on discrimination in modern medicine http://www.boa.ac.uk/resources/knowledge-hub/where-i-come-from-a-reflection-on-discrimination-in-modern- medicine.html

17. Childhood mortality rates Viner 2019 [Query – check: This links to 'Child mortality in England compared with Sweden: a birth cohort study' by Zylbersztejn A, et al] https://www.thelancet.com/ action/showPdf?pii=S0140-6736%2818%2930670-6

18. Schon D, 1983. The Reflective Practitioner. New York. Basic Books.

19. Playdon Z, 2009. A principled approach to practice and a practiced approach to principles. http://www.zoeplydon.com

20. Hippocratic oath

    https://en.wikipedia.org/wiki/Hippocratic_Oath

21. Padua medical school and modern medicine https://www.ncbi.nlm.nih.gov/pmc/articles/PMC3963738/

22. Duffy T, 2011. The Flexner Report – 100 years later. Yale J Bio Med; Sep 84(3): 269–276.

23. History of the NHS. https://www.nuffieldtrust.org.uk/health-and- social-care-explained/the-history-of-the-nhs

24. The Shipman Inquiry. Dame Smith, 2003 https://assets.publishing.service.gov.uk/government/uploads/system/uploads/ attachment_data/file/273227/5854.pdf

25. Medical error is third biggest cause of death in the US, experts say, 2016 The Guardian on-line access https://www.theguardian. com/society/2016/may/03/cause-of-death-united-states-medical- error

26. Surgeon who burned initials into livers of two patients fined £10,000. https://www.theguardian.com/uk-news/2018/jan/12/surgeon-burned-initials-livers-two-patients-fined-simon-bramhall- assault-transplant

27. Fish D, Coles C, 1998. Iceberg of professional practice. Developing Professional Judgement in Health Care.

28. News insight: Safeguarding – Baby P and the lessons for the children's workforce, 2008 https://www.cypnow.co.uk/other/article/news-insight-safeguarding-baby-p-and-the-lessons-for-the-childrens-workforce

29. Independent inquiry into child sexual exploitation in Rotherham (1997–2013)https://www.rotherham.gov.uk/downloads/download/31/independent-inquiry-into-child-sexual-exploitation-in- rotherham-1997---2013

30. NHS and Department of Health investigations into Jimmy Savile, 2014 https://www.gov.uk/government/collections/nhs-and- department-of-health-investigations-into-jimmy-savile

Quotes:

"The hardest part of any journey is the first step." John W Hayes https://john-w-hayes.medium.com/the-hardest-part-of-any-journey-is-the-first-step-4c55dd6c357c

"Travel doesn't merely broaden the mind. It makes the mind." Bruce Chatwin https://www.azquotes.com/quote/858197

"It's a funny thing about coming home. Nothing changes. Everything looks the same, feels the same, even smells the same. You realise what's changed is you." F Scott Fitzgerald https://whatever-you-write.tumblr.com/post/122435154500/its-a-funny-thing-coming-home-nothing-changes

"Failure is success in progress." Albert Einstein https://www.goodreads.com/quotes/424937-failure-is-success-in-progress

"It is good to have an end to journey towards; but it is the journey that matters, in the end." Ernest Hemmingway https://www.passiton.com/ inspirational-quotes/7023-it-is-good-to-have-an-end-to-journey- toward

"Life can only be understood backward; but it must be lived looking forward." Soren Kierkegaard.https://sweatyourassets.biz/collection- of-the-best-quotes-sweat-your-assets/

Printed in Great Britain
by Amazon